Prison(er) E

STORIES OF CHANGE AND TRANSFORMATION

David Wilson is Professor of Criminal Justice at the University of Central England in Birmingham. He is the author of several books and numerous articles on criminal justice—including *The Longest Injustice* (also Waterside Press), *The Prison Governor: Theory and Practice* and *What Everyone in Britain Should Know About Crime and Punishment*. He is the Co-Editor of the *Howard Journal of Criminal Justice*.

Anne Reuss is a lecturer in sociology at the University of Abertay Dundee, specialising in crime and deviance and penology. Involved with adult, further and higher education for over 20 years, she 'served a five year stretch' in HM Prison Full Sutton between 1993 and 1998 lecturing and conducting research on the University of Leeds Full Sutton project, researching the claim that attendance on Higher Education courses whilst imprisoned can lead to 'change'. She is also a member of the Editorial Advisory Group for the *Howard Journal*.

Prison(er) Education
Tales of Change and Transformation

First edition 2000

Published by
WATERSIDE PRESS
Domum Road
Winchester SO23 9NN
United Kingdom

Telephone or Fax: 01962 855567
E-mail: watersidepress@compuserve.com
Online catalogue and bookstore: www.watersidepress.co.uk

ISBN 1 872 870 90 2

Catalogue-In-Publication Data: A catalogue record for this book can be obtained from the British Library

Printing and binding: Antony Rowe Ltd, Chippenham

Prison(er) Education

STORIES OF CHANGE AND TRANSFORMATION

Edited by

David Wilson
Anne Reuss

WATERSIDE PRESS

WINCHESTER

The Contributors*

Stephen Duguid is Associate Professor of Humanities and Department Chair at Simon Fraser University, Vancouver, Canada. He has had extensive experience teaching in and administering education programmes in prisons and has published widely in the field. His most recent work is *Can Prisons Work?: The Prisoner as Object and Subject in Modern Corrections* (Toronto, 2000)

Ross Gordon was born in Glasgow in 1958, brought up in Salford, left grammar school to work without sitting any exams and was given a life sentence for murder in 1977. He studied for a Mathematics Degree and did teacher training on day release before being returned to closed conditions from a pre-release hostel after struggling with drink and drug problems. He completed a Masters Degree in Mathematics Education, gained a number of ABE teaching and assessing qualifications and is currently helping with the delivery and assessment of Basic and Key Skills Education in Littlehey prison whilst waiting for a Judicial Review to be heard.

Emma Hughes studied at Stanford, Columbia and Cambridge, most recently earning an M. Phil. degree in Criminology. The thesis examined the role of the arts in prisons and was followed by research at the Unit for the Arts and Offenders. She is currently a doctoral student at the University of Central England in Birmingham, writing a dissertation on prisoners' experiences of distance-learning

Petra MacGuinness has taught Basic Skills, Key Skills and ESOL at HMP Whitemoor since 1992. Her first degree was in Social Work, and she also possesses an MA in Criminal Justice from the University of Central England in Birmingham. She is married, and has three children.

Ray Pawson Dr Ray Pawson is Reader in Social Research Methodology at the University of Leeds. His main interest is research methodology and he has published widely on the principles and practice of research, covering various methods—qualitative and quantitative, pure and applied, contemporaneous and historical. He is author of: *A Measure for Measures: A Manifesto for Empirical Sociology* (1989, Routledge); *Realistic Evaluation* (with N. Tilley, 1997, Sage); and over 50 journal papers and book chapters. He has held appointments as the President of the Committee on Methodology of the International Sociological Association, as the UK Chair of the International Forum for the Study of Education in Penal Systems and as senior research fellow of the Economic and Social Research Council. He is currently involved in the evaluation of the New Deal for Communities and writing another book on sociological method.

Elizabeth Waller Liz Waller is Open University Co-ordinator and teaches GCSE History and Religious Studies at HMP Whitemooor. She has a BA (Hons) from the Open University, and an MA in Criminal Justice from the University of Central England in Birmingham. She is married with three children.

* *Details of the editors appear on page i.*

Prison(er) Education

CONTENTS

CHAPTER

1. Introduction 9

2. The Researcher's Tale *Anne Reuss* 24

3. Theory and Correctional Enterprise *Stephen Duguid* 48

4. The Evaluator's Tale *Ray Pawson* 62

5. Dealing With Time: Factors That Influence Prisoners to Participate in Prison Education Programmes *Petra MacGuinness* 83

6. Disjunction and Integration in Prison Education *Elizabeth Waller* 106

7. An Inside View: Prisoners' Letters On Education *Emma Hughes* 138

8. Prison Education: One Inmate's Experience *Ross Gordon* 158

9. The Way Forward *Anne Reuss and David Wilson* 172

Index 183

*This book is dedicated to Mrs. Glenn Cruickshank – the best
Maths teacher ever employed by the Prison Service.*

Acknowledgements

Barbara McCalla for typing the manuscript with her usual speed and efficiency; Anne Maguire for her support; my colleagues at UCE, especially Chris Painter, John Rouse, Basia Spalek and Kester Isaac-Henry; former colleagues in HM Prison Service, especially Tim Newell, Shane Bryans, Terry Knight and Martin Lomas.

David Wilson
University of Central England in Birmingham

Grateful thanks to all family and friends 'on the out' and still 'doing time' with special thanks to Ted, Lawrence, Mostyn, Darren, Vince, Rosan, Mo, Allan, Bunny, Dudley, Andrew, Brian, Tim, Duke and Patrick and many others too numerous to mention and to all the education staff who work so hard in our prisons—and to Fred Astaire, Ginger Rogers and Ally McBeal who helped the research process more than they could ever know.

Anne Reuss
University of Abertay Dundee

CHAPTER 1

Introduction

David Wilson

This *Introduction* seeks to achieve three inter-related aims. First, as is traditional with introductions, to guide the reader through the book drawing attention to the chapters that follow, and what makes them different from each other and other work within this particular genre. In one sense this is quite a simple task, for very little has been written about education in prisons in the United Kingdom, and that which has is rarely based on primary research. Much of this book is written by those who have a direct experience of working or researching inside prisons—especially within Prison Education Departments—and as such it is perhaps the first, concerted attempt to draw together a body of research dedicated to this subject. As such the book also reveals, perhaps for the first time, the often hidden tensions within which prison educationalists have to operate if they are to be successful.

Second, in charting the relatively undiscovered world of education within prisons the book seeks to do more than simply draw the contours of the landscape. Rather, it takes as a starting point the transforming power of education (whilst acknowledging this means different things to different people) both at the level of so-called 'basic skills' but more importantly beyond that level, including the provision of degree courses). Thus it explores the potential that education has to change offending behaviour. The book will cite two different but complementary rationales for this belief—Reuss's 'Education for Empowerment' model, and the realist, empirical work of Pawson and Duguid—all set within the discourse of 'What Works' within prisons. Above all the book seeks to actively engage in a debate about 'who prison education is for'. In doing so—a theme running throughout the book—we will attempt to give prisoners a voice about what education means to them, and *Chapter 8* has been written by Ross Gordon, a serving prisoner at HMP Littlehey. This theme is tentatively introduced within this *Introduction* by citing some examples of prisoner autobiography.

No book about prison or the services provided within prisons—especially education—can fail to recognise the political dimension in which prisons operate. So whilst much of the book relates to the institutional context within which education is offered to prisoners, the book also addresses broader political pressures. Indeed, the third task of this *Introduction* is to offer some insight into these two contexts so as to remind the reader that education within prison has to be seen as legitimate to a variety of audiences, many of whom would fundamentally disagree with the direction that education within prison should take. How the needs of these different audiences are balanced is the challenge faced by the educationalist who works in prisons, or those who seek to champion education's cause. Within the context of this *Introduction* some of these themes will be explored by looking at the process of 'contracting out' education provision in 1992.

EDUCATION IN PRISONS: RECENT TENSIONS

It was Anne Reuss (1998) who most recently championed the 'transforming' power of education in prisons in the United Kingdom, and as a consequence—and just as importantly—she began to question 'Who prison education is for?' By entitling her research 'Prison(er) Education' she reminded us that there is a largely unspoken tension between the prison's view of what education's contribution is to the institution's overall regime, and the many and diverse—often very personal—motives of those prisoners who enrol on education classes. This tension was being described as far back as 1979, when Mike Fitzgerald and Joe Sim reminded us that 'Education is a tool for living and is also a weapon for control in the hands of the prison authorities' (Fitzgerald and Sim, 1979: 69). Whilst all of this is rooted at the level of the institution, it should also be remembered that there is a political dimension to the provision of education in prisons, which exists beyond the institutional level. As Sir Stephen Tumim, a former Chief Inspector of Prisons has pointed out, for example, ' . . . in 1995 in particular government policy appeared to involve saving money and looking for votes by cutting down on education and the arts in prison' (Tumim, 1997: 39).

The need for education, like prison itself (c.f. Cavadino and Dignan, 1992), to appease different audiences—the prison, the prisoner and prison educationalists within the prison, and politicians and the public outside of the prison's walls—has important consequences. A failure to openly resolve this question within the prison leaves the prison expecting measurable results from the classroom in the form of a contribution to Key Performance Indicator (KPI) 5's 'purposeful activity', and thus often seems to encourage a 'pile it high, and sell it cheap' mentality, with an emphasis on basic literacy and numeracy skills. This might not meet the needs of either the prisoners or those who have to teach them, and nor does it necessarily appease a political or public agenda outside of prison which oscillates between punishment and the desire to rehabilitate all offenders.

Nonetheless there is a great deal of evidence which suggests that basic numeracy and literacy skills are lacking in the prison population (c.f. Coyle, 1994; Devlin, 1995; Maguire and Honess, 1997; Wilson and Ashton, 1998), which underscores the need to provide education at this level. However a policy based solely on this approach also implicitly suggests that those with literacy and numeracy skills do not commit crime, and leaves a void in regime provision for development beyond this level. Moreover the desire to offer basic literacy and numeracy skills seems to stem not so much from a wish to understand why the prisoner has offended, and what will help him or her to change, but from a more atheoretical interest in managing the prison population. Thus education becomes a way for 'doing time', and preventing idle hands from making mischief. In describing why they enrolled on education classes in interview, or in autobiography some prisoners do indeed describe a desire 'to pass the time' (c.f. Cohen and Taylor, 1972; Devlin and Turney, 1999; Maguire and Honess 1997). However even if this was so, it is rarely acknowledged that education staff working in prisons are expected to input skills to students who have 'failed' in traditional educational environments. Prisoners lack basic skills because they have often been excluded from school, and this simple fact requires education staff in prisons to adopt different techniques and approaches to help the prisoner to learn. But what is it that encourages prisoners to enrol on education, and does our knowledge of what motivates them offer any help to teachers in schools and colleges?

PRISON VOICES—STRAIGHTS AND CONS

Some of the answers to these questions can be gleaned from listening to prisoners themselves. Morgan (1999) has most recently commented upon the strategy of secrecy within prisons as a means of exercising power and control. Whilst this of course also applies to staff who have to sign the Official Secrets Act, it is all the more relevant to prisoners—in one sense the 'consumers of prison'—in that they are often without a voice. Those who do break the culture of secrecy in speaking out, or through autobiography, are often denied validity and legitimacy as an authoritative source on the culture of prisons. Yet, as Morgan (1999: 337) has argued prisoner autobiographies 'represent some of the most extended narratives and analyses of a particular social experience' and may thus reveal 'the meaning of prison and its practices'.

Morgan attempts to infuse his analysis by dividing the autobiographies that he uses into two groups—'Straights' and 'Cons'. Straights are those prisoners who produced autobiographies and who had no long-term criminal history, and thus a 'lack of recognition of a criminal identity' (Morgan, 1999: 334). In contrast, Cons are those prisoners who produced autobiographies and who had a long-term history of imprisonment, and 'a clear identification with a criminal lifestyle and identity' (Morgan, 1999: 332). Thus Morgan uses these accounts to create 'insider' and 'outsider' perspectives on prison life, although he comes to no firm conclusions as to which account is more credible and valid. By using aspects of Morgan's analysis to present a Cons' account of education—the autobiography of Frank Cook, and its impact upon him—and comparing it with observations made by John Hoskison, a Straights' description of life inside—ways of thinking about prisoner education are 'opened up'.

The difficulties of using this methodological approach relate primarily to validity and generalizability. For example, some people will argue that as interesting as these accounts are they are merely anecdotal, and lack authority. Yet this view seems too shortsighted, and fails to accommodate a potentially rich source that can add to the discourse of the sociology of imprisonment. Nonetheless in attempting to overcome these problems some measure of triangulation will be used by accessing more formal published sources, and in particular by reference to the autobiographies of Nelson Mandela and Vaclav Havel. Both are former political prisoners who became leaders of their countries, and who wrote insightfully about their incarceration. As such they provide a distinctly authoritative account of the part to be played by education within their respective penal systems, whilst also casting an international dimension onto the themes described above. In short their 'voice' would become formal and legitimate—a reality denied to most ex-prisoners.

Prisoners are motivated to engage with education for a variety of reasons and some—many of who already possess basic literacy and numeric skills, and are capable of degree level study—clearly want to enrol for more personal reasons. Frank Cook's (1998) autobiography (an example of a Con's account) for example, is particularly revealing for it describes several of the themes already mentioned. Namely, that he had failed at school; was a discipline problem within the penal system, and therefore had to be accommodated in unconventional ways by education staff; and, finally, was transformed by the experience. Firstly he describes his primary school education, and the impact that it made on him:

> Because I lived on gypsy camps until the age of eight, I had missed the majority of my primary schooling and so I was put in the bottom set. The set, known as the 'dunces class', comprised of maladjusted children, immigrant Asian kids who couldn't speak English and the usual odds and sods who couldn't be fitted into the normal framework of the education system. I was more intelligent than the other members of the set and willing to learn but, as I couldn't read or write, the lessons were of no benefit to me. School offered me little stimulation and I turned to mischief, both in and out of school, to amuse myself and the other members of the class. Incidents, including lobbing paving slabs over motorway bridges, setting farm animals loose and, on one occasion, herding sheep into the local hospital, secured my

popularity with the pupils but amongst the teachers I built up a reputation as a bit of a trouble-maker (Cook and Wilkinson, 1998: 11).

Several years later—in 1989—with a string of convictions for violence behind him, he ends up at the Special Unit at HMP Hull.[1] Cook explains that his original motivation to engage in education was being 'bored out of my skull' and so he 'wandered into the art and craft studio' (p.91), but it is his description of the impact that this made on him which is worthy of repeating:

> I went down to the classroom and demanded aggressively that the door be opened. The screw[2] looked uncomfortable but, after the nod from a cordial colleague, he hesitantly opened the door. I stormed into the room and plunged my hand into a vat of terracotta clay. I pulled out a big lump and began to manipulate it roughly. The sensation of the clay in my hands was incredible and, although it was a new experience for me, deep down it felt familiar … I plunged into this new world and was simultaneously puzzled and intrigued by it. I still had reservations and worries but I had an even stronger feeling that this was something more important than I had ever done and this conviction spurred me on (Cook and Wilkinson, 1998: 92–93).

This passage is very revealing, and the language used suggests the force and dynamism of the transformation that Cook was experiencing. He 'demanded', 'stormed', 'plunged'—words from his old, violent past— and then, having put his hands in the clay experiences a feeling of difference. He later describes that difference as the emergence of his 'conscience'. Not only that, Cook also informs us that by setting this example 'other lads on the unit had also started to take up various hobbies' and that 'the scum of the country' were 'actually beginning to achieve something' (p.93). In doing so he also reflects that some of the staff were uncomfortable with this transformation, and how their discomfort would impact upon the unit.

He states that some staff 'were used to treating us like shit and we responded by acting like animals which, in their minds, justified their behaviour', so this new positive approach by the prisoners created tension on the unit—in short that the staff 'were unable to accept that inmates could accomplish anything worthwhile' (p.93). This tension was resolved, according to Cook, in that '. . . the tools, paintbrushes and materials, mysteriously began to vanish and it always happened when

---

[1] Special Units, sometimes known as CRCs—the initials of the committee that managed them (the Control Review Committee) were established in the mid-1970s to accommodate a small, but growing number of disruptive prisoners who could not safely be housed within the mainstream prison system. Three such units were established—at HMPs Lincoln, Hull, and C wing of HMP Parkhurst. A fourth was established at HMP Woodhill in the early 1990s to replace the CRC at HMP Lincoln.

[2] Prison slang for a prison officer

we were locked up. It was obvious that it was deliberate sabotage on the part of the screws' (p.93). Some measure of support for Cook's description of how education in more traditional prison settings could be sabotaged comes from a former Deputy Education Officer at HMP Lewes, who states that 'some prisoners are not unlocked in time to attend classes. Frequently this depends on the goodwill of officers and, although matters have improved, many officers are still reluctant to co-operate' (Matlock, 1995: 30). Whilst not necessarily accepting Cook's analysis as to why prison officers refused to co-operate (and see Hoskison's account below), Matlock at the very least suggests that 'goodwill' rather than the rights of the prisoner, or the needs of the prison's regime were a determining factor in whether or not education was provided. Indeed, in the same year, a national survey of education contractors undertaken by the Prison Reform Trust (Flynn and Price, 1995: 28–29) found that one of the main barriers to prison education was 'the reluctance or unavailability of prison officers to escort prisoners to education'.

These rarely publicly aired views reveal one aspect of the tension which education has to face in its attempts to appease different audiences within the prison. Cook's Cons' account dramatically reveals the impact that education can have, and whilst many outside of the prison's wall would support the transformation that occurred in him, this change subtly impacts on the culture of the discipline staff, and the rationale—at least as he sees it—that they have for doing their job. Whether we support Cook's analysis or not in relation to prison staff, we can at least accept his insight into his own development and growth through education. Indeed he has subsequently been released from prison, and is happily crime free. More than this, we can compare the impact that education had on him and his fellow prisoners, with a Straights' account of how prisoners can learn from each other but in a negative rather than in a positive way.

John Hoskison was a professional golfer who was sentenced to three years imprisonment in 1995 for killing a cyclist in a road accident whilst under the influence of drink. His description of his time inside at HMP Coldingley conforms to Morgan's definition of a Straight's account. Whilst he did not formally enrol on education—despite a desire to—he comments that 'I shall always be indebted to the teachers of the education department'. The reasons for this indebtedness relate to their manipulation of the internal job market at the prison so that he could become the Chapel Orderly, and in providing him with the support that he needed to complete a correspondence course in journalism.

'After weeks of scrounging paper they came up with a way that I could get access to the computer room and use one as a word processor. Early in the mornings I've been meeting them at eight o'clock and they've been letting me in to type. I owe them a debt of gratitude'

(Hoskison, 1998: 204). In short, the education department became both a haven from the reality of the rest of the prison, and the teachers people who were able to get things done. He describes the fact that education was 'actively promoted by enthusiastic staff', but that they 'faced an impossible task' given that 'their obvious commitment to helping to educate prisoners was in direct contrast to that of the prison, and the prison service in general' (Hoskison, 1998: 137). As evidence for this statement Hoskison cites the way that prisoners are paid:

> It is a simple fact that a prisoner's ability to survive in jail is linked directly to the wage that he earns at work. Every single penny is vital—and I mean every penny. Wages for a 40 hour week in the metal shop averaged out at about £10. For taking a full-time education course we were paid £4 a week. The £6 shortfall constituted three extra phonecards for those who wanted to phone home, or half a bag of heroin for those who didn't ... There were many who wanted to enrol in full-time education, but very, very few could afford to do so (Hoskison, 1998: 137).

In contrast to the education staff's enthusiasm, and 'can-do' mentality, Hoskison comments on the fact that the discipline staff 'were paranoid about making decisions', and that the prison was 'out of control'. It was awash with drugs, home-made 'hooch' (alcohol), and fights were common (Hoskison, 1998: 180). However, what is of greater interest is his description of the informal culture of the prison that was able to develop in these circumstances, whereby prisoners learned criminogenic rather than law-abiding skills from each other. For example, commenting on the proposals contained within the Crime (Sentences) Act 1997 that would introduce mandatory minimum sentencing—popularly described as 'three strikes and you're out'—he describes 'the strange effect' that this had on the prison:

> Suddenly education was available in Coldingley. Pockets of inmates sprang up, swapping techniques and *modi operandi* so that they couldn't be nailed for the same crime ... It was Terry the armed robber who spoke to me ...'Just gotta show these guys something', he said, and went on to explain all he wanted me to do was stand behind a pretend till in a make-believe jeweller's and serve a customer ... 'Afternoon Sir, how can I help you?' I said to Jim, who stood before me. After a brief conversation he nervously glanced round, reached behind his back and rather clumsily produced a sawn-off broom handle. Suddenly he was all over me. 'On the floor, on the floor!' he screamed, his face contorted with anger, the sawn-off pressed to my throat, pinning me against the back wall. Even though I was acting a part, me heart-rate rocketed. 'No, no, no, no, no!' cried Terry. 'For Christ's sake, you're not Starsky and Hutch, the guy would have shit himself—panicked—you've gotta be much more casual'. Now it was teacher's turn and this time Terry entered my shop ...Terry glanced around nonchalantly, made a few casual remarks, then with lightning speed reached behind his back, swung the

hissed 'Do as I say or I'll blow your fuckin' head off ... his whole manner exuded professionalism ...'Got it?' he asked the other two. (Hoskison, 1998: 129–130)

This is an interesting passage for at the most basic level it confirms the official view of a government Green Paper in 1988 that prison can be 'an expensive way of making bad people worse', and that in relation to young offenders sending them to prison, even for a short period of custody, was 'likely to confirm them as criminals'. This was made all the worse 'if they acquire new criminal skills from more sophisticated offenders' (Home Office, 1988: para 2.15). Indeed the most recent prison statistics reveal that for all the prisoners who were discharged in 1994 56 per cent were re-convicted within two years (Home Office, 1998: 156). More than this, Hoskison reminds us that prisoners as much as staff working within HM Prison Service will react to changes initiated at the macro level where 'the politics of law and order' shapes penal policy, and develop strategies accordingly.

Finally, Hoskison's Straight account can be used to reflect on Frank Cook's understanding of the tension that exists between staff and prisoners. Reflection here is important, for Cook seems to define this tension solely from the perspective of the staff frustrating positive inmate initiatives, whereas Hoskison offers a different analysis. For example, he remembers a situation in which he exchanged pleasantries with a member of staff who had been playing golf that morning.

> Moments later he disappeared onto the wing and within seconds I was grabbed from behind and thrown back against the wall. A white hand grabbed my chin in an excruciating grip. 'Don't ever let me catch you smiling at a screw again,' said one of the drug baron's henchmen. 'If you do, I'll cut you so fuckin' bad your bird will never want to set eyes on you again' ... prisoners are not meant to show anything but the utmost contempt towards officers. (Hoskison, 1998: 142)

In short, the battle-lines are drawn by both sides, although each wage war in different ways.

INTERNATIONAL PERSPECTIVES

The autobiographies of Nelson Mandela and Vaclav Havel are of interest both in relation to their different experiences of education whilst in custody, and also in further pushing Morgan's use of Straight and Cons' accounts as sources. They offer a form of triangulation for the accounts used above, and unlike Cook or even Hoskison—who is now a sometime Inspector of Prisons for HM Chief Inspector—both Mandela and Havel were ultimately to have status and power at the highest levels. So despite both Mandela and Havel being arrested and imprisoned on several occasions—one test of Morgan's definition of a Con—their incarcerations stemmed not so much from a criminal identity, but from the ability of their countries' respective legal systems to define political dissent as criminal. As such their accounts must be seen as Straights' accounts, and their incarceration should remind us that crime is not a fixed entity, but rather something which changes and evolves, and which varies between cultures. Of note, both describe similar transforming experiences through education.

In the absence of formal education provision on Robben Island, Mandela, for example, remembers that 'at night, our cell block seemed more like a study hall than a prison'; that, 'in the struggle Robben Island was known as "the university"'; and that 'we became our own faculty, with our own professors, our own curriculum and our own courses' (Mandela, 1994: 489; 556). Mandela himself advises that he taught a course in political economy and Marxism, and that there were seemingly endless disagreements with the prison authorities about the provision of books, desks, writing materials and paper. All of this would echo Hoskison's concerns about finding paper and a word processor for his journalism course, if not his negative views in relation to what prisoners could learn from each other. Mandela also describes how within a week of the appointment of a new commanding officer at the prison—Piet Badenhorst—who is described as 'brutal', all his study privileges had been removed. (Mandela, 1994: 543).

Whilst it is undoubtedly true that conditions in apartheid South Africa, or communist Czechoslovakia for that matter, do not relate directly to conditions within British prisons what is of interest is the way that education is perceived in all these different cultures as being a threat, and thus the various strategies that the prison authorities could use to undermine it. As such, Mandela describes the simple removal of his study privileges, whereas Cook in HMP Hull talks of 'sabotage'. In this sense the difference between South Africa and England is not so much about the nature of democracy and apartheid, but of how a macro political reality shaped the respective institutional responses. Indeed it is tempting to see Mandela's circumstances as a classic example of how education could be used, in the words of Fitzgerald and Sim who were writing about education in prisons in this country, as both a tool for living and a weapon of control.

Vaclav Havel was imprisoned between 1979 and 1983, first in Hermanice and thereafter at Plzen-Bory. In his autobiography—largely consisting of letters that he wrote to his wife—he describes the fact that he was forced to do manual labour in the absence of formal education provision, but that nonetheless he had constructed a six point plan for his stay inside. In a letter dated 17 November 1979 he summarised his plan for his imprisonment as follows:

1. to remain at least as healthy as I am now (and perhaps cure my haemorrhoids);

2. generally reconstitute myself psychologically;

3. write at least two plays;

4. improve my English;

5. learn German at least as well as I know English;

6. study the entire bible thoroughly

If I succeed in fulfilling this plan, the years may not be entirely lost (Havel, 1988: 51).

Of note, four of the six elements of this plan relate directly to education—albeit self-education, and the phrases to 'reconstitute myself psychologically' and 'to remain healthy' are also indicative of the use that he would make of learning. For example, just over two years later he is again writing to his wife having all but abandoned his six point plan, which he now describes as 'immensely naïve'. However he comments that 'the fact that I so often return to themes of identity, responsibility, etc in my letters is certainly no accident'. They were no accident for identity and responsibility relates to the first two points of his plan, a fact that he illuminates more fully:

I am merely defending my own identity in conditions I did not invent, and doing so in the only way possible, by attempting to be responsible and dignified. Not to do so as a matter of course and in a sporting spirit, as it were, would mean giving up on myself, merging with my surroundings, losing my dignity, ceasing to be ... one can therefore defend one's dignity anywhere, at any time; it is not a onetime decision, but a daily and demanding 'existential praxis': the danger of becoming a doormat is always there, just as there are always opportunities not to become one. (Havel, 1988: 301–302)

This passage must surely be seen as a crucial description of the need to maintain a personal, non-institutional identity; a depiction of the self that transcends the prison walls, and cultural barriers. Havel here reminds us of Cook, plunging his hands into clay and developing a conscience; of Hoskison enrolling on his journalism course; and of Mandela teaching his course in Marxism. (It also echoes descriptions covered in the chapters by MacGuinness, Waller and Hughes, and in what Russ Gordon writes in *Chapter 8.*) None were prepared to become a 'doormat', and education was the means by which they could express their identity. However, as the word implies, choosing not to be a doormat inevitably poses challenges to those in authority.

In all of this there are echoes of what Reuss describes as 'education for empowerment', whereby education in prisons is thought of in terms of the personal value of learning, and thus as something which helps prisoners 'retain a degree of choice and control in what they do whilst in prison' (Reuss, 1999: 125). She sees a model for assessing education's worth as being based on the ability of education to encourage prisoners to make informed and responsible decisions about their lives, and as working through the social process of acquiring knowledge; learning over time; the affect that education can have on a prisoner's identity, and in particular counteracting a negative sense of self; and finally by fostering what Elias (1987) characterised as 'detour thinking'. In short, for her the value of education relates to what works for the prisoner, not for the prison, and as each prisoner is different what works for one will not necessarily work for anyone else. Shoe-horning all prisoners into basic skills is thus not the answer, for even if that 'works' for the prison—it can be measured against a KPI (being introduced in 2000)—it does not ultimately guarantee anything in relation to how those prisoners will behave when they leave prison. What might be more significant are the transformations described by numerous prisoners in that their exposure to education has allowed them, in the words of Frank Cook to develop a conscience.

CONTRACTING OUT

So far we have largely been concerned with the tensions that exists about education at the institutional level—the tension between prisoners and prison staff, between education staff and discipline staff, or indeed between education staff and prisoners. However education within prison also has to accommodate external audiences, and their views about the service that should be provided. This was especially apparent throughout the 'contracting out' process ushered into prison education through the Further and Higher Education Act 1992, which separated colleges of further and higher education from Local Education Authorities (LEAs) and allowed them to become independent corporations as of 1 April 1993. Prior to that date education in prisons had been supplied by the LEA through a local college of higher or further education, and the Home Office paid the salaries of the teachers, plus a 5 per cent handling charge (c.f. Matthews, 1999; Koppitt, 1999). There had been no formal contract between the Home Office and the LEAs, and often as Helen Matthews has observed prison educators 'appeared to be the least capable [and] shunted out of harm's way' (Matthews, 1999: 17).

In short Governors had very little control over education staff, or how they were chosen, and who in turn had working arrangements related to their colleagues teaching within the local college of higher education, which did not necessarily meet the needs of the prisoners, or of the prison. The Tory government also believed that this process would introduce fresh ideas and encourage innovation, thus bringing about increased efficiency and value for money (c.f. Flynn and Price, 1995).[3] So contracting out the provision of education within the prison seemed like one way of resolving some contractual difficulties, and buying a service that more closely met the needs of all concerned, but, as one governor observed, how this was done amounted to 'a sorry tale' (Coyle, 1994: 201).

The mechanics of the process of contracting out were long and complicated. Initially it had been envisaged that the contracting out process would take eight months to complete, and that contractors would be offered contracts for three years. This was later extended to five years, and in the High Court two lecturers from HMYOI Thorn Cross won a case against their future employers—South Manchester College—over whether the European Acquired Rights Directive (ARD) would apply to the new contracts. This was an important victory as ARD ensured that new employers would have to honour the terms and conditions of employment provided under previous contracts of employment. All of this meant that only 16 of the 125 contracts that had been put out to tender started on 1 April 1993, and the remainder did not come into operation until 31 August of that year. In total there were 45 contractors, with nine contractors delivering to more than half of all prisons (Benson, 1994: 42). Even when these contracts eventually began they were marked by controversy and resentment, and the Chief Inspector of Prisons—Judge Stephen Tumim—commented in his Annual Report for 1992–93 that the morale of teaching staff had been severely dented, and that the management of the change was conducted without sufficient consultation and with unseemly haste. Teaching staff faced months of uncertainty and anxiety about their future employment' (quoted in Flynn and Price, 1995: 6–7). Nonetheless the Chief Education Officer at the time, Ian Benson, believed that as a result of this process 'we have secured a better means of delivering education in prisons. At both a national and local level, we now have the opportunity to exploit these arrangements and to develop a service in which all can feel a justifiable sense of pride' (Benson, 1994: 43).

The views of the Chief Inspector and of the Chief Education Officer cannot be reconciled. Of interest what they reveal for our purposes is a fundamental disagreement about the future direction that the

---

[3] This account follows that provided in Flynn and Price's national survey of prison education undertaken in 1995.

management of education in prisons should take. On the one hand Benson seems to endorse a bureaucratic, management and efficiency model—similar to what Andrew Rutherford (1994) in his discussions with 28 criminal justice professionals has characterised as 'an efficiency credo'. Indeed all of this neatly dovetailed with HM Prison Service becoming a Next Steps Agency in April 1993. The benefits of this move to Agency Status were described by Brian Caffarey, the Head of the Agency Unit for HM Prison Service as 'in essence about setting clear objectives for an organization and giving it greater autonomy to deliver better services and better value for money' (Caffarey, 1992: 40), and by the current government as encouraging a 'more business-like focus on management and service delivery' (Home Office, 1998: 13). Here is the language and culture of Business Plans and Mission Statements and Key Performance Indicators, and expedient managerialism.

On the other hand, the Chief Inspector of Prisons would more closely resemble those criminal justice professionals who have what Rutherford describes as a 'humanity credo', which essentially means that they empathise with offenders. They are the 'human face' of criminal justice, not in any soft-headed way, but in that the basis for doing their work is essentially moral. It seeks to engage with, rather than manage prisoners, and by getting to know them as people encourage them to change their offending behaviour by encouraging self-responsibility. This process inevitably takes time and is very difficult to 'measure' in the way that one can measure the numbers of prisoners who have completed, for example, a basic skills course.

There is no doubt that Benson forecast the future much more accurately than the Chief Inspector of Prisons, and in 1998 there was a further tendering process undertaken in relation to prison education provision, with contracts awarded for five years with a view to renewing them for a further five years. Currently there are 27 contractors—a reduction of 18 from 1993—made up of 24 further education colleges, two LEAs and one charity. Similarly, in 1995, HM Prison Service drew up a Core Curriculum that was to be delivered, which included literacy and numeracy, IT and social and life skills, and which will be the subject of a KPI being introduced in 2000 which seeks to reduce by 15 per cent the numbers of prisoners discharged without basic skills at Level 2 or above. This has concerned several prison educationalists, and one has suggested that 'this emphasis on basic skills may mean that the wider curriculum could be restricted [and] could vastly reduce the wider opportunities for inmates which is a real cause for concern' (Koppit, 1999: 19). She goes on to explain why this is so:

> Many inmates who have low self-esteem are attracted to prison education by the craft/art classes where they often find that they can achieve positive results and are then tempted onto the more academic classes where they

have previously failed. These students may well be frightened and intimidated if only the core curriculum classes were on offer (Koppit, 1999: 19).

This short history of contracting out is clearly not exhaustive, but has been included to further illuminate the various pressures on education within prisons beyond those tensions at the institutional level. Space does not allow more detailed analysis of how these external pressures became further complicated by the escapes from HMPs Whitemoor and Parkhurst in 1994 and 1995, which resulted in a penal culture of 'security, security, security' (c.f. Bryans and Wilson, 1998), or of the impact on education as a result of the sustained growth in the prison population since 1993. However these two external factors meant that with the increase in prison numbers by some 14,000 between 1995 and 1998 when one might reasonably have expected spending on education to have risen, in fact it was reduced by £1 million. More than this, for example, art is not on the Core Curriculum. Art classes were scrapped during this period because 'they are often the first subject to go when there are budget restrictions' (Ruthven, 1998: 24). Indeed there are many prisons where nothing but the Core Curriculum is provided, particularly in those prisons where workshops need staffing, or where offending behaviour courses take priority. Nonetheless Penny Robson, the new Chief Education Officer is optimistic about the new Core Curriculum which she believes 'has developed a transparent and systematic quality assurance procedure [which] can only be of benefit to prisoners' (Robson, 1996: 18). She does not tell us how a 'quality assurance procedure' benefits prisoners, or even if they were asked for their views. Prisoners have again become silenced, and official voices speak on their behalf. In fact there is a simple presumption that just by managing the system better, and being able to demonstrate that management then everyone gains. What Frank Cook or Vaclav Havel would have made of this no one knows, but the remainder of this book is a sustained, realistic, passionate and pragmatic attempt to build a case for education in prisons beyond the language of managerial efficiency.

LOOKING INSIDE THE BOOK

The chapters that follow have all been written by practitioners who have worked—in one way or another—with education in prison. The 'Researcher's Tale' tells the tale of what it's like to conduct research in a maximum security dispersal prison with groups of prisoners studying at degree level. Reuss describes 'what she did and how she did it' in the hope that it will provide an indication of the 'highs and lows' of conducting research in a prison environment without losing sight of the prisoner at the heart of the study. In describing her methodological approach Reuss offers insights into the conducting of a classroom ethnography in a prison setting which hints at the complexity of attempting to analyse the effectiveness of prison education programmes in terms of reducing recidivism.

Stephen Duguid and Ray Pawson contribute the next two chapters. Both have long-established and outstanding reputations as academics interested in education in prison. Offering 'Theorist' and 'Evaluator's tales', they tell stories of how theory in relation to crime, deviance and education, and how educational programmes in prisons can be evaluated which will push academic debate in this area onto a new level. Both chapters deserve to be widely read, debated and form the basis of policy in the years to come.

Petra MacGuinness and Elizabeth Waller—both educationalists at HMP Whitemoor—offer practical and theoretical insights into the mechanics of prison education. In *Chapter 5* Petra MacGuinness looks at those factors which influence prisoners to participate in prison education programmes—an interesting subject given prisoners' often poor experiences of education in schools; whilst in the following chapter Elizabeth Waller investigates the issue of race, learning and disjunction amongst black prisoners at HMP Whitemoor. In doing so, she returns to a key theme of the book: namely, that prisoners are transformed by their experience of engaging with education programmes.

Chapters 7 and *8* are very directly concerned with what prisoners say about prison education. In *Chapter 7* Emma Hughes uses a unique research resource at the Prisoners Education Trust of letters kept by the Trust from prisoners applying for course funding. Building on the work of Reuss, Duguid and Pawson she attempts to give prisoners a voice in discussions of evaluation and success. In *Chapter 8* Ross Gordon tells his own compelling story of education's transforming power. Few who read his testimony could fail to be moved by what he describes, and the challenges he still has to face.

Building on all of what has gone before 'The Way Forward'—our concluding chapter—offers a vision of prison(er) education in the future. It seeks to encourage and chide; to plead and provide evidence about the stories contained within this book. It is also realistic, for we know—all of us who work in prisons, or have had experience of prison either as a researcher, teacher or as an inmate—that ultimately the way forward in prison education is to transform the penal system itself. This is no small undertaking but we hope that this book and the stories that this book tells will be a modest contribution.

BIBLIOGRAPHY for *Chapter 1*

Benson I. (1994), 'Education in Prisons', *Prison Service Journal*, July 1994, No 94, pp. 41–43

Bryans S. and Wilson D. (1998), *The Prison Governor:Theory and Practice*, Leyhill: *Prison Service Journal*

Caffarey B. (1992), 'Agency Status', in *Perspectives on Prison: A Collection of Views on Prison Life and Running Prisons*, London: HMSO

Cavadino M. and Dignan J. (1992), *The Penal System: An Introduction*, London: Sage

Cook F. and Wilkinson M. (1998), *Hard Cell*, Liverpool: Blue Coat Press

Coyle A. (1994), *The Prisons We Deserve*, London: Harper Collins

Devlin A. (1995), *Criminal Classes*, Winchester: Waterside Press

Devlin A. and Turney R. (1999), *Going Straight: After Crime and Punishment*, Winchester: Waterside Press

Duguid S. and Pawson R. (1998), 'Education, Change, and Transformation—The Prison Experience,' *Evaluation Review*, Vol. 22, No 4, August 1998, pp.470–495

Fitzgerald M. and Sim J. (1979), *British Prisons*, Oxford: Basil Blackwell

Flynn N. and Price D. (1995), *Education in Prisons: A National Survey*, London: Prison Reform Trust

Havel V. (1988), *Letters to Olga*, London: Faber and Faber

Home Office (1988), *Punishment, Custody and the Community*, London: HMSO

Home Office (1998), *Joining Forces to Protect the Public—Prisons-Probation: A Consultation Document*, London: HMSO

Home Office (1998), *Prison Statistics 1997*, London: HMSO

Hoskison J. (1998), *Inside: One Man's Experience of Prison*, London: John Murray

Koppit D. R. (1999), *Young Offenders and Their Educational Experiences Past and Present*, unpub MA Thesis, University of Central England

Maguire M. and Honess T. (1997), *Supported Distance Learning in Prisons*, London: Prisoners' Education Trust

Mandela N. (1994), *Long Walk to Freedom*, London: Little Brown and Company

Matthews H. (1999), *The Effectiveness of Prison Education*, unpub MA Thesis, University of Central England

Matlock G. (1995), 'Breaking Down the Barriers to a New Prison,' in *A Good and Useful Life: Constructive Prison Regimes*, London: Prison Reform Trust

Morgan S. (1999), 'Prison Lives: Critical Issues in Reading Prisoner Autobiography,' *The Howard Journal*, 38 (3) pp. 328–340

Reuss A. (1999), 'Prison(er) Education', *The Howard Journal*, Volume 38, No 2, May 1999, pp. 113–127

Robson P. (1996), 'Learning from Scratch,' *Prison Report*, Issue 36, Autumn 1996, pp.18–19

Rutherford A. (1994), *Criminal Justice and the Pursuit of Decency*, Winchester: Waterside Press

Ruthven D. (1998), 'In a Class of its Own,' *Prison Report*, Issue 45, December 1998, pp. 24–25

Tumim S. (1997), *The Future of Crime and Punishment*, London: Phoenix

Wilson D. and Ashton J. (1998), *What Everyone in Britain Should Know About Crime and Punishment*, London: Blackstone.

CHAPTER 2

The Researcher's Tale

Anne Reuss

For a number of years, whilst working as a lecturer in sociology at both Further and Higher Education levels, I became interested in what happened when people 'returned-to-learn'. So many students, on completion of a course, would say 'I feel different'/'I wish I'd known that before'/'This has really changed me'—that I wondered what was *really* going on in the classroom. My curiosity became the foundation for my doctoral thesis on *Higher Education and Personal Change in Prisoners* (1997)—a teaching/learning and research experience that was to prove fairly unique in the history of prisoner education in the UK.

What became apparent however, as I embarked upon this somewhat lonely road, was that conducting the research was not going to be easy. In fact, it became, as most dedicated researchers will know, a lengthy, time-consuming learning process for myself, and so, this chapter will focus on the reality of conducting research with maximum security prisoners about their experiences of studying at degree level whilst serving their sentences. My research was carried out over a period of five years whilst lecturing on degree level sociology and social policy on a project which began in 1989 between the University of Leeds and a maximum security dispersal prison. The project ran until funding for the course—from the Prison Service—was withdrawn in August 1998. I was involved with the 'Leeds Course', as it became known, as lecturer and researcher between 1993 and 1998, examining the idea that attendance on education courses and especially Higher Education courses whilst imprisoned, could somehow lead to 'changes' in offending behaviour.

The research took the form of a classroom ethnography, documenting 'classroom talk' and analysing the learning experiences of groups of male prisoners, learning together as a form of social interaction (Reuss, 1997). I was interested in examining exactly how these 'changes' occurred, if indeed they did occur and what the implications would be for penal practice, particularly as the types of programmes being introduced to prison regimes at the time of the study focused primarily on addressing offending behaviour, sometimes, it seemed, at the expense of more traditional education courses which prisoners *chose* to attend whilst doing time. My interest stemmed from ideas that education programmes undertaken whilst in prison *may* be rehabilitative, but what was unclear was *how* the potential for a possible change in offending behaviour might occur.

However, before I begin to describe some aspects of my own experiences of conducting research in a prison, I believe that it has to be acknowledged that there are over 60,000 people in prisons in England and Wales of whom a small percentage have access to education at any level whilst serving their sentences. They are in fact the 'real' specialists whose experiences of prison education programmes are far more telling than anything studied or written by prison civilian staff, uniformed staff or those 'academic tourists' who visit prisons for a short period of time. By contrast, my own research became a 'five year stretch' during which I gained a fairly unique view of life inside, working with the people who are *actually* imprisoned, who live, breathe and experience imprisonment over periods of time which may stretch from months to multiple life-sentences; people like Ted who I met in prison, who has spent most of the last 30 years inside, like Lawrence too who will be way beyond retirement age when he gets out—both now in their fifties, 'classic examples' (and I know they will not object to my saying so) of our ageing prison population.

With the exception of prison autobiographies, rarely have 'research insiders' written about what they did *and how they did it* when it comes to prison research. By 'research insiders' I refer to those who, like myself, spent all day, four days per week working with the same group of prisoners over a number of years. Those 'academic tourists' referred to earlier are in a sense 'research outsiders', who visit prisons and are funded to conduct research for short periods of time. Such research contracts may well be shaped and influenced by a particular political ideology and/or agenda thus ensuring that the researcher has less of an opportunity to 'tell a tale-from-the-field'. This is why anyone wanting a detailed 'picture' of prison life simply has to keep going back inside, short of actually living in the place. Unfortunately, those who do, tend to wish on occasion that they did not have to keep returning to an environment not renowned for its propensity to welcome. However, as someone who did manage to survive the rigours of conducting research in a prison over a relatively long period of time, it seems that it would be useful to share some of those research experiences for those thinking of pursuing a similar course.

Most recent studies conducted in prisons cannot claim to be the definitive account of prison life in the twentieth century, and certainly any studies which are conducted on education in prisons provide only a 'snapshot' of one part of the experience of imprisonment—for *some* prisoners *some* of the time. Describing any aspect of prison life is a complex undertaking; similarly, a good prison classroom ethnography could incorporate the widely differing perspectives of those who transgress society's norms, those who enforce those norms and those who study and work with the transgressors, but in depicting something of the reality of classroom research within a prison, what should emerge is a more *realistic* account of the experiences of the researcher and those with whom she is working.

An account of the actual experience of conducting research in a maximum security prison education department provides a 'tale' from a fairly remote 'field' so this chapter will endeavour to describe what happens when you decide to conduct research involving prisoners and education programmes in that particular setting. Most people are aware that one way of finding things out about the world is to simply go out there and ask other people questions—which sounds relatively easy. If you try and do this in a maximum security dispersal prison to find out whether 'doing' a degree course in sociology brings about any kind of 'change' in prisoners, then things are not going to be that straightforward.

What I hope to show in 'The Researcher's Tale' is the importance of involving *prisoners as people* in an in-depth and sensitive research programme which would have borne little or no fruit without their consent, co-operation, expertise and specialist knowledge of an environment which, for the most part, remains unseen, barely acknowledged and preferably not thought about or reflected upon by most of us. The first section of this chapter will therefore discuss some of the experiences of gaining access to a prison.

The second section will consider some of the methodological techniques employed to cope with researching a most sensitive area of social life—i.e. the long-term imprisonment of individuals by other individuals. Whatever method is chosen by a prison researcher, it will be rigorously scrutinised by penal practitioners, academics and not least, by the prison authorities concerned as issues of security will always take precedence over the researcher's 'unique contribution to knowledge'. My choice of the ethnographic approach does not imply the 'rightness' of this particular method for conducting research into prisoner education, nor does it imply that the outcomes will be absolutely valid, rational, objective or even value-free. As a result of involving the prisoner-students themselves with the research, discussions on validity and the consequences of respondent validation are included as a means of casting a realist (Pawson and Tilley, 1997) interpretation on the study.

Thirdly, the issue of generalizability has to be addressed—to what extent do the findings transfer to other classrooms within the prison system and how far does the fieldwork present a picture of the reality of prison classroom practice? This is because conducting fieldwork in a prison education department produces findings that may be assessed and considered by a diverse group of practitioners and policy-makers. These concerns form the final section of 'The Researcher's Tale'.

ACCESS TO THE PRISON: A 'WAY-IN' TO THE RESEARCH

Classroom ethnographers often find themselves attempting to explain that which is intangible, elusive or even obscure because they often *teach* the people who, in other research studies, might be loosely described as 'research subjects' or 'respondents'. In most classroom ethnographies, the subjects are pupils, students or teachers themselves and the status attached to those labels may colour the research findings. In my own classroom ethnography, the research 'subjects' were first and foremost and in the eyes of most people, serious criminals serving long sentences in an English maximum security dispersal prison.

Conducting research within a prison context means dealing with the kind of distractions that give hardened research practitioners nightmares: Can I do that? Should I say this? Will it cause trouble if …? As a prison researcher you may well find yourself working with *one* small group of prisoners 'selected' by those in authority in *one* prison. The prison may be a single sex prison, it may be, as in my own study, a maximum security dispersal prison, which means that there is a very real likelihood that your research respondents will 'disappear' overnight because they have been 'shipped out' as a matter of security. You will not know where they have gone to and there will be little opportunity to follow up any work you may have started with them. The whole range of carefully premeditated methodological strategies and designs disappear one by one in such a context, but you still have your hypothesis, your classroom and your working relationship with a small core of students who, hopefully, will know exactly what your research is all about.

I had visited the prison once only prior to commencing work as a prison lecturer/researcher, after having been 'cleared' for security purposes. This in itself can be a daunting prospect for the keen researcher who may suddenly begin to imagine all manner of skeletons in cupboards. I regarded my first visit as essential in order to meet the students and give them some indication as to why I was about to spend, initially, the next three to four years 'inside' and had consciously chosen to do so. As I have indicated, it turned out to be a five year 'stretch'. Prisons become obsessive places. The group of male students with whom I would be working were part of an already established programme of higher education within the prison, so I was fortunate in that it was relatively easy to join the course as an additional tutor and draw on my own previous experiences of teaching mature students over several years. This made access easier than it might have been.

On that first visit, the men asked me any questions they wished—about myself, about the research, my reasons for 'being there', the things

I would teach. The idea was to maintain open working relationships, again in an environment not necessarily reputed for having the best of relationships between service provider and client. It seemed important to avoid a situation where the men would feel anxious about the research and so we discussed the outline of the study and my reasons for wanting to carry it out.

To attempt to describe what actually took place in the classroom on each single teaching day is an impossibility. The most one can hope to achieve on that score is to provide a physical description of the prison classroom with its barred window (the prison was built in the late 1980s), single blackboard propped against the reinforced glass corridor window—'to stop the nosey bastard officers from spying on us'—as one student intimated, 12 chairs and tables, partitioned beige walls between the classrooms, three filing cabinets, teacher's desk and bright green alarm bell marked 'No. 9' placed strategically on the wall—'in case of trouble'. The amount of class contact time was substantial and so the rapport which developed with the prisoner-students became in itself a 'way-in' (Hammersley and Atkinson, 1983: 82).

The compartmentalised social world of the prisoner—and it is a social world despite stereotypical views to the contrary, is not an easy world to become accustomed to. Perhaps the most telling description of this world comes from one who inhabits it 24 hours a day. As with all good descriptions, the following is a highly personal account which provides a wider context for my own research, telling us a little of the prison regime beyond the classroom walls in the education block:

> After tea in the evenings the jail becomes a veritable minefield. Screws shouting to each other, doors banging, Brixton Blasters at full volume, blokes who have drunk too much "hooch", who are approaching on a collision course with such endearments as "Aveyergorrafagmate" (Please do you have a cigarette), and the inevitable nutter with a head full of heroin and serious attitude problems. This prevails until 8p.m., when everyone gets locked up ...
>
> Once locked up for the night, decisions have to be made ... what needs doing and in what order it will be done. Typically this would include letter to the wife, Leeds essay and readings, legal work on court cases pending, listen to the news on the radio, washing, cups of tea from the thermos flask ... all this has to be done against the usual background of the ubiquitous Ghetto Blasters, blokes hammering on their doors for the attention of the night watchman (who is probably watching TV and cannot hear the cell alarm bell) ... or some poor enlightened soul telling the world a mile away that Jesus still loves him (even though his neighbours don't) ...
>
> Weekends are much the same as weekdays ... without the benefit of the peaceful interlude in the Education Department ...
>
> In addition to the foregoing, time has to be found for changing library books, showers, canteen, cooking the occasional meal, visits, standing in

queues for everything ... and running around like a blue-arsed fly to remedy the numerous cock-ups that can be taken for granted on a regular basis ...

The fabric of a prison, be it Victorian or modern, is insignificant, it is merely a repository ... a place where people interact with others.

At the top of this hierarchy is the Number One Governor ... usually a timid little man who shuffles papers for his lords and masters in Whitehall, ... beneath the Number One are the junior grades ... and beneath these the screws proper. The Bananas ... yellow, bent and inclined to hang around in bunches. These are the true "governors" of a jail. If they are basically decent, it is a good jail. If they are bastards ... be prepared for the worst.

Finally there are the prisoners themselves ... fools, misfits, drunks, drug addicts, miscreants ... plus whatever offence they may be in for ... penny pinchers at one extreme, paedophiles at the other.

Mix all these ingredients together in a concrete repository ... and you have a British jail.' (Ted, 1995).

To attempt to 'fit into' this world is a time consuming process, because mistrust and suspicion frequently underpin any form of social interaction. One of the first things I had to do was explain to the men why I was there and who I was working for because they asked. The fact that my work was not dependent on Home Office funding contributed in no small measure to gaining access, in the sense that the prisoners did not feel that they were being scrutinised.

What became important was to build on and develop the positive relationships which were formed as part of the 'way-in'. I believed that a high level of 'subject involvement' would be the most successful in providing the evidence to build a more complete understanding of the experience of studying degree level material whilst imprisoned. The men were invited to read any sections of the research that they wished; their involvement was grounded in trust; an important consideration when researching in a prison. With hindsight, I still believe this to be the case. Interpreting the classroom context, the interactions, analysing the complex human processes of understanding information and knowledge and comprehending how individuals distil it all into the structure of personality, meant 'getting to know' the men well and simultaneously abandoning any preconceived ideas I might have had about prisoners or the crimes they may have committed. There would be many who would 'drift' in and out of the course but always a solid core of students committed to their studies and aware of the research. There were, however, those 'on education' who would not join the course *because* research was being undertaken on the grounds that they believed it to be 'something to do with the Home Office' which it was not. As previously stated, this fact in itself became one of the methodological strengths of the research.

I explained to the men that I would be analysing their conversations, their 'talk' in the classroom. They were intrigued as to how this would be done. I explained that I would not be taping the conversations because this presented firstly, a practical problem in terms of prison security and also made demands on the availability of the tape-recorder each day when other teachers needed it. Tape-recording also made some of the men feel uncomfortable and inhibited in their learning or more general classroom behaviour. I simply wrote down what had occurred in some of the sessions and documented the discussions which took place focusing on the subject-matter of sociology. The men became accustomed to my 'scribbling', as they described it, whilst they 'talked'. I worked with complete blocks of conversations in order to convey more of a sense of context than would be possible with pages of transcription symbols, rather than transcribe each and every conversation.

The following 'classroom conversation'—as the 'bits' of data became known—illustrates the kind of discussion that was looked at throughout my research. This particular example was used to show that student-teacher interaction in a prison setting is complex because it involves more than simply passing on new knowledge. It is about 'openness' or trust between teacher and student for one thing, especially with regard to what is being said in the classroom context. The men were discussing what was current Conservative Government policy with regard to family responsibility and child delinquency:

A: I believe it should be partly the State and partly the family who has responsibility. You see, you can educate the kids at nursery schools when they're very young.

B: But that doesn't mean anything, it's gotta be down to the individual ...

A: You see I've worked with young kids in Belfast, on the estate, they get into joy-riding, stealing electrical goods and so on. Then what happens? They bring the police back to the estate, we don't want that; we, the community should deal with it. We try and explain this to the kids, but then it's coming up to Christmas say, and they've no money and they want things for presents and so on. In some ways you can't blame them.

A: Do you think adults have a moral responsibility—as parents—towards ensuring their kids don't do these things?

B: You can't—never mind the New Right and what they say. If you have a kid on the streets in London making five grand a day from selling crack, that, for a kid from an inner city area, is more than he might get in a year, so you can't just take that away from him. What alternative can you give him? What is there? There's got to be something else to replace that, he's not going to give it up that easily. It's about money and survival.

What this brief example also shows is that the men would 'disclose' knowledge in the course of classroom conversations which they might not have done in other circumstances—not that this is in any sense incriminatory—it simply highlights the fact that, in the context of learning on this kind of course, a student's own life experiences are full of social comment. That social comment, in a prison setting, offers insights into a world that most people might choose to ignore, but it is no less valid for that. An obvious comparison can be made with adult students in adult educational settings who also 'use' memory and the recalling of personal life experiences to enhance their learning and make sense of their world.

Researchers have to sometimes concede that they mentally become part of the 'world' being studied and so the prison researcher's dilemma becomes grounded in the question 'Am I truly a part of the world I study?' This cannot be answered with the desired candour of the 'total participant'. To have been truly a part of the world of a maximum security prison would quite simply have meant being there 24 hours a day, seven days a week—and serving a five to 35 year 'stretch'. As both researcher *and* teacher, becoming 'accustomed' to the closed, highly regulated prison environment where some people are detained indefinitely due to the nature of their alleged offence, takes a while. It presents the kind of challenge that places unconsidered and occasionally unheard of demands upon both teacher/researcher and prisoner/student. The demands of both the prison (for the researcher/teacher) and imprisonment (for the prisoners) underpin subsequent research relationships which are also social relationships, which in turn shape the research itself and hence the degree of respondent involvement.

Those relationships, ideally, are also based on perceiving prisoners as people because the cultural 'baggage' associated with the label of prisoner/criminal/offender can be as damaging to the research project as any other factors which may affect the validity of the work. The quality and quantity of information received from the men in my own study would not have been forthcoming at all had there been the slightest attempt to deny them their individuality, autonomy and humanity—a vital component when it comes to gaining 'access' to the prisoner's world.

A mutual working relationship was built up with prisoners throughout the period of the research which in some respects contrasted with the differing attitudes of prison officers towards those imprisoned, some of whom believed that they worked with 'the dangerous garbage of society', as one officer informed me. Adapting to these contradictory attitudes and perceptions means that diplomacy plays a key role in prison research. Being diplomatic becomes second nature as you satisfy both the demands of the prison and the demands of your students. Diplomacy above all, if conducting a case study with prisoners, means spending time talking to your respondents about your research. It means for example, explaining why you are writing certain things down, asking if there are any objections to the inclusion of particular remarks, making judgements about certain statements in terms of their 'sincerity', veracity or degree of potential to cause offence or be misconstrued. It also means 'removing' data if someone asks you to, either for reasons of security or peace of mind. Diplomacy and being tactful are therefore crucial tools for the prison researcher. Together with trust, they form the basis of wider access and positive research relationships.

Other useful tools, as I discovered, were flexibility, adaptability and empathy which helped create an informal, facilitative learning atmosphere that countered the negativity experienced elsewhere in the prison. 'In here, Anne, you can just be yourself', was a sentiment frequently expressed about the classroom. Access to prisoners can be construed in a number of ways. Not only has the actual physical difficulty of gaining entry to a prison to be considered, i.e. facing the 'gate' each morning, removing items from pockets, removing shoes, outer clothing etc., but there is also the difficulty of building up sufficient trust to form the positive research relationships already mentioned. Perhaps a brief example illustrates the point. Some men would literally become bored either with discussing research matters or the subject-matter under discussion and would leave the class for 'association' (meeting with other prisoners from other classes whilst down on education). This would not be tolerated or expected in a 'standard' educational setting. In prison, it was the norm—depending on which prison officers were on duty.

Tact again plays an important role. The 'blankers-off' as one member of the group christened these prisoners, often had more important things to think about, were 'newcomers' to the prison or group and felt insecure, or, realistically speaking were too busy dealing with drug problems or even drug dealing/dealers. Disruption and interruption were characteristic of prison routine and awareness of this in the classroom was also essential. It formed the context of the study as did awareness of group dynamics. Murderers, terrorists, armed robbers and 'drug barons' do not necessarily agree on all things and the 'way-in' can close up very rapidly if people do not 'gel' as a group in any research setting. If some 'class-mates' vacated the classroom, this was as much respected, by other class members, as noted or commented upon.

It rapidly became clear that the prisoners had 'knowledge' about their own setting which I did not share. This, as it would in all kinds of similar research studies, shifted the power-balance in their favour according to which 'role' was being played, i.e. teacher/researcher, prisoner/student/respondent. Often the men would 'talk' and I would 'listen', a 'mirror-image' of the (stereo)typical student/teacher relationship. There would invariably be a few moments of unease in the classroom as new parameters of behaviour or new 'role-sets' (Merton, 1957) became established. As Willis states, 'The ethnographic account ... , records a crucial level of experience ...' (1993: 94) and awareness of how research relationships impact upon research forms as much a part of that 'crucial level of experience' as does the subject-matter being investigated. The flexibility, adaptability and empathy mentioned above were grounded in diplomacy, tact and trust to the extent that 'listening' to individual prisoners discussing their life experiences either against a background of sociological knowledge or simply 'just talking' provided a unique experience in itself.

The prisoner-students in my study were said to 'weave' their learning processes together into a synthesis of outcomes which had a potentiality for 'change' (Reuss, 1997). It seemed to make sense that I too, was involved in a form of weaving together the teaching and researching experiences and practices into a fuller or broader account of what actually takes place in a prison classroom in order to 'flesh out' the actual research. This provides a realistic account and makes others aware of the circumstances of the research (Pawson and Tilley, 1997: xiv). It also shows that building up a 'working' set of research relationships alongside a 'working' set of teaching relationships is important because one set has a 'knock-on' effect on the other. The two sets of relationships have to be worked in tandem, they form the totality of the classroom interactions and are continuously developing throughout any research period. In the interests of maintaining positive working relationships with the prisoners, I would abide by their requests not to discuss research matters if officers entered the room. As Diesing observes, the task of the field work researcher:

> ... is to become part of the community or group he is studying. This task imposes an essential requirement of permissiveness on the researcher; he must make himself acceptable, allow himself to be socialised, accept the point of view and ideology of his hosts. (1972: 144).

Field relations were an important consideration in my study where the 'messages' which were 'passed' to the prisoners via clothing, spoken language, body language, personal demeanour and so on were of great significance—metaphorically speaking. In a prison context they can mean the difference between obtaining vast amounts of data or none at all:

> Impressions of the researcher that pose an obstacle to access must be avoided or countered as far as possible, while those that facilitate it must

be encouraged, within the limits set by ethical considerations. (Hammersley and Atkinson, 1983: 78).

Acceptable relationships with the group had to be maintained, not least as a female researcher conducting research in an all male prison. Dress, demeanour, adoption of language codes and particular types of behaviour all become additional tools in the ethnographer's resource bank. If the researcher in prison 'gets it wrong', the whole project can be jeopardised on a number of levels, from simply gaining security clearance, to prisoners refusing to join the class. In such a setting, impression management counts for a great deal. The choice of 'what to wear for work' takes on a whole new significance when working in a prison as was pointed out to me by other education staff and prisoners when I wore a short skirt!

Issues of gender neutrality must be considered by those wishing to conduct research in prisons but only because the research process is inevitably coloured by the adoption of stereotypical male and female roles—rightly or wrongly as a strategy for survival in a prison setting. The reason for this is because the work is being undertaken in a setting where role-playing as a strategy for survival is honed to a fine art by penal practitioners, prisoners and civilian staff alike. It becomes a form of 'normalising' one's behaviour and the adoption of particular roles offsets the symbolic representation of the total institution of the prison. The roles both normalise and regulate the social situations and experiences which individuals create there. From a realistic perspective, being a female researcher in an all male prison not 'working for the authorities' did ensure a willingness on the part of respondents to co-operate. I would however, be loathe to consider that I had presented myself to the prisoner-students as a '... socially acceptable incompetent' (Hammersley and Atkinson, 1983: 85).

Self-presentation is a sensitive issue for the prison researcher impacting upon matters of subjectivity and objectivity and compounded by gender relations. Empathy with the prisoner can mean the difference between gaining results or not and throughout my own fieldwork it became apparent that interaction *was* coloured by gender relations which simply became part of the reality of the classroom experience. This in turn became an essential dimension of the research relationship contributing to the 'way-in'. It is extremely difficult under the circumstances of this kind of research, for the researcher to remain 'neutral'.

Understanding the culture of the participants in prison ethnographies is another crucial aspect of any research to be undertaken there. Assuming the prior existence of a prison (sub)culture can be dangerous though because, if nothing else, it encourages the development of even more stereotypical ideas about those who have allegedly offended. However, that is not to say that such a culture does not 'exist' in the minds and hearts of those sentenced and the sentencers. It quite patently does; just as cultural attitudes, beliefs, customs and ideals pervade wider society so too, do they characterise prison communities.

I quickly had to 'learn' the maximum security prison culture from the perspective of the prisoners; a culture which has a long 'history' both written and oral (Bryans and Wilson, 1998; Boyle, 1977; Muncie and McLaughlin, 1996; Cavadino and Dignan, 1997; Morgan, 1999) which shapes and re-shapes interaction within the prison . It was in my interests to do so to produce results and build up a close rapport but one which hopefully did not deteriorate into 'over-rapport' (Hammersley and Atkinson, 1983: 98-104). Achieving a balance between insider-outsider relationships or 'familiarity' and 'strangeness', in order to maintain validity contributes to the pattern of research rather than detracts from it. 'Going native' in a maximum security dispersal prison is perhaps not the best recommended approach; equally the adoption of a 'marginal position' and the maintenance of that position is not easy in such an environment. Balancing the many roles and subjective feelings about imprisonment, long sentences, punishment, justice and injustice with the more objective task of conducting research was something of which I became acutely conscious, for not only does a prison contain individuals—in every sense of the word—it is a place of work for many others who firmly believe that they are simply doing a job.

There are observable and highly visible differences in the distribution of power between individuals within a prison. The prejudices, hostilities, tensions and stigmatisations which exist between groups and individuals have become the fabric of the prison itself and as such are definitive of it. The prison researcher has to adopt specific strategies for dealing with the divisions, inequalities and sometimes injustices which stem from them. As such the strategies and techniques adopted shape the research itself.

METHODOLOGICAL TECHNIQUES

What are the techniques that one can hope to employ both to facilitate and develop research into a realistic account of what takes place in a prison classroom? It seemed to me that there were three important things to consider:

- 'ice-breaking';
- whether the research was 'contaminated by sympathy';
- the role of the respondent in the research or 'respondent validation'.

Ice-breaking

As I began my research, I was acutely aware of how difficult it would be to maintain the equilibrium between a 'detached' account and a highly 'subjective' tale from the field. The issue of validity posed quite a problem initially but the extent to which 'bias' or 'contamination' would be present in the research findings, was addressed by taking the view that the methods I used would add a dimension to the work in reproducing and creating the reality of classroom practice. Again working the teaching and research relationships in tandem, presenting the research findings back to the men produced positive 'feedback' on what had occurred in the classroom. Their knowledgeability, their expertise in relation to the situation they were in proved to be invaluable in fleshing out the context of the research. It also added humour and humanity to, what at times, appeared to be a very 'de-human' environment.

Reading the first 'instalment' of the research to the first group of prisoner-students with whom I worked was the most difficult aspect of the entire research project—akin to 'stealing souls' or the absolute embarrassment of hearing oneself speak for the first time on a tape-recorder. I wondered at the time, how many prison researchers had ever felt more 'criminal' than their respondents. They were quiet, anticipatory, a little tense and I was under the spotlight. Would they approve? Had I recounted things accurately? Would they really feel embarrassed? The only voice I could hear was Tony's, from three months earlier:

Everything you do and say is written down in here.

Then Dudley broke the ice, giggled and said:

That sounds really posh, man. It don't sound like us ... but that's okay.

And the research relationship survived.

Research 'ice-breaking' is not easy, but worth the effort in a prison context. Throughout the study, as I gave sections of the work to the men to read, their reactions varied from humour, 'Eh, Allan, you were going on a bit there'—to the more poignant 'I really miss Darren, you know, he brought a spark into the group, even if I didn't always agree with him. Reading that through has brought it back as if it were yesterday. I wonder where he is now?' 'Bloody Winston Green, the bastards,' came the reply.

Reading or going through one's research with one's respondents is reminiscent of the account Willis provides of how his research role was seen by the 'Hammertown Lads' after they had read his early drafts:

Bill: The bits about us were simple enough.

John: It's the bits in between.

Joey: Well, I started to read it, I started at the very beginning, y'know I was gonna read as much as I could, then I just packed it in, just started readin' the parts about us and then little bits in the middle.

Spanksy: The parts what you wrote about us, I read those, but it was, y'know, the parts what actually were actually describing the book like I didn't … (Willis; 1993: 195)

If the men requested that an item be removed because it was of a 'sensitive' nature, then the request would be complied with, as previously stated, keeping the proceedings as 'democratic' as was possible and helping to develop the project into one of open involvement and interaction between researcher and 'researched'.

This was evidenced by the fact that when the whole of the first chapter of the research was read by the men involved with the study, they were highly critical in that they felt that much more ought to be said about the prison, and could be said, from their perspective. Despite this, they agreed it was the best thing they had read about prisons. They were anxious to ensure, for example, that I had the exact and accurate times of the daily regime and movements, and there was considerable debate about the different regimes on different wings until consensus was reached. This kind of 'detail' mattered a great deal, in that it had to convey a 'sense' of the place. Similarly, when looking at 'the prisoners language', there were so many regional variations, that a great deal of time had to be spent working through and refining the definitions that characterised 'prison talk'.

Overall however, responses to my research differed according to the following criteria:

(a) their concerns for myself as researcher in such an environment

(b) embarrassment—i.e. 'Did I really say that?'

(c) any possible 'knock-on' effects from the research in terms of their sentence duration, self- preservation and survival within the prison system; and

(d) facing up to their own situation, as research of this nature confronts the individual with the 'truth' of their position and life-experiences; in a prison environment, many inmates will 'deny' this in order to 'survive'.

These responses highlighted a further dimension of conducting prison research which neither myself nor the men had thought about, i.e. the 'sensitivity' of reading the work in terms of its personal effect on both parties. Not so much 'sensitive' because we were in a prison and were constantly aware of security matters, but it was more a deeper sensitivity which grew towards the situation of imprisonment as a means of punishment and towards the implications of criticising penal policy and practice. In this respect the men's concerns for me as researcher were quite marked, particularly where any criticism of regimes was either explicitly or implicitly made. They would say, 'Can you say that? Watch yourself—you know what the system is like, don't you go losing your job 'cos of us'.

The responses of each man were coloured by his own interpretations of what had been written, particularly if named in a classroom conversation. Ted, for example, would often say, 'Is that what I said?' and Allan would add, 'Yes, come on Ted, you know you did!' Others would say, 'It's a good job only you hear us saying these things—we hope!', then light heartedly dismissed with, 'Wait till she's famous, then everybody will know what you said'.

Facing up to their situation of imprisonment was something which the men had to do with not a little courage and honesty when they chose to be involved with the research project. In a sense they had to be made aware that this would happen from the start—confronting prisoners with work which describes 'their' prison, 'their' imprisonment, its routine, its practices and in particular discussing elements of research which, in this instance concerned personal change, is no easy task. As a prison researcher, I was aware of a degree of contradiction and tension with this aspect of the work which deepened as the work progressed, but then dissipated as I learned (from the men themselves) that 'going soft' on prisoners does not achieve anything.

Being realistic about imprisonment by balancing one's involvement and detachment (Elias, 1987) achieves more positive results; what the men responded to in my research, was respect for each of them as an individual. If anyone did not wish to be present in the classroom when research matters were being discussed, then that choice was respected. If things were tense in the prison and the men were 'up tight', the research was simply left alone. Alternatively, if the men started to discuss research spontaneously, then teaching was discarded and we had a 'research session'. The different responses and the reasons for them, were important and had to be 'managed' for work to proceed.

Where the level of respondent involvement is high as it was in my work as a prison ethnographer, what has to be learned and dealt with is the fact that 'prisoner paranoia' runs high and is very infectious. However, this dissipates over time too, as ultimately, one accepts that a higher authority will probably decide what may or may not be included in the research anyway. The success or failure of 'ice-breaking' highlights only one dilemma for those choosing to undertake prison research—ice-breaking is only one 'tool' in the prison researcher's tool kit, and as all successful robbers tell me, 'You have to go properly tooled-up, Anne'.

Contaminated by sympathy?

As Cohen and Taylor (1972: 180) pointed out after conducting research in Durham prison, when a researcher enters a 'deviant's' environment, any work produced is often assumed, by those who take the time to scrutinise it, to be tainted by bias. The researcher needs to be aware that the 'weaving' and 'interweaving' of interactions between the researcher and researched is not something that can be lightly dismissed as 'bias'. Efforts have to be made to find the links and connections which bind people together in social situations. Just as Cohen and Taylor 'walked into the wing each week for over three years', finding it 'difficult not to feel sympathy with the prisoners' situation' (1972: 181), I too felt that my involvement with the prisoner-students and my account of classroom practices could be open to criticism in terms of researcher bias.

'Taking sides' when conducting research, particularly with those designated 'offenders', presents its own peculiar set of problems, often best described as 'moral dilemmas'. I felt that one way of resolving the issue was to have recourse to empathy rather than sympathy. The individual moralities and courses of action taken by prisoners, prior to imprisonment and even whilst imprisoned, have to be 'overlooked'. They cannot and perhaps should not, be judged by the researcher, for judgement has already been made at the moment of sentencing. A degree of 'moral distancing' has to take place. The empathy arises from awareness of any human qualities and mutual respect between researcher and researched, and from both parties being fully aware of each other's capabilities as human beings. Empathy can also develop if a researcher in prison *listens* to the prisoner.

In addition, the researcher who also teaches cannot fail to notice that some kind of 'transformation' may be occurring in students throughout the teaching and learning process. Any commentary on this, as part of the research process may well be misinterpreted as bias. Education courses in prisons create a potentially favourable 'climate' for the students who attend them, a climate in which there is plenty of room for personal growth. Commenting on the positive outcomes of that process does not amount to bias in favour of prisoners; although it may be interpreted as such by those with a more cynical approach.

'Contamination by sympathy' can be also avoided if the 'discovery and depiction' (Becker, 1963: 168) of what occurs in a prison classroom is portrayed in such a way that it is seen as contributing to existing literature on crime and deviance in a positive manner. Much of this literature seems devoid of 'people'; not only does exclusion and marginalisation dog offenders once sentenced, there seems to be little remembrance of the social networks in which they are embedded and are capable of creating and re-creating anew—whether in prison or beyond release. Becker reminds the researcher of the difficulties of the task:

It is not easy to study deviants. Because they are regarded as outsiders by the rest of society and because they themselves tend to regard the rest of society as outsiders, the student who would discover the facts about deviance has a substantial barrier to climb before he will be allowed to see the things he needs to see. (1963: 168).

Ethnography in general creates *and* reproduces reality. It is about more than 'discovering the facts' for it reproduces the reality of a world that is meaningful to those who inhabit it. Imprisonment is certainly a 'meaningful' experience to prisoners, but that 'meaningfulness' can be either positive or negative for individual prisoners. Undoubtedly for many, it tends to be negative and one of the more interesting aspects of having conducted research in a prison is the fact that when others realise that your research describes *something positive* that can occur to people whilst in prison, then it seems to stand at odds with the stereotypical view of prisons as 'nasty' places where the last thing you do is acquire degree level qualifications. The ethnographic researcher in prison may have to face criticism of her work for no other reason than, in 'reproducing reality', it depicts people—who are supposed to be 'being punished'—actually 'enjoying' the social activity of learning. It seems that anyone who contributes to such a process must be biased in favour of the wrong-doer; but such assumptions are misplaced. Prison classroom ethnographies where teaching and researching go hand-in-hand invariably contain detailed documentation of prison life and prison classroom practice. This means that there are both 'good' and 'bad' tales to tell about what goes on in prisons and about what constitutes an 'effective' programme of learning within a prison environment. As yet, there is no law in place which states that learning is a crime and that it should not be enjoyed.

Research findings from the prison classroom should define prisoners as people *and not solely as prisoners.* It does not automatically follow that bias will colour those findings because what the researcher does is simply obtain, in Becker's words, '... an accurate and complete account of what deviants do', (1963: 170)—at least what they 'do' in the prison classroom.

The conducting of a prison classroom ethnography *does* mean 'gaining the confidence of those one studies', spending months building up research relationships, working out how best to 'gain access' and committing oneself to research over a fairly long period of time. It means making 'moral shifts', challenging many moralities, accepting that one might have acquired certain kinds of 'new' knowledge that was not consciously sought—for example, robbing a bank is *never* quite tackled as depicted in the movies! The prison classroom ethnography must be taken *for what it is.* It is not a tale of moral condemnation on the actions of individual prisoners. They have already been judged by their peers at the moment of sentencing. A prison classroom ethnography is an account of meaningful interaction between individuals in a highly regulated environment; the appeal to validity lies in the depiction of the reality of the experience for those involved. As Becker indicates:

> If we study the processes involved in deviance, then, we must take the viewpoint of at least one of the groups involved, either of those who are treated as deviant or of those who label others as deviant. (1963: 173).

The research I conducted attempted to ' ...capture the perspectives of ... participants' (Becker, 1963), either with respect for their views on prisons or with regard for their interpretations of the outcomes of learning, but my analysis moved beyond Becker's approach of seeing the world from the 'viewpoint of the deviant or labeller', because it examined the context, mechanisms and outcomes from the perspective of researcher/respondent/teacher/student/prisoner. The capturing of perspectives and viewpoints in a prison classroom where students were engaged in the task of evaluating and assessing the perspectives and viewpoints of others (through studying sociology) is a multi-dimensional process. One of the dimensions of that process in my own work was the realisation that my viewpoint became firmly embedded in the prisoner's own critique of imprisonment; I therefore had to 'learn' to be both 'involved' and 'detached'—'contaminated and uncontaminated' in my approach.

Respondent validation—a building block?
A full understanding of *prisoner* education can only be achieved by asking the prisoner—as student—what perceptions he or she had of the experience of learning the subject in question. Hence there has to be a focus on subject-matter being taught, classroom interaction, issues relating to the way in which the prisoner sees himself or herself and ultimately on learning outcomes—if there is indeed to be any assessment of what constitutes a successful programme of education in a prison.

The depiction of classroom practice has to be 'fleshed out' and this was done by showing the 'research subjects' the accounts I collected of their learning processes and experiences. Their comments contributed towards a more holistic view of those learning processes which, in turn, balanced my own. As a form of respondent validation, this lessened any perceived 'contamination'—by sympathy or otherwise, simply because the participants too had knowledge *of the context* (in this case the prison classroom), that I did not possess.

In a prison, it is undoubtedly the case that one's students will have access to what Hammersley and Atkinson (1983) describe as 'information networks ... more powerful than those accessible to the ethnographer'.

These have to be drawn on despite the criticism that one's research 'subjects' will only be concerned with personal interest and may be over-anxious to re-interpret anything that the researcher may present. This is a falsely naïve view. As Hammersley and Atkinson indicate, respondents react to research in ways which are inevitably ' ... coloured by their social position and their perceptions of the research act ...' (1983, 197).

Suffice it to say that most people in prison are *acutely* aware of their social position and much can be gained from their insight and reactions to other people's interpretations of their situation. This forms yet a further dimension to the interactive research process and lends itself well to the conducting of research in a prison environment.

In my own research, as the work progressed, the men would pick up on different group dynamics as revealed in conversations, different memories of other events taking place within the prison and different emphases placed by each other on the same basic subject-matter. Frequently their remarks would run along the lines of 'Oh yes, I remember when we did that,' or 'That was a bloody good rant we had then,' or 'That was just before so-and-so got moved' or 'We were doing that before the riot.' Such comments reinforce the claims that the experience of learning can be meaningful *because* it is located and embedded in a much wider social and interactive context. It does not occur in isolation from other experiences and events.

The expertise of both respondent and researcher when combined, contribute to the findings of the research. The contributions of the prisoners as students to my own research lay in the extent to which they accepted or agreed with my claims. Those who had been present in the group for longer periods of time, were better able to do this than those who were 'new' to the course and 'new' to the prison because their level of 'expertise' was greater—both in terms of the course, the research and in assimilating the prison culture.

The 'final product' of the research, however, rests with the researcher. It cannot rest with the respondents because the 'flow of (research) understanding' (Pawson and Tilley, 1997: 166), comes to an end as the research nears completion. In short, the researcher who presents final drafts to her subjects finds that the response is more likely to be as follows: 'It sounds really hard, I don't really understand it', 'It looks really good, it sounds like the books we have to read'. Flattering though this may be to the researcher, it again reinforces the claim that respondent validation is more to do with the fact that their views are a *part* of the research method, they form a 'building-block' (Reuss, 1997) towards putting together a more complete and realistic picture of the research. The end product does remain 'distanced' from the respondents—it moves beyond their involvement and their concerns.

However, in 'showing' one's research findings to one's research subjects, it does mean that there is more than one set of data available because this kind of 'feedback' ensures that the original data is not taken at 'face value', although this would be highly unlikely for anyone conducting research in a prison environment. It also has to be remembered that the researcher's interpretations of what happens in a prison classroom will not necessarily coincide with the prisoner-student's. There is a degree of 'selection' attached to the process which is inevitable when observations are being carried out (Bloor, 1987)—respondents do organize their worlds differently from researchers, but it can be said that a certain amount of 'self-recognition' is also taking place. The entire research process is therefore meaningful to both parties as active participants engaged in the construction of social reality and its validity is assured as such.

My own research was not 'controlled' or 'manipulated' by outsiders as stated earlier, a fact which was to become something of an issue for Cohen and Taylor writing approximately thirty years ago (1972). In the time which has elapsed since they conducted their research, not that much has changed in terms of psychological survival for those serving long sentences and their work is permeated with the kind of psychological stories with which anyone working with long-term prisoners is all too familiar. There is a hint of pessimism in their understanding and analyses of the effects of such sentences on those who receive them and in their depiction of survival. It depicts a kind of human tragedy on a vast and much misunderstood scale. Beneath the angst encountered in a prison and the perceived amorality, the basic human interactions are grounded in the *social* and by focusing on some of those interactions in the classroom from a researcher's point of view, it can be shown that there is also present, in the prison, a degree of mutuality and reciprocity which can be drawn upon and which moves beyond the pessimism of 'nothing works' in prisons.

GENERALIZABILITY

As a final assessment of having conducted ethnographic research in a prison environment, the remaining question I had to address centred on whether or not the findings of the study and the concepts explored were readily transferable to other educational programmes in prison settings. My findings seemed to indicate that a course of higher education in prison could bring about change or transformation in prisoner-students who assimilated the course material in a complex process of learning and social interaction which is 'woven', or synthesised into their life-experience. Elements of this process are retained by individual prisoners through time and become embedded in their conscience, if interpreted as *meaningful*. The learning process thus acquires the *potential* to influence or direct post-release behaviour. The learning is also, for some prisoners, a process of empowerment. (Reuss, 1997). Not all prisoner-students *have* to study degree level sociology for this to take place and potentially affect post-release behaviour. *What is of significance is to explore the actual context in which those unique processes are embedded and through which prisoners mediate their learning experiences.* If those experiences are, or have been interpreted, as worthwhile then the potential exists for personal development and possibly a change in offending behaviour. (Reuss, 1999: 117).

The most significant question underpinning my research was undoubtedly 'To what extent do people care about change in prisoners?'; i.e. in the sense that prisoners may 'change' their offending behaviour, or 'stop' it altogether as a result of attending some educational course whilst imprisoned. The extent to which a prison classroom ethnography can throw light on this is difficult to assess because the question masks the real issues for some within penal policy and practice who are far more concerned with the kind of evaluation that focuses on whether or not 'prison works' as an effective form of deterrence in a much more general sense.

It has to be acknowledged that the 'desire' of each prisoner to 'change' is subjectively motivated irrespective of what anyone else may desire of offenders as a whole. To some extent, therein lies the problem because prisoners are frequently perceived as a homogeneous group rather than as individual people with individual tastes, preferences and life-styles, whose commonality lies *only* in their incarceration. With this in mind, then it can be said that findings from my own study which show that learning processes within a prison classroom have significance and can potentially affect post-release behaviour, *are* transferable to other courses and other educational programmes within prisons. As stated above, if researchers investigate the actual context of learning in prisons and focus on the structures, interactions and interdependencies which weave together on courses to form observable phenomena, then the reality of prison classroom practice can be better understood and the way paved for more appropriate and effective regimes.

The complexity of each prisoner's 'life-course', the memories, ideas and existing knowledge streams brought to each class meeting can only be hinted at; future life beyond prison remains uncertain and unknowable and so the focus of the classroom ethnography has to remain on the *potential* of each learning experience to assist prisoner-students in defining their situation in relation to wider social contexts and networks that bind people together. Learning in any context is not simply a uni-directional, linear process, despite the fact that it is useful to construct such a 'temporal sequence'. This is merely a useful 'device', an analytical tool, to show that prisoners cannot and should not be seen as *temporally* constrained within the prison. There has been a life prior to imprisonment and for all but a small minority, there will be one beyond.

CONCLUSION

To enter a maximum security prison and conduct research may not be something to which most people aspire. To have done so as a 'research-insider' provided me with a unique opportunity to describe a relatively little-known 'world' and yet one which is still central to the understanding of punishment in a modern society. Whilst my research does not furnish details of every single aspect of prison life, it depicts the minutiae of classroom practice and offers an approach to understanding the potential capacity of education in a prison setting to re-invest offenders with some measure of social and cultural capital when they may otherwise have none. Furthermore, in describing 'The Researcher's Tale', others may be provided with an insight into how best to approach a prison setting, research it and survive the experience.

There are complex ethical issues to consider for any researcher engaged in this kind of work, issues which have to be confronted on both a personal and public level. Evaluations and assessments of one's approach are ever present, and sometimes the question of whether it is all worthwhile is more than apparent, meaning the research, the education of offenders, the imprisonment of offenders and so on, because sadly, there is always the issue of whether anyone else really cares about what happens to those who are imprisoned.

Observing those 'we study' does not seem to be the most politically correct of approaches in this day and age, but the classic studies of interaction in the classroom (Hargreaves, 1967; Lacey, 1970; Keddie, 1971; Willis, 1977) stand as testament to the importance of simply being aware of 'what goes on' in a classroom between student, teacher, institution and home (Entwhistle, 1987). 'What goes on' in a prison classroom is, of course, so intimately bound up with questions of rehabilitation and recidivism that there is a tendency on the part of practitioners to overlook the prisoner and what he or she gets from the experience as a *person* and as an *individual learner*. It is also worth remembering that most people have a fairly negative attitude towards the prison population; the prisoner is seen as the 'other', the 'outsider', someone who is taken 'out' of society and who certainly does not 'belong' in it. The exclusion and marginalisation of those who have offended and been imprisoned is a well known fact, but it perhaps has to be acknowledged that:

The need to learn the culture of those we are studying is most obvious in the case of societies other than our own. Here, not only may we not know *why* people do what they do, often we do not even know *what* they are doing. (Hammersley and Atkinson,1983: 7)

The sad truth is that for most people, 'studying' the prisoner as the 'other', as a member of a 'society other than our own' is exactly what many prison researchers do in order to 'make sense' of behaviour perceived as 'abnormal' What is often overlooked is the fact that prisons are culturally acceptable institutions 'containing' people who are not culturally acceptable. This poses something of a problem when prisoners have to 'rejoin' society, because they are not seen as 'people'.

At the risk of being labelled 'con-lover'—and one has to be realistic here—the well-being of those imprisoned *should* be of concern to a wider public, in much the same way as the well-being of victims of crime. The programmes and activities which prisoners are expected to attend are now focused on addressing offending behaviour at the expense of traditional education programmes which have also been shown to have considerable benefits for the prisoner (Duguid, 1997; Davidson, 1995; Flynn and Price, 1995; Reuss, 1997; West, 1997; Williford, 1994; Woolf, 1991). Researchers should be given every opportunity to develop methods of understanding what 'goes on' in prison classrooms because prisoner education is not to be lightly dismissed as something that simply keeps inmates 'occupied' for a few hours each day. It offers, potentially, a 'way forward' whilst doing time and it is hoped that this chapter has given some indication of one approach to studying how that process occurs.

BIBLIOGRAPHY for *Chapter 2*

Atkinson P. (1990), *The Ethnographic Imagination*, London: Routledge

Becker H. (1963), *Outsiders*, New York: Macmillan

Bloor M. (1987), Shorter Report: 'On The Analysis of Observational Data: A Discussion of the Worth and Uses of Inductive Techniques and Respondent Validation'

Bryans S. and Wilson D. (1998), *The Prison Governor: Theory and Practice*, Leyhill: *Prison Service Journal*

Cohen S. and Taylor L. (1972), *Psychological Survival*, Harmondsworth: Penguin.

Davidson H. S. (ed.) (1995), *Schooling in a 'Total Institution', Critical Perspectives on Prison Education*, Westport, Conn.: Bergin and Garvey

Diesing P. (1972), *Patterns of Discovery in the Social Sciences*, London: Routledge and Kegan Paul

Duguid S. (1983), 'Origins and Development of University Education at Matsqui Institution', *Canadian Journal of Criminology*; July, 295-308

Duguid S. (1986), 'What Works in Prison Education?', *Adult Education*, Vol. 58: (4), 329-334.

Duguid S. (1995), 'People Are Complicated and Prisoners are People—Using Recidivism to Evaluate Effectiveness in Prison Education Programmes'.

Duguid S. (1997), 'Education Change and Transformation: The Prison Experience, Humanities Programme', Vancouver: Simon Fraser University.

Flynn N. (1995), 'Criminal Classes', *Prison Report*, The Prison Reform Trust Magazine, vol. 33, Winter 1995, London: Prison Reform Trust

Flynn N. and Price D. (1995), *Education in Prisons: A National Survey*, London: Prison Reform Trust

Garland D. (1990), *Punishment and Modern Society*, Oxford: Clarendon Press

Hammersley M. and Atkinson P. (1983), *Ethnography, Principles in Practice*, London: Routledge

Kaplan A. (1964), *The Conduct of Inquiry*, New York: Chandler

Mitchell J. C. (1983), 'Case and Situation Analysis', *Sociological Review*, Vol. 32, (2), 187-211.

Pawson R. and Tilley, N. (1997), *Realistic Evaluation*, London: Sage

Pawson R. (1989), *A Measure for Measures*, London: Routledge

Prison Reform Trust; (1995), *'A Good and Useful Life'*, Constructive Prison Regimes, London: Prison Reform Trust

Ragin C. and Becker H. (eds.) (1992), *What is a Case?: Exploring the Foundations of Social Inquiry*, Cambridge: Cambridge University Press

Reuss A. (1997), *Higher Education and Personal Change in Prisoners*, Unpublished thesis, University of Leeds

Reuss A. (1999), 'Prison(er) Education', *The Howard Journal of Criminal Justice*, Vol. 38, (2), 113-127

West T. (1997), *Prisons of Promise*, Winchester: Waterside Press

Williford M. (1994), *Higher Education in Prisons: A Contradiction in Terms?*, Phoenix, Ariz.: American Council on Education, Oryx Press

Woolf Report (1991), *Prison Disturbances April 1990*, London: HMSO.

CHAPTER 3

Theory and the Correctional Enterprise

Stephen Duguid

What kind of tale should a theorist tell? A 'tall tale' the cynic might well respond or at least one that explains why so often in the public policy realm in which prisons exist the theory-ridden tail so often seems to wag the dog. The pessimist might call, on the other hand for a tale about the impoverishment of theory in prison work, a recounting of the dismal series of failures that flow from flawed theories of crime causation and cure. The pragmatist, though, would ask for a tale explaining why the means are never sufficient to implement the theories that are generated in our universities, institutes, think tanks and government offices. This tale, alas, must be more modest, being a brief review of the role of theory in the prison/correctional enterprise followed by a recounting of my own encounter with theory.

If notions of unity, holism and continuum can be said to characterise the mental world of many cultures, in the West, by way of contrast, the cultivation of opposites in the form of dualisms has held sway. Starting with the Cartesean division of mind and body we travel daily through a maze of oppositions such as self and other, nature and culture, male and female, good and evil. Following a now internalised dialectic we are persuaded to frame these dualities as either/or choices, as in the currently popular 'Jobs versus the environment' or the perennial 'men versus women'. One of the more popular dualisms in Western culture is the juxtaposition of 'theory' with 'practice', the implication being that there are people who 'do things'—practitioners, those who practice—and people who think about the doing of things—theorisers. And, of course, there is the old homily that 'those who can, do and those who can't, teach'.

This dualistic worldview or 'way-of-seeing' is a kind of theory, perhaps a meta-theory, a way of organizing perceptions of the world that can be a guide to action and understanding.

The single-minded focus on choosing—on being 'us' or 'them' for instance—makes a fetish of simplicity and it is in this making of theory the handmaiden of simplicity that we begin to encounter serious difficulties when moving into the realms of policy and practice. In the criminal justice field, the Cartesean approach too often leads to either/or thinking in the solving of social problems, current examples being boot camps for juvenile delinquents, three-strikes and you're out for repeat offenders, and an 'eye for an eye' approach to sentencing. Lured by the siren call of simple solutions to complex problems, politicians, practitioners and the public call forth theories that explain and make a virtue of these solutions. These theories—the most current in corrections being that criminal deviance stems from deficits in so-called 'cognitive skills'—contain valuable truths but are too often forced by the engines of duality and simplicity to extend their claims beyond their reach. Practitioners are forced by policy-makers who have been convinced by professors that the latest theory, if applied with vigour and thoroughness, will finally give them the results they need to satisfy the public. The result is failure and public disillusionment. The Medical Model of the post-war era met this fate in the 1970s and one lives in expectation that the current 'tough-love' and 'tit-for-tat' theories that ground boot camps, three strikes and the death penalty will meet the same fate. For prison educators it seems just as likely that 'cognitive skills' will share that fate.

Theory, then, has a bad reputation. That eminently practical statesman, inventor and empiricist Thomas Jefferson (Matthews, 1984:1) warned us as early as 1787 that '... the moment a person forms a theory his imagination sees in every object only the traits which favour the theory.' Thus Aristotelians viewed the universe through the theory/lens of crystalline spheres with an unmoving earth at the centre and though despite his telescope Galileo was eventually forced to submit to the theory, he was rumoured to have muttered under his breath, '... and yet, it moves'. Some of the greatest and most tragic delusions of the twentieth century have their roots in such theory-driven perceptions. As well, novelists, artists and humanists in general warn us on a regular basis that no 'theory of human behaviour' can hope to capture the individual's inner world of assumptions that provide meaning and propel one to action.

And, of course, since every theory is met by a counter-theory and since both seem to change as often as the weather there is a great deal of popular cynicism about the whole theory-business. This popular cynicism is mirrored in contemporary intellectual circles by the post-modernists with their focus on 'difference', 'relativism' and 'subjectivity', making the idea of theory itself seem oddly out of date—despite the fact that post-modernism itself is a theory!

Adding to their fragility in the face of reality, theories often make claims to universality, to holding across cultures, across time and across genders. One thinks of the 'categorical imperative' of Immanuel Kant and the more modern moral development theory of Lawrence Kohlberg. Yet each claim to universality was countered by a claim of particularity— David Hume in the case of Kant and Carol Gilligan in the case of Kohlberg. Hume insisted that moral rules were reflective of conditions and since conditions changed, rules must change as well. Gilligan demonstrated that Kohlberg's universal stages of moral development were in fact gender specific, that women existed in a moral universe derived more from the realities of gender than from some hypothetical universal human nature. Increasingly, claims for the universality of a theory are greeted with suspicion, even in science where not only evolution and the 'Big Bang' remain 'theories' open to dispute but even gravity and the motions of the planets are viewed by some as grounded as much in supposition and language as in laws.

Still, despite these faults, correctives and suspicions, theoretical frameworks remain the essential lenses or filters through which people view information, select facts, study social reality, define problems, and eventually, construct solutions to those problems. Even when theories are wrong they can be useful—Aristotle's theory of the structure of the heavens, for instance, was able to predict the seasons, tides, eclipses and other important phenomena even with an unmoving earth at the centre of a crystal sphere. The world of crime, the criminal, prisons, and corrections provides especially fertile ground for such theoretical frameworks since it has historically been a world in which solutions to important human problems are at once intractable and yet jut as essential as knowing about the seasons, tides and eclipses. Unfortunately, it has proven to be highly susceptible to theories resembling the Aristotelean spheres—structurally neat, marginally functional but wrong.

For those of us involved in prison regimes or correctional systems (both 'regime' and 'system' implying approaches to the problem that are mired in theory, the one having military or governance roots and the other rooted in modern bureaucratic and systems theory) theory plays a role in at least three areas:

(1) diagnosing the problem of crime and deviance
(2) understanding the context of prison and imprisoned
(3) prescribing cures and predicting outcomes.

For those of us engaged with the more specific function of prisoner education, the theoretical perspectives that swirl about all three of these areas have a direct impact on how, what and whom we teach and in some cases whether we can teach at all. While such theories may emanate from universities and research centres and seem therefore far removed from the prison and the prison classroom, they in fact permeate the prison/correctional bureaucracy, have advocates in political circles and may at times even gain favour or earn disdain from the general public. They might, as well, enter the mental world of the classroom teacher, melding with existing educational theories in mysterious, sometimes fruitful and sometimes disastrous ways. Thus teachers can end up defining themselves as 'correctional educators', joining teams of experts dedicated to 'rehabilitation', transforming their classrooms into part of the punitive experience, or becoming the social worker or comrade of the oppressed prisoner—all in the service of a theory. While the predisposition of the teacher and the moral atmosphere of the prison play an important part in bringing about these shifts, they are as well grounded in the various criminological, sociological and psychological theories to which teachers in prison are exposed.

THEORIES ABOUT THE PROBLEM OF CRIME AND DEVIANCE

There are two basic sets of assumptions at work here, which one might think of as 'meta-theories' or theories-about-theories which generate sub-sets of theories which in turn lead to actions. On the one hand there is the approach to crime and deviance stemming from Plato (and Confucius) that starts from the position that humans are basically good, moral beings who commit evil acts either through ignorance or because of social conditions. From this assumption flow a series of theories by educators and sociologists about what should be done about crime and criminals. The opposite approach, central to much Christian teaching, holds that humans are fundamentally flawed, ego-driven, and perhaps even evil and hence must be restrained and, if possible, reformed or converted if they are to live a moral life. From this position flow a series of theories by moralists and psychologists about what should be done about crime and criminals. This is obviously one of the 'great divides' in human culture, and which of these approaches the prison educator finds affiliation with will have a great impact on all subsequent action in the classroom.

The 'man is good' theory—and it is a theory in the sense that it provides a framework with which the senses and the intellect organize reality—is based on the existence of a conscience or its genetic equivalent. While Socrates believed in the innate goodness of humans, he also placed great stress on the impact of nurture and especially education, arguing consistently that no one willingly acts wrongly and that when one knows enough, is able to reason well enough, conduct inquiry well enough and discern a logical series of ideas well enough then one's actions ought to be and generally will be socially appropriate and morally correct. Even so, he acknowledged that despite education the 'inner voice' (conscience) could sometimes only provide warnings about wrong decisions and could not in fact prevent them (Dihle, 1994: 175). This theory of innate human goodness survives the two millennia since Plato, surfacing with particular vigour during the era of the Enlightenment in the eighteenth century. David Hume, Adam Smith, Jean-Jacques Rousseau, John Locke, Mary Wollstonecraft, Thomas

Jefferson and William Godwin all argued for an 'instinctive benevolence' in humans that was antecedent to reason or education and rooted in feelings of sympathy for other sentient beings and thereby leading to the potential for virtuous action in the world. In the nineteenth century the theory moves from this philosophic base to a scientific grounding in Darwin's theory of evolution, reinforced in the twentieth century by modern genetics and evolutionary psychology. Thus altruism, compassion, empathy, love, conscience, the sense of justice eventually finds their origin in theories about 'reciprocal-altruism genes' (Wright, 1994: 13).

But what about crime? What about all the evidence of bad behaviour? For many, Plato's answer that it simply resulted from ignorance or the occasional lapse of conscience was never very convincing. Likewise the Enlightenment philosophers' explanation often seemed suspiciously based on notions of class, manners, and mores rather on the universal attributes that such a meta-theory seemed to imply. From the Darwinians, on the other hand, the approach gained in credibility. A genetic predisposition toward altruism, sympathy and co-operation was seen as having its roots in natural selection, a theory that seemed grounded in empirical truths. According to Darwin, empathetic and co-operative humans (i.e. 'good') had better odds of surviving and flourishing compared to selfish non-co-operators. This empathy can, however, readily be switched off if social conditions allow or encourage the same benefits to be gained by other means such as aggressive action, another innate disposition. 'Sympathy' is thus an option, not a given. Supporting the dominant sociological view that poverty or desperate social conditions produce crime, the new evolutionary psychologist/neo-Darwinians argue that such conditions lead directly to an inhibition of altruism as the organism (the young male presumably) anticipates a short life span in the ghetto unless aggressive steps are taken (Wright, 1994: 222).

So whether from God or from genetic evolution, the theory that humans are fundamentally disposed to 'do the right thing', first by looking after themselves and then by empathising with others, confronts crime or other anti-social behaviours by looking first at the context rather than the individual. From this approach various sociological theories have risen to prominence in responding to crime and deviance. While this is no place for a full-scale review of these theories (see George Void and Thomas Bernard, 1986, for an in depth survey) some examples may illuminate the trend. In the nineteenth century, for instance, Durkheim theorised that crime was normal and indeed essential to the workings of any healthy society built on the division of labour and its inevitable differential (i.e. unequal) distribution of wealth and resources. Thus in a society in which equality of opportunity is the ideological norm but unequal distribution of such opportunity the social reality (i.e. due to racism, sexism, regional disparities, etc.) the resulting structural stress will result in attempts by individuals to assert the ideological norm, by deviant means if necessary (e.g. Taylor, 1975: Clinard (ed.), 1964).

Carrying this theoretical approach to crime one step further, the development of labelling theory by Howard Becker, David Matza and others puts an even greater distance between the character or personality of the individual 'deviant' and the nature of the acts being committed. Thus for Becker '... social groups create deviance by making the rules whose infraction constitutes deviance, and by applying those rules to particular people and labelling them as outsiders' (Manders, 1975: 54). The classic illustration, of course, is the ever changing rules about substance abuse and narcotics and the 'creation' of criminals through the outlawing of specific items, from alcohol to heroin. Likewise the currently popular label 'sexual offender' derives as much from the shifting sexual mores of a culture as it does from any specific set of actions.

The influential social theorist Michel Foucault, while accepting much of the spirit and substance of labelling theory, moved this theoretical approach even further into the realm of context by arguing that the bureaucratic institutions of modern society—in this case the prisons—created and perpetuated deviance by creating the 'criminal'. Once created, the label remained forever and one entered the 'carceral archipelago' described so vividly in the autobiographical works of Jean Genet. Perhaps the most challenging reach of this genre of argument was Zygmunt Bauman's 1989 book *Modernity and the Holocaust*, a powerful argument that the greatest deviance of the twentieth century stemmed from the very modernity that most had presumed stood in the way of such 'primitive' behaviours: 'The Holocaust was born and executed in our modern rational society, at the high stage of our civilisation and at the peak of human cultural achievement, and for this reason it is a problem of that society, civilisation and culture' (Bauman, 1989: x). While not intending to excuse or forgive the acts of individuals who committed 'crimes against humanity', neither is Bauman prepared to understand those acts via the character of those individuals or the supposed flaws of a specific community.

Translated into policy, such a theoretical approach to deviance and crime occupies the 'liberal' ground of the political spectrum, insisting that social changes rather than individual 'correction' is the only reasonable approach to the problem of public safety and individual well-being. Prisons become unfortunate containment institutions in which little 'correcting' can be done since the causes of an individual's incarceration are in most cases outside that person's control. All that one can hope for in such institutions is the provision of a humane environment and possibly education and training programmes which can provide a means for greater access to the levers of power and control in society and possibly a way to break the hold of the label 'criminal' by acquiring a new language, a new set of skills and thereby a new identity.

The 'human as good' approach certainly contains within it the possibility of an individual experiencing a social crisis or catastrophe significant enough to result in a 'bad' person. Even Jefferson admitted some people were beyond redemption—but the bias is clearly toward social causation and therefore the application of social rather than psychological solutions. The approach that 'humans are bad', to pose the dualism in the crudest way, reverses poles and posits that only rules, moral systems, religions or other 'systems' can restrain deviant behaviour which is perceived to be quite 'natural'. Grounded in the Christian concept of Original Sin, this approach posits that humans are by nature sinners who need salvation, beasts who need taming, or pleasure-seekers in need of restraint. Manifested in both psychology and sociology, this approach has a long history and has resulted in a number of theories that have had a direct impact on the criminal justice system.

Freud set the modern tone with his notion that we are at base primitive pleasure-seekers constantly being required to repress these ego-driven instincts in the face of 'civilisation'. At his most outspoken he agreed with the ancient proverb that 'man is a wolf to man', defying us to deny it in the face of observed reality (Freud, 1961: 65). This repression leads in some cases to illness and a need for psychiatric intervention and in other cases to deviance or subversion and a need for psychological or even pharmacological intervention. An equally strong tradition in anthropology argued that humans were not by nature social and therefore had to be '... broken to group living ...' by socialisation and the imposition of social controls (Goldsmith, 1978: 14). The behaviourist H. J. Eysenck insisted that we needed to stop asking why some people behave badly and ask instead why all of us do not do so since selfish, aggressive and immoral behaviour is so clearly to our individual benefit (Lickora, 1976: 108). The criminologist James Q. Wilson seals the argument by declaring simply that 'wicked people exist', an idea picked up eagerly by politicians such as Ronald Reagan who speculated that some men are prone to evil. In the popular press, taking their lead from professors and presidents, journalists concluded that 'we have to accept that some people are broken' and cannot easily be repaired (Lamothe, 1996: 62).

As in the more optimistic or beneficent approach to human behaviour, several important theories are generated on the basis of this more cynical or pragmatic—take your pick—approach. The primary focus of all these theories was on 'difference'—what it was that seemed to make deviant juveniles and adults different from their rule-following peers. From the RAND Corporation's studies of career criminals to research on the origins of juvenile delinquency to work on the nature of 'authoritarian personalities', research increasingly began to isolate a distinct group whose deviance, it was argued, was based on either biological factors or on severe personality and cognitive deficits or disorders whose origin lay in early childhood (cf. E and S Glueck, 1968). Either way, the result was a severely damaged individual who required intensive therapeutic, educational, pharmacological intervention or in some cases preventative detention. The various theories linked with this psychological and biological way of explaining deviance and prescribing solutions all had the effect of shifting the gaze of society away from structural or systemic problems and onto the individual deviant. Or, in my preferred way of conveying the point, transformed the deviant/offender from a 'subject' to an 'object'.

SUBJECTS AND OBJECTS

Within the prison/correctional systems of most Western nations this latter approach with its ever-shifting sets of theories has held sway for the past 50 years. But this hegemony was not without its ups and downs. In 1974, what was until that time proudly referred to as the 'Medical Model' of corrections (a set of theories based on criminal deviance being an 'illness subject to cure') was challenged in a fundamental way. The famous 'Nothing Works' essay by Robert Martinson essentially argued that the 'Emperor had no clothes on', that the evidence supposedly holding up the theories was not there or worse, that the evidence in fact refuted the theory (1974). It was at this point that I entered the world of prison education, hired by the University of Victoria to teach history to inmates at two federal prisons in British Columbia and that my 'Theorist's Tale' begins in earnest.

As an historian, I perceived myself in 1974 to be without theory, interested more in facts, stories, perceptions and memories. In fact, of course, I was riddled with theoretical notions of cause and effect, steeped in the then popular Marxist or at least materialist theories about what made history 'move'. The university programme I taught with, however, had a very public theory, having been designed by a psychologist as an experiment to test whether very traditional liberal arts courses could lead to individual moral and cognitive growth among prisoner-students and, if so, whether this growth or 'development' would result in a reduced incidence of return to crime after release—i.e. lower recidivism (Ayers, 1980). At first I was resistant to this experimental approach to what I saw as my 'craft', an approach so transparent that I was convinced it would undermine my position as teacher and that the subjects—my students— would either abandon the programme or simply comply with whatever the experimenters wanted in order to enhance their chances for release.

Eventually—as I have described elsewhere (Duguid, 1997)—I abandoned these fears and for several years embraced the 'cognitive-moral development' theory—indeed becoming one of its more outspoken supporters.

My path from sceptic to acolyte is illustrative of the powerful attraction of theories as both models for explanation of observed realities and as a means of buttressing one's position within a given field of endeavour. I did observe clear effects after several years of immersion in the prison liberal arts programme. The prisoner-students were clearly more literate, thought more critically, were more aware of and had a more sophisticated understanding of social, political and moral issues, and were in many cases obviously considering non-criminal post-release careers. They had been exposed to a great many instructors from the university, met other people through their coursework who were foreign to their usual social world, and were adopting habits and aspirations that implied integration with rather than antagonism to 'straight society'. Clearly, the educational experience was having an impact. The education programme, however, depended on more than these potentially only cosmetic effects if it was to remain in the prison. It was in constant competition for resources (and inmates!) with other programmes making similar claims and needed constantly to fend off those inside and outside the prison who questioned the appropriateness of educating criminals. To be able to show a reduction in recidivism and to link that with the education programme via an externally validated theory was one path toward providing the necessary protection.

The theory, then, of cognitive-moral development had two qualities that attracted me and several other members of the programme staff, none of whom had been wedded to the theory in any intellectual or academic—one might say 'authentic'—way. On the one hand, we needed a frame or model within which we could understand the changes we were observing and a developmental theory made particular sense in assessing the impact of education. Secondly—and this grew in importance over time—we needed a shield to protect us from the proponents of other theories and competing interests. For a few years this latter function of our theory came to dominate my own work as the education programme in which I was employed and later became 'responsible' for came under increasing attack in the form of budgetary restrictions, bureaucratic interference, and pressure from other programmes.

'Theory', then, can fulfil a crucial protective function. It reinforces the morale of programme staff by providing an externally validated rationale or reason for their activity. In doing this it must be sophisticated enough to withstand competition from other theories being used for the same purpose. Thus the cognitive-moral development theory that was utilised by the education programme in British Columbia in the 1970s and 1980s had to compete with behaviourist theories that called for special therapeutic communities, with other psychological approaches that focused on intensive counselling and group therapy, with theories that claimed learning disabilities were at the core of deviance and with other theories that made claims for training, skill acquisition, pharmaceutical interventions, deterrence by punishment and so forth. Strangely, while all of these theoretical approaches anchored their claim to validity on a rehabilitative or reformational outcome, few of them actually attempted to establish that claim with empirical research. It seemed enough in the highly politicised atmosphere of the prison to simply have strong advocates within (and sometimes outside) the system, advocates whose careers were in some way linked to the success of the theoretical approach.

Being outsiders to the prison, we were not in a powerful position to defend either the education programme or the cognitive-moral development theory that was its rationale. As a first line of defence myself and other academically-minded folk in the programme began to give papers at academic conferences, policy seminars and practitioner workshops, hoping that by sheer volume of 'noise' concerning the strength of the theory and its link with our practice we would help ensure our survival. As well, we hoped to interest people outside of the prison in the efficacy of the programme by linking it, via this theory, to education in the community at large.

It early on became clear to us that this would not be sufficient, that our links with other 'outsiders' would be unable to withstand competitors for money, space and subjects who had equally sophisticated theories but were more closely linked to the prison hierarchy. To meet this challenge we decided to buttress our position by seeking empirical data to support our theory. That is, since we argued that educational experiences that stimulated cognitive and moral development would result not just in improvement in test scores but in behavioural changes as well, we set about to prove it by following up our students after release. An initial study completed in 1980 and a subsequent major research effort in 1993-96 provided the data we needed to establish the credibility of the theory and the programme it supported (Duguid and Pawson, 1998). There were dramatic reductions in predicted recidivism for the former students in the education programme as well as indications of significant changes in other aspects of their lives. The research design, for instance, went to great lengths to establish the connection between these results and the students' participation in the academic programme. In 1993, just as this data was emerging, the education programme was cut by the Correctional Service of Canada. What had gone wrong?

Ironically, the education programme was done in not by its traditional competitors and opponents, but by a programme based on a more elaborate and ecumenical version of the same developmental theory—the cognitive skills programme. Indeed, the education programme and the new 'Cog-Skills' programme had been on parallel tracks for several years within the federal Correctional Service of Canada. The originators of the cognitive skills initiative, Robert Ross and Elizabeth Fabiano, had been supporters of the education programme and proponents of both initiatives saw them as complimentary rather than competitive (cf. Fabiano and Ross, 1983; Ross, 1985).

Two things had gone 'wrong' by 1993. First, the theory supporting the education programme had changed, and had become more 'complicated'. The initial theoretical premise behind the programme had suggested that positive behavioural changes would result from increases in levels or stages of cognitive and moral development stemming from taking education courses in the humanities. Those of us involved with the programme were confident that these changes in behaviour were occurring, but were less sure of the singularity of the theoretical explanation. In attempting to explore this in the 1993 follow-up study, researchers utilised a 'theory-driven' methodology developed by Ray Pawson which posed the more complex question of 'What works, for whom, and why?'. In other words, it was presumed that several theories might be at work in explaining behavioural changes. The resulting research made the case that different components of the education programme worked for different students at different times—a 'theory' to be sure, but not a simple one.

Meanwhile, the Cognitive Skills proponents took a more traditional approach, arguing that offenders shared a specific range of 'criminogenic factors' that each needed addressing and that this was most efficiently done via a series of standard modules administered by experienced prison staff (e.g., rather than by outsiders). While the educators argued that human complexity made it too difficult to predict 'in advance' what would work for whom, the cognitive skills programme insisted that individual needs could be diagnosed and therefore individual 'prescriptions' efficiently and cost-effectively administered. In terms of simplicity and efficiency there was no contest. There was also, of course, no substantive evidence that the cognitive skills theory was correct but as in the case of the Aristotelean crystalline sphere there was a strong conviction that it should work and it as well served some very specific needs—whether it worked or not.

These specific needs comprised the second thing that had 'gone wrong' with the education programme. By the 1990s it was clear that the Correctional Service of Canada no longer wished to have prison programmes in the hands of outsiders. The Cognitive Skills Program had as its central premise the desirability of using prison staff as teachers/coaches in the delivery of the various modules utilised in the programme. This had a positive impact on prison staff morale by adding teacher/counsellor/trainer to their sense of identity and at the same time served to eliminate the often-troublesome presence of outsiders in the prison.

But enough about me! What does this tale have to tell us about theory and prison education? The most obvious lesson we can learn is that theories do not have to be 'true' or even 'reasonably true' to be powerful. For instance, there is a theory of sorts behind the idea that the authoritarian regime of military-style boot camps will reform young offenders and many correctional jurisdictions have developed such facilities in response to that theory. Despite the fact that virtually all evidence we have shows that these boot camps do not reduce re-offending, the camps and the theory that supports them thrive (cf. Mackenzie, 1995; Wright and Mys, 1998). A recent follow-up study assessing the effectiveness of the Cognitive Skills Program in Canada has shown it to be contra the theory—ineffective in reducing recidivism for high risk offenders, yet 'Cog-Skills' thrives and its theory is regarded as robust (Robinson, 1995). Faced with empirical data that calls a theory into question, proponents typically fall back on the need for more time, resources, staff or whatever other component promises the expected breakthrough—in the case of cognitive skills the cure was seen as an 'increased dosage'. This process of 'escalation', to use a tired term from the Vietnam War era, dates at least from Aristotle whose cosmology was constantly being refined by the addition of ever more epicycles explaining each erratic movement of the heavenly bodies that violated his theory of the cosmos.

Perhaps more important, these empirical failures and the constant feeling that the various theories of deviance and correction are grand in design but faulty in practice may stem from the fundamental premises of the two meta-approaches described earlier. Both the 'man-is-good' and the 'man-is-bad' approach end up having us focus on the offender/inmate/prisoner as the primary object of concern. The first approach does so somewhat reluctantly but in the end the theories it spawns presume that the potentially good individual has in the case of offenders been so damaged by society that specific reformational and rehabilitative steps are required. The second approach lustily zeroes in on these flawed humans and prescribes a series of corrective interventions that will end up coercing them toward lawful behaviour— bending them to the 'yoke of necessity' some might say. Michel Foucault's central insight about the prison regime—its intense observational gaze directed toward the deviant offender—revealed this fundamental symmetry of modern approaches to corrections. The individual prisoner in all the various theories that stem from these two fundamental approaches to the 'problem of deviance' ends up as the 'problem', either because the social causes of deviance are deemed too complex to address or because they are held to be irrelevant. In either case, once the deviant individual is in the grasp of a theory-driven intervention complexity tends to disappear as the individual assumes the shape of his diagnosed problem—he becomes 'addicted', 'untrained', 'violent', or 'learning disabled'; a 'sexual offender', 'career criminal', 'sociopath', or 'young offender'; is shunted into 'anger management', 'group counselling', 'job training', or 'psychotherapy'. The theories and their attendant programmes are hence more powerful than the individuals they address, imposing an identity on those individuals—in a word turning them into objects.

The central insight derived from my years in prison as teacher, researcher and amateur theorist is that authentic and lasting change in the form of rehabilitation, reformation or transformation can only occur if individuals are dealt with as subjects rather than objects. As a result of this insight in my current research in the area of prison education I have utilised a theory, the realist evaluation methodology developed by Ray Pawson, that acknowledges the complexity of individuals and of contexts and accepts the essential subjectivity and uniqueness of the individual. By seeking to discover what aspect or component of a given intervention is effective with which sub-set of the subjects concerned and under what kinds of circumstances or contexts, such a theory preserves the essential integrity and complexity of the process of education.

To be both functional and true to the complexity of the human body and spirit a theory designed to understand and influence human behaviour must approach its subjects—in this case the offender/prisoner—in full acknowledgement of their subjectivity. Any change process, including education, that is imposed via a subject-object relationship will, almost inevitably, be overthrown or abandoned once the individual sheds the objectified identity of prisoner and regains his or her identity as citizen, father, husband, worker or even criminal—in other words once again becomes a subject.

BIBLIOGRAPHY for *Chapter 3*

Ayers J. D. *et al* (1980), *Effects of University of Victoria Progam: A Post-Release Study*, Ministry of the Solicitor General of Canada

Bauman Z (1989), *Modernity and the Holocaust*, New York: Cornell University Press

Clinard M. (ed.) (1964), *Anomie and Deviant Behaviour*, New York: Free Press

Dihle A. (1994), *A History of Greek Literature*, London: Routledge

Duguid S. (1997), 'Cognitive Dissidents Bite the Dust—The Demise of University Education in Canada's Prisons,' *Journal of Correctional Education*, Special Issue, Vol 48: 2

Duguid S. and Pawson R. (1988), 'Education, Change and Transformation: The Prison Experience,' *Evaluation Review*, Vol 22: 4

Fabiano E. and Ross R. (1983), *The Cognitive Model of Crime and Delinquency: Prevention and Rehabilitation*, Planning and Research Branch of the Ontario Ministry of Corectional Services

Freud S. (1961), *Civilisation and its Discontents*, New York: Norton

Glueck E. and Gluek S. (1968), *Delinquents and Non-Delinquents in Perspective*, Boston: Harvard University Press

Goldsmith E. (1978), *The Stable Society*, Wadebridge: Wadebridge Press

Lamothe L. (1996), 'Getting Away with Murder', *Next City*, Fall

Lickona T. (1976), *Moral Development and Behaviour*, New York: Holt, Rinehart and Winston

Manders D. (1975), 'Labelling Theory and Social Reality,' *The Insurgent Sociologist*, Vol 6: 1

Martinson R. (1974), 'What Works? Questions and Answers about Prison Reform,' *Public Interest*, Spring

Matthews R. (1984), *The Radical Politics of Thomas Jefferson*, Lawrence: University of Kansas Press

Mackenzie D. (1995), 'Boot Camp Prisons and Recidivism in Eight States,' *Criminology*, Vol 33: 3

Robinson D. (1995), *The Impact of Cognitive Skills Training on Post-Release Recidivism Among Canadian Federal Offenders*, Correctional Service of Canada

Ross R. (1985), *Time to Think: A Cognitive Model of Delinquency, Prevention and Offender Rehabilitation*, Johnson City, Tennessee: Institute of Social Sciences and Arts

Taylor I. (1975), *Critical Criminology*, London: Routledge and Kegan Paul

Vold G. and Bernard T. (1986), *Theoretical Criminology*, New York: Oxford

Wright D. and Mys G. L. (1998) 'Correctional Boot Camps, Attitudes and Recidivism: The Oklahoma Experience,' *Journal of Offender Rehabilitation*, Vol 28

Wright R. (1994), *The Moral Animal*, New York: Vintage.

CHAPTER 4

The Evaluator's Tale

Ray Pawson

The 'Evaluator's Tale', like many others in this volume, is one of great expectations and thwarted ambitions. Great expectations flow because we live in an age of 'evidence-based policy-making' and a unique opportunity is at hand to actually show that prisoner education works. Thwarted ambitions follow, alas, because research on the education of offenders has hardly registered as part of this process, and one sees only an absence of evidence and a vacuum in policy.

INTRODUCTION: THE PROMISE OF EVALUATION

There is a story, probably apocryphal, about a set of flip charts being produced in Whitehall in 1999 bearing the legend, 'What counts is what works'. The idea was that in their every meeting on reform and policy change, politicians and civil servants would have in their eyeshot this reminder that pragmatism rather than dogmatism was the order of the day. This notion is reminiscent of the 'Great Society' movement in the US in the 1960s, in which rational decision-making was promoted as the great engine of public policy (Campbell, 1969). The guiding principle was that all publicly-funded programmes should be made to face the court of empirical evidence. A new breed of applied social researchers, going by the name of evaluators, was drafted in with the task of determining 'what works' in the world of social intercessions. The premise, simply put, was that since there is a huge speculative element in all policy development, the systematic use of research evidence would enable a weeding-out of ineffective interventions and a fine-tuning of those initiatives that were able to demonstrate their mettle.

Adherence to this stratagem has waxed and waned over the decades and evaluation's fortunes have chopped and changed from country to country and from government to government. At century's turn it seems that evaluation research in the UK is, once again, *de rigueur*. As with all incoming administrations, the Labour government has seen itself as a storehouse of innovation. Programme after programme has been mounted. There have been *New Deals* for the unemployed, for disabled people, for communities and so on. There have been national programmes on burglary reduction, housing allocation, traffic congestion and so on. There have been targeted interventions on failing schools, regional government, health action zones and so on. These are, moreover, *New* Labour initiatives. Consequently, some are launched allowing the recipients a degree of control, many are mounted on the basis that they become self-sustaining, and all are commissioned in the knowledge that they have to demonstrate their utility and cost their benefits via the process of audit and evaluation. The result of this bustle of policy making is a bonanza for applied social research. Each initiative has a little army of evaluators in tow (at a going rate, by the way, of one per-cent of the total cost of the programmes) charged with doing the counting so that we may know what is working.

We reach my opening case. In the light of this maelstrom of activity, after this Lord Mayor's show, we cast our eyes on public policy on the education of offenders. If one scans the Whitehall white papers, scrutinises the Home Office research bulletins, immerses oneself in the outpourings from the think tanks, one is hard put to come across any significant innovation in penal policy. One discovers no *New Deal* for prisoners and, despite 'education, education, education' being another favoured motto, one confronts not a scrap of government interest in prisoner education. My first task in this chapter, however, is not to explain this lacunae, nor to point fingers at culprits, but simply to make the case that, somehow, those responsible for prisoner education have got to catch the evidence-based policy train before it leaves the platform.

The cause of offender education needs the support of hard evidence because, otherwise, its practitioners have to fall back on anecdote—and anecdote, quite simply, is insufficient. Every contributor to this book actually 'knows' that prisoner education works because they will have seen it working and can tell the tale. My hunch is that these tales add up to quite a comprehensive claim. Thus there will be declarations about education's benefit to the *individual*—via character building and confidence raising, via the acquisition of basic skills and employment credentials, via changes in self-reflection and moral judgement, via improvements in social skills and cultural aspirations etc. There will also be assertions about education's contribution to the *institution* in terms of—improvement in regime order and control, development in sentence-planning, enhancement in staff-inmate relations, progression in the well-being of lifers etc. Even that is not the end of it, for I believe that few practitioners would actually shy away from the grandest claim of all, namely that education is able to slow the revolving door of incarceration and reincarceration.

All of this knowledge, in all of its particulars, is based on vast experience and has been delivered time and time again in the testimony of the 'reformed'. But this leaves us with a problem. However vast that experience, however eloquent that testimony, it leaves us well short of the bottom line of being able to *show* that education is the great agent of rehabilitation. What is required is something easy to say, but something that has thus far eluded the capabilities of penal researchers and reformers. We need to be able to *demonstrate* clearly that the experience of education has actually changed the thinking of inmates, in sufficient numbers, so that on release they are able to resist the return to a life of crime.

We thus come to the plan of the chapter—the tale proper. I want to recount the story of a successful but thwarted adventure in evaluation of prisoner education, which did indeed attempt to get to the bottom line. The main body of the chapter will thus provide an account of the evaluation of the Simon Fraser Prison Education Programme, a study that, I believe, provides the best evidence yet of the rehabilitative potential of prisoner education. But I also need to top and tail the tale with the 'health warning' that the case under study was, note again, successful *but* thwarted. My little homily to the need for a powerful evidence-base on the link between education and rehabilitation is thus made in full awareness of the many difficulties that lie in wait of those attempting to construct the evidence-base. And I begin by acknowledging some of them.

CAVEAT: THE PITFALLS OF EVALUATION

'Does it work?'. This is the blunt question that evaluators are charged with and, in truth, it is a challenge to which they are often unable to give a straight answer. This is no place to conduct a full examination of the hazards of evaluation methodology (see Pawson and Tilley, 1997: Ch. 1 and 2) but I do want to give some preliminary sense of what is possible and what is not possible in the domain of evaluative research on offender education.

Evaluation research has its origins in agricultural and medical science. In these fields, the 'what works?' question is a relatively simple one, the interventions under scrutiny are:

(a) singular 'treatments'
(b) applied to a well-defined set of 'subjects'
(c) targeted at specific 'outcomes'.

Thus in the health field, evaluation might take on the task of investigating a new drug aimed at patients suffering a particular form of cancer and seeking the goal of preventing or delaying cancer deaths. In agriculture the task is typically one of evaluating a new fertiliser designed for a specific crop with the aim of increasing yields. In such cases relatively straightforward modes of investigation are available. Researchers use a beautifully simple design, known as the randomised controlled trial (RCT), in order to capture evidence on these three basic elements of an intervention. The RCT divides 'subjects' into two groups known as the experimental and control groups, the 'treatment' is applied only to the former but not the latter, and 'outcome' differences are measured by comparisons of changes in the treated and untreated group. A programme under evaluation thus may be said to 'work' by virtue of the simple test of whether the experimental group has 'outperformed' the controls

Such a research strategy is untenable when trying to decipher the effects of programmes such as prisoner education. The above, three-step formula of RCT investigation breaks down in the face of complexity after complexity. Thus, in the initiatives in which we are interested here:

(a) education is not a 'treatment' applied in dosages but a multifaceted and prolonged social encounter involving a range of ideas, curricula, aptitudes and personnel

(b) the 'subjects', namely inmates, are hardly uniform and whilst they do not represent an exact cross-section of society, they do present a mighty range of social backgrounds, a positive jumble of prior educational experience and, indeed, an unfortunate array of offences

(c) the rehabilitative 'outcome' of prisoner education is rarely perceived in simple, therapeutic terms but is considered to work *indirectly* via building character, raising self-confidence, acquiring competence, gaining credentials, promoting self-reflection, creating moral standards, improving social skills, enlarging cultural aspirations and so on.

Now, in the face of such complexity the very question, 'Does prisoner education work?' becomes a dangerous oversimplification. There is an educational and training presence at the root of almost every career, profession, institution and economic sector in modern society. Such ubiquity suggests that education is capable of performing many, many different functions. This capacity is not always realised, however. Every teacher, including those who work in prison, will have tales of those untouched by years in the classroom. Every educational reformer, including those responsible for the expansion of nursery provision, the introduction of comprehensive schools, the widening access to higher education and so on, will have felt disappointment at education's inability to produce major social transformations. In this respect education is no different from any other major social intervention, in that it offers no instant solutions and no universal panaceas.

In the recognition of this state of affairs we glimpse the resolution to the evaluator's dilemma. The way forward in the evaluation of complex programmes such as education is not to abandon the 'does it work?' question, but to ask it more sensibly. The evaluation task is thus to take on a more measured and conditional question about 'why' prisoner education might work and then move on to inquire 'for whom' and 'in what circumstances' and 'in what respects' it does work. This new agenda is becoming the norm in evaluation methodology (see Pawson and Tilley, 1997: Ch. 4) and in the following section, we will come to some of these crucial details in exploring the 'why's' and 'wherefores' of the Simon Fraser programme.

At the risk of this becoming a pedant's tale of the evaluator's problems, there is one further preliminary that must be mentioned. Apart from the philosophical limitation on the nature of evaluation knowledge just mentioned, there is also a barrage of practical problems facing the intrepid researcher entering the prison walls. By their very nature, prisons are secretive and unco-operative places. By instinct and training, prison officers and officials are suspicious and circumspect. By dint of lack of funding and poor conditions, prison educators tend to be thin on the ground and not too long around. And last but not least, by the time-honoured demands of inmate culture, prisoners are particularly keen to keep from surveillance at least one aspect of their lives—namely what goes on in their heads.

All this is by way of saying that many of the basic activities of social research, which are routine and familiar in the outside world, become alien and benighted when attempted on the 'inside'. This applies across the entire research act from getting past the gatekeepers, obtaining funding, gaining access to records, drawing adequate samples, getting straight answers in data collection, publishing results and analysis openly, and so on. I will not go through these points chapter and verse (but for some lurid tales see Cohen and Taylor, 1977 and Finckenauer, 1982). Rather, since we are in confessions mode here, I will rest content with the single example and tell the engaging little tale of a failure of my own research.

The research in question was conducted in HMP Full Sutton and was intended to investigate the personal changes experienced by inmates when undergoing a higher education course offered by the University of Leeds. A fuller and more sophisticated analysis of how such research should be, and eventually was, undertaken is provided by Reuss (1997 and in *Chapter 2* of this volume). I am referring here to the early days of the programme and to some initial, pilot work attempting to get to grips with the research task. The standard, text-book way of charting change in individuals is to conduct some before-and-after measurement of attitudes, beliefs and behaviours. In this instance the plan was to conduct some pre-course and post-course measurements for inmates proceeding through the eighteen month programme. And so at the very start of the initiative, indeed on the first occasion that the inmate-students clapped eyes on the Leeds team, yours truly entered the prison classroom armed with a battery of questionnaires and personality tests.

As a veteran researcher, I was of course aware that in answering questions, subjects respond to much more than the questions on the page. They take into consideration the purpose of the research (as they understand it), the demeanour of the researcher (as they perceive it), the legitimacy of the sponsor (as they consider it) and so on. Here, I also remind the reader of the bit of prison folklore mentioned above about the inmate's desire to retain control of their thoughts in an otherwise totally superintended world. I was thus not expecting a particularly smooth ride and indeed suffered a bit of leg-pulling about whether I was a Home Office spy as well as some rather well-informed banter on why they were doing psychological tests rather than the course as advertised—namely, sociology. I had hoped to get by with charm, grace, humility, docility, and besides, as the old joke goes, this was a captive audience. So how did it go?

Well, in fact all the questionnaires got completed, but in a way which led me directly back to the methodological drawing board. The expected grilling I received about the purpose of the questions, included the unexpected thoughts of one prisoner that one could actually see dawning on his face, 'You'll do these again at the end of the course to see if we have changed, eh?' It became obvious even at that early stage that my respondents would be in charge of whatever patterns emerged from the data. This feeling was reinforced by the rather articulate questionnaire response of another inmate-student who remained stubbornly silent throughout that first session. Another classic way in which respondents can win control over the research process is through a procedure called 'faking-good'. This occurs when the research subject sticks deliberately to 'socially desirable' answers rather than admitting the researcher into their true thinking. It is a familiar enough problem, but one that was also taken to new heights on this occasion. One of the attitude tests used a set of strict, fixed-answer boxes for each question posed as shown in *Table 1*.

Strongly Agree	Generally Agree	Somewhat Agree	Somewhat Disagree	Generally Disagree	Strongly Disagree
0	1	2	3	4	5

Table 1

This was designed without a 'neutral point' in an attempt to ease the subject into a point of view, one way or the other. But so keen was this particular respondent to appear as 'Mr. Average' that he invented an answer box of his own and went through the questionnaire recording almost all the items as two and a half.

The point, I trust, is made. Evaluation research in a prison context is rarely simple and neither are the conclusions to be drawn from it. But let us be quite clear of the moral of this particular tale. The difficulties confronting evaluation have, in some radical circles, prompted a sceptical reaction to the whole enterprise of evidence-based policy making. Building the evidence-base is a slow and considered business. Most governments, as we have seen, prefer to make policy at pace. In order to keep in rhythm, a new style of research, known to proponents and opponents alike as 'quick and dirty evaluation' has evolved. In this mode, researchers can become political puppets and end up seeking only the data that supports particular policy assumptions, rather than give a balanced picture of the winners and losers as suggested above.

So what is the way forward? Imprisonment is a hidden industry and a state-controlled industry to boot. It is, therefore, very difficult to influence from outside the policy mainstream. Thus despite evaluation being open to immense difficulties and potential abuse, prison reformers would be quite wrong to line up with the cynics who deny the possibility of providing hard evidence linking education to rehabilitation. The alternative, the education-for-education's-sake argument, will bring not a single further teacher into the prisons. Prisoner education has few allies. It thus has to grasp the double-edged sword of evaluation in order to make the prudent and cautious case that, applied in the right circumstances to appropriate offenders, prisoner education works.

THE SIMON FRASER PRISON EDUCATION PROGRAMME

I want to turn now to my nugget of evidence on education and rehabilitation. I was responsible for the research design on this particular study. All the fieldwork and analysis was undertaken (and all the political flack was endured) by a research team led by Steven Duguid. Duguid himself was part of the team of practitioners who had pioneered the prison education programme from its beginnings in the 1960s. More detailed accounts of the research may be consulted in Duguid and Pawson (1998) and Duguid *et al* (1998).

This particular initiative was, by a considerable margin, the biggest higher education programme ever attempted in a prison context. It ran in four different federal prisons in British Columbia, Canada, having a huge life span of over 20 years. Each year the university offered a humanities programme with some social science modules, so that it was possible to collect enough credits to get a Simon Fraser University degree. Men would spend anything from one semester up to five years on the course, sometimes cascading from prison to prison. The programme involved well over 1,000 men, with 690 being registered for two semesters or more and it was this group who became the subject of the research.

It is impossible to convey the atmosphere and facilities of the initiative in a short space. Suffice to say that there was an attempt to create a 'mini campus' or 'learning centre' in the four penitentiaries. Each prison had a university block with its own library. There was a full-time co-ordinator in each institution who organized specialists in the various disciplines (many of whom were existing Simon Fraser 'profs') to deliver the programme. There was an 'open door' policy; anyone who wished to enrol could enrol for induction courses. The inmates themselves played a role in the delivery programme, having a student council, and acting as assistant tutors and librarians. The underlying idea, insofar this was possible behind penitentiary wires, was to imitate the educational provision at Simon Fraser. Tutors got on with their *Introduction to North American History*, their *Creative Writing*, their *Shakespeare* and so on with ne'er a thought for rehabilitation and certainly no moralising about crime.

Even from this brief description one gets the feel of an extraordinary programme. It is, however, very important to note that Canada is the land of 'mass' higher education, so the very idea of confronting large numbers of inmates with university access is not as unusual as it might be in the UK. Moreover, it transpired that the success of the programme had little to do with elite provision for high-flying students. Rather, as we shall see, its secrets lie in unleashing some of the standard benefits of life-long learning and some of the traditional powers of adult education

How the programme was evaluated

The basic idea, of course, is to see if the educational experience of the men impacted on recidivism rates. This paper describes just one fragment of the strategies employed in the attempt to answer that question. It covers the main quantitative aspects of inquiry but it should be noted that there were more qualitative elements as well, employing 'life-stories' of inmates and 'mini histories' of classroom events. The main data bash took the form of a 'tracking exercise' following the 690 men through their home background, criminal, prison, prison-education, and post-release history. Our aim was to go beyond crude aggregate measures of success or failure and to try to find what was it about certain inmates and their educational experience that distinguished the recidivist from the non-recidivist. The final data set thus consisted of 60-odd variables following through each man's life. These were collected from correctional and educational records. The project involved unparalleled access to some of the dustiest files of the Correctional Service of Canada (CSC), two years of research assistant time being required to collect the data.

The core analytic logic is illustrated in *Figure 1*: We describe our research design as 'sub-group' method. Its first ingredient is 'practitioner theory'. We asked those who had taught/administered the course our baseline question about 'What types of men in what types of circumstances are likely to be changed by the course?' We wanted to know from them what combination of type of provision and type of prisoner they considered to be the key to successful (and unsuccessful) outcomes. Educators, the world over, tend to be very good at this. They can tell tales galore of 'A has really improved as a result of being on the X programme', that 'It was a complete bloody waste of time for B to take Y' and so on. Our practitioners, too, were full of ideas. The most instructive quotation I unearthed from these interviews went as follows:

> The men who are more likely to be changed are best described as 'mediocre'. You shouldn't look for high-flyers. They're likely to come from a deprived background with a poor and maybe non-existent school record. They will be mediocre criminals too. They'll have gone on from petty crime, street crime to drugs or armed robbery or something. Then when they come onto the program, they're mediocre or worse. They just survive the first semester but gradually they build up getting Cs and Bs. So by the end, they've actually come a long, long way. And that's what changes 'em. It's not so much a case of 'rehabilitation' as 'habilitation'.'

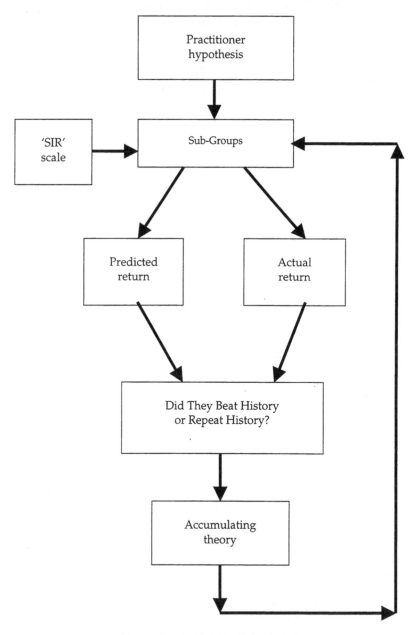

Figure 1: Design Logic—Sub-group method

This was one of those moments when as a researcher one prays 'Please God make sure that the tape recorder worked' for it was propositions like this one that went on to form the backbone of the investigation. Practitioners proceeded to identify a whole range of further mechanisms and context, which they saw as vital ingredients in making the programme work. Our task was not only to unearth such testimony, but to go beyond its anecdotal usage and formalise such hypotheses so they could actually be tested.

Step two was to thus identify some of these interesting sub-groups in the data set. So, if for some reason, our practitioners had said 'this programme was good for the rehabilitation of armed robbers' or 'the Shakespeare module was crucial in going straight'—we could indeed focus in on a group of gun-toters who had read Macbeth and examine their post-release fortunes more closely. As the reader might imagine, this fictional piece of folk wisdom is chosen merely for illustration's sake. The vital point is that that our data set allowed us to identify *any* sub-groups of inmates capable of revealing vital clues on 'for whom' and 'in what circumstances' the course was particularly effective. These could be defined either in very broad terms (prisoner students over '30 years') or identified by a quite particular admixture of characteristics (prisoner students who were 'school drop-outs' *and* 'young offenders' *and* 'drug users' *and* 'social science majors' *and* with 'improving course grades').

Step three was to look at the actual rate of return to prison for the particular group under scrutiny, thus testing out the practitioner theories according to their ability to identify sub-groups who avoided reconviction and reincarceration. Note that our sample was limited, by definition, to prisoner students who had been released from prison. They also had to have the *opportunity* to complete three years on parole without being reincarcerated. This gave us our baseline measure (the CSC standard definition) that a recidivist was someone who returned to prison for an indictable offence within three years of being released on parole. As we suspected, there was considerable variation in the return rates between subgroups and our educationalists showed considerable acumen in being able to predict particular groups with low recidivism rates.

Identifying a group liable to reform is, of course, only half the battle. What we are interested in here is whether the experience of education does something to change the destiny of inmates. So, for instance, merely predicting and procuring low recidivism rates means little if one is working with a group that is already prone to reform. In methodological terms, we had to find a way of dealing with a 'counterfactual'. We had to find a way of comparing the actual rates of return to prison with those that would obtain if the inmates had *not* undergone the programme.

Our actual yardstick for comparison was a 'reconviction prediction scale'. It is terribly important that evaluation trades on previous knowledge of the process under study and we already know great deal about re-offence. There are very clear aggregate patterns linking reconvictions to marital status, type of offence, number of offences and so on (Cormier, 1997). These key predictors have been rolled together into a statistical instrument that provides a reliable estimate of the probable rate of return to prison for any inmate. In Canada this is known as the SIR scale (statistical information on recidivism scale) and a crucial variable in our data collection was to collect the 'SIR score' for each Simon Fraser inmate. Such information was compiled routinely by CSC for the later cohorts in our study but we also calculated them for many of the earlier generations of prisoner students.

This brings us to our key calculation—our actual measure of 'success'. All the following data analysis is based on the same, simple formula—*Did a particular sub-group of inmate students beat its SIR prediction?* SIR tells us what would have normally happened to such a group. We obtained the data on what actually happened. Thus the research asks—*Did they beat history or do they repeat history?* What we discovered as we delved into the sub-groups was an enormous variation in SIR-beating. What we tried to do was to identify those particular pathways or sub-groups or sub-sub-groups that were most strongly associated with rehabilitation. This is illustrated in the feedback loop in *Figure 1.* By slightly refining and redefining the composition of the groups we hoped to identify some really key winners (jocularly known as the 'the mastersirbeaters') who we hoped would provide transferable lessons for other programmes. The evaluation was thus initially driven by the hunches of the practitioners but we were able to refine this starting point by building in more general criminological theory and growing empirical wisdom into the composition of the groups selected for analysis.

Some key findings

Our analysis began with an overview of the entire cohort of the prison education programme students. Six hundred and ninety men attended the course for two semesters or more and met the release date qualification mentioned above. We managed to get complete records on 654 of them and these became our 'total group'. SIR predicted 58 per cent of this group would not return to prison within three years. The actual rate was 75 per cent—a relative improvement of 30 per cent (see *Table 2*). This was obviously a finding of considerable promise, it is a particularly pleasing result in an area of the criminal justice system that gave birth to the 'nothing works' lament (Martinson, 1974). But, on the basis of what I have already argued, it is only the start of the story for the modern evaluator. This aggregate estimate is drawn over a long time period and from a data-base compiled by many different hands. There is bound to be a degree of error in the precise estimate of programme success. Besides, the programme has many, many distinctive features of time and place and we want to get away from any simple message that on the basis of a particularly successful result one can declare that prisoner education 'works'. Our main task was to try to discover some transferable lessons by seeking further pointers about 'what it was about the course which had worked for which inmates in what circumstances'. Much more was to be leaned by paying attention to the fate of the sub-groups within the initiative and the following excursion, identifying some of the key winners (and losers) on the programme, gives a pointer to some of the prize assets of prisoner education.

Total Group (n=654)	Predicted Non-Return (%)	Actual Non-Return (%)	Relative Improvement (%)
	58	75	30

Table 2: **Total Group**

The Improvers

One mechanism that was identified time and again by our practitioners was the value of the 'hard slog'. They argued that life-change came with gradual progress, which in turn pulled in the work ethic, built confidence, increased skills etc. Education's benefits are not felt overnight but are cashed in over a lifetime. The 'theory' at work here suggested that many offenders have preferred the quick buck but that this characteristic may be changed by the need to wrestle to gain the longer-term rewards education has to offer. We identified a group of 'improvers' to test this out (measured, somewhat crudely, by an improvement in grades over their tenure on course). The result was that for the 119 who had managed to shift up by a grade, there was indeed an increased rate of SIR-beating over that obtained by the group as a whole (see *Table 3*). This result moves us in a positive direction but is hardly earth shaking. We use it as a first illustration of the method, in that it shows how we can give an instant picture of the relative progress of different clusters of inmate students. The hypothesis explored however is rather unrefined and a shade tautological, saying little more than those who work hard on a course may take that resolve forward. What we need to know much more about is what produces the aptitude for hard-slog in the first place and in which situations does academic improvement turn to life change.

Improvers (*n*=119)	Predicted Non-Return (%)	Actual Non-Return (%)	Relative Improvement (%)
	56	77	37

Table 3 'Improvers' Sub-group

We can introduce these questions by traversing the feedback loop in *Figure 1* and introducing more finely-grained, sub-sub-groups into the analysis. We wanted to know if the 'hard slog' had more significance according to the different circumstances of the inmate. Where would improvement really pay off? This led to a range of other comparisons three of which—'improvers by age bands', 'improvers by educational background', 'improvers by further education at release'—are depicted in *Table 4*.

Table 4: **Improvers Sub-sub-groups**

Subgroups	Predicted (%)	Actual (%)	Relative Improvement (%)
17-21 Years (*n*=15)	55	93	69*
22-25 Years (*n*=29)	52	66	26
26-30 Years (*n*=29)	55	66	18
31-35 Years (*n*=24)	57	88	54*
36+ Years (*n*=22)	65	86	33

Table 4(a) **Age of 'Improvers' at Current Conviction**

Subgroups	Predicted (%)	Actual (%)	Relative Improvement (%)
grade10 or less (55)	48	65	36
grade11/GED (22)	59	91	54*
grade 12 (18)	70	89	27
post-sec (24)	63	83	33

Table 4(b): **'Improvers' by Education at Prison Entry**

Subgroups	Predicted(%)	Actual (%)	Relative Improvement (%)
Further Ed. (52)	56	90	61*
No Further Ed. (53)	59	74	25
Withdrew (13)	50	38	-23

Table 4(c): 'Improvers' by Further-Education After Release

Table 4(a) breaks down the group of 'improvers' into sub-categories according to their age at their most recent convictions. Two particular clusters of such inmates (marked*) were strongly associated with rehabilitation. In the case of our 31–35 year-olds, we had a ready-made explanation. Many practitioners fostered a 'maturity' hypothesis, arguing that it was the 'calming-down set' who had learned from bitter experience of time-served, and thus might be rather more prepared to put in hard-slog and to derive benefits from it. One hears similar sentiments across many other programmes with offenders and this is a useful fragment of evidence to support it. Note that we are not merely repeating popular wisdom here about old lags loosing their bottle or their ability to flee. We know already that the revolving door of reincarceration begins to slow for the over-30s, but the key point is that it is already factored into the SIR scale. The improvement in rehabilitation rate we unearth here is thus *over and above* its natural decline for older offenders. Though they may be better disposed to going straight, the over-30s still need a lifeline to pursue that goal and this is what education can provide.

The shining performance of the very young 'improvers' (17–21 year olds) was somewhat harder to figure. Our best, if tenuous, shot at this was in terms of a 'shelter' or 'protection' mechanism. Some practitioners argued that the SFU course was sought after deliberately by young inmates who, by dint of a serious crime, found themselves in a federal prison but who were not yet ensconced in criminal culture. Serving their time by deliberately keeping heads down at study was an alternative choice to the prison norm of being dragged further into criminal association. Note that 'age' is not acting mechanically as an explanatory variable here—both of our findings support 'cultural' hypotheses. They identify this middle patch (22-30 years) as the age of the 'crim', the 'con', the 'hard-man' and indicate that these are the identities that dominate prison life and against which education struggles to make an impact. The periods around the edge, however, are the really supportive contexts for rehabilitation through hard slogging.

We turn next to a breakdown of the progress of 'improvers' according to their educational experiences prior to entering prison.

One needs a little local knowledge of Canadian educational grades to figure out *Table 4(b)*, which shows that improvement has its strongest pay-off (marked*) for those with just the most basic previous qualifications. We are probably dealing with a 'second chance' thesis here. It is widely known that mature students who benefit/change most from a return to learning are the ones who have missed out on or been denied educational opportunities. What, perhaps, this data shows is that it is easier to build on faint promise (GED is the equivalent of some modest GCSE passes) than no track record whatsoever. Education offers no modish magic bullet, no *dernier cri*, and sometimes it is the very fit with the experience of the mainstream that gives us confidence in these results

Table 4(c) is a further example of a well-worn educational path. The table follows our 'improvers' through to post-release and, unsurprisingly, we see a classic 'continuity' mechanism at work. SIR-beating is enhanced considerably for those inmates (marked*) who follow further education after release. Statistically speaking, this is a startling result but one has to keep in mind the old adage that data never speak for themselves. I have argued all along that education can work in wondrous many ways and that the method here only reveals the outline footprint of these inner workings. Further information is needed before the significance of this particular result is fully apparent. In this instance, we asked some former students why this particular pattern was so marked and they offered much food-for-thought, no doubt all of it having a grain of truth.

The simplest 'theory', and the most humbling, was that the finding is true by definition. It is tautologically true that if the ex-convict is attending further education in college, then they cannot be in prison. A rather more positive idea was the 'keep 'em busy mechanism'. The period immediately after release is known to be a particularly fragile time for ex-convicts, who often lack the support to resist the very pressures that took them into crime in the first place. Going to college or university may establish a legitimate and familiar routine instead of being simply cast adrift. A third possibility, was an 'identity change' hypothesis, which suggests that education can play a crucial part in a conscious effort to 'go straight'. Education is one of the few relatively open and lawful avenues for the ex-offender. What may also be happening is that these Simon Fraser inmates follow up their prison education experience deliberately in order to build respectable, post-release identities as 'mature students'. In social science terms, this is known as 'reference group affiliation', which in ordinary parlance might be rendered as the strategy of making step-by-step progression to eventual membership of the chattering classes.

These brief examples show how research can begin to fill out some of the inner workings of the 'black box' programme. The 'improvement hypothesis' is thus refined from a general appreciation of 'hard-sloggers' to a more subtle set of processes that could be built into a variety of programmes. One might summarise this by saying that— 'what work's best is hard-slogging, applied at an age pre or post the inmate-culture bulge, by offenders who have only the faintest speck of previous educational achievement, and who go on to build a post-release identity around their new-found prowess'.

The hard cases
We come to my final example in which I want to pursue the same method to make a rather different point about the nature of rehabilitation. I have repeated, tortuously, the point that programmes do not work universally but that success depends on context. Lives of crime and years of imprisonment, in and of themselves, leave huge marks on the offender. We should not expect education to wash away all such traces and indeed we might expect some aspects of this socialisation to be indelible. Another aspect of the research was to examine the traditional bugbear of prison programming, namely the 'revolving door brigade', the 'perpetual returnees'. We termed them the 'hard-cases' and operationalised them as a sub-group using an amalgam of three key indicators of recidivism—these inmates were school 'drop-outs', from 'broken homes', with a large string of 'juvenile convictions'. Their propensity to re-offend was reflected in a SIR score that was a full 16 points worse than prisoner students as a whole (see *Table 5*).

We tried to see if there was any particular feature of the university programme that impacted upon them. This was a frustrating task in that the relative improvement for SFU 'hard-cases' was the same as for the SFU group as a whole (c.f. *Table 2* and *Table 5*). Moreover, they seemed to respond to variations in educational experience as for the group as a whole. Thus hard-case, hard-sloggers did as well as 'improvers' in general. The only minor difference in educational impact that was in terms of the relative successes of hard-cases who choose theatre courses. The performance arts course requires a great deal of collaboration and it might be that its collective nature finds resonance with this particular group. However, numbers were small in this respect and make us reluctant to pronounce upon a trend. As with much else in our work, it should be regarded as a hypothesis worthy of further investigation (details in Duguid *et al*, 1998).

Hard cases (n=118)	Predicted non-return	Actual non-return	Relative improvement
	42	55	31

Table 5(a): 'Hard Cases' sub-group

Subgroups	Predicted (%)	Actual (%)	Relative improvement (%)
One year (169)	57	70	22
Two years (199)	59	78	33
3-4 years (165)	57	73	29
5 or more (121)	59	80	36

Table 5(b): 'Total Group' Gap between Prison Education Program and Release

Subgroups	Predicted (%)	Actual (%)	Relative Improvement (%)
One year (29)	41	34	-15*
Twoyears (32)	41	56	36
3-4 years (31)	41	61	50
5 or more (26)	46	69	50

Table 5(c): 'Hard Cases': Gap between Prison Education Program and Release

Subgroups	Predicted( )%	Actual (%)	Relative Improvement (%)
(27)	43	70	62

Table 5(d): 'Hard Cases' with Further Education after Release

Our inquiry into the hard cases did not draw an entire blank, however, for it revealed the importance of education programmes working in harmony with other aspects of the prison regime. We had become interested in this idea of 'continuity' between the programme and post-release activity (recall *Table 4(c)*) and further hypothesised that groups with shorter gaps between attending the programme and release would further improve their chances in the rehabilitation stakes. The thinking was very much along the lines of the importance of 'maintaining progress' and of maximising the potential for transferring success from 'inside' to 'outside'. This proved too simplistic a hypotheses and for the 'total group' (see *Table 5(b)*) there was no clear relationship between 'time out of education' and 'rehabilitation'. The case of the hard-cases was even more bizarre in this respect. Extreme disaster, in the form of a quick return to prison, awaited the vast majority who studied on the programme shortly before release (see *Table 5(b)* marked*).

Why the paradoxical result? Never should anyone investigating prison programmes forget that inmates spend relatively little 'programme time' as compared to 'doing time'. It turned out that the 29 impending disasters here contained a high proportion of 'sentence-expiry' cases. In other words, these inmates were those who had been pitched directly out of medium/maximum security prisons without any of the benefits of preparation for release offered by the more usual process of 'cascading' down to the lower security regimes. What we see here is that education cannot compensate for the mechanics of the penal system. Hard-cases, with no basic preparation for release, tend to come straight back through the prison gates. Note as a post-script however, that even for hard-cases another aspect of 'continuity' thesis remains true. Few hard-cases make it to post-release education, but for those who do—rehabilitation awaits (see *Table 5(c)*).

CONCLUSION

And so to the conclusion of the 'Evaluator's Tale'. Modern social science methodology has abandoned the search for magic bullet solutions for the complex problems that beset major societal institutions such as the criminal justice system. Evaluation research has started to ask the right question and requires the investigator to compile an evidence-base founded upon understanding the varying outcomes of programmes, over a number of trials, for subjects from a variety of backgrounds, and in a range of different institutional circumstances. Alas, on this criterion, it follows that there are simply not enough sustained inquiries around to make the political/policy case for an expansion of prisoner education. However, it is undeniable that the scatter of results presented here, and elsewhere, are encouraging. So let me try to emphasise, once again, the key message.

Although the case studied is one of a higher education initiative in a 'corrections' regime geographically and culturally distant from the United Kingdom, it contains lessons for all programming with offenders. Although the course 'worked' at the aggregate level, if one begins to ask 'why did it work?,' it transpires that success can be attributed to a range of specific processes that were particularly appropriate to identifiable groups of offenders. What emerges as important are features such as:

- the longevity and continuity of provision

- the close linkages between courses and teaching personnel across several prisons

- the opportunity to begin attendance without the recognised entry qualifications

- the institutional fortitude to allow low achievers to develop slowly

- the use of specialist, non-prison, teaching staff

- the award of high-status, nationally-recognised qualifications rather than corrections certificates

- the prospect of playing a part in organizing the initiative

- the value of the identity of 'mature student', and so on.

None of these attributes are unique to the Simon Fraser programme. Indeed they can, and should, play a part in all education and training from basic skills onwards.

Perhaps above all, what counted in our case study was the measure of 'choice' afforded to the offender. A systematic education system with *all* its potential benefits was widely available over a long time period and offered an alternative to the latent, school-for-crime syllabus that pervades the contemporary prison. Inmates were thus free to volunteer for the course (or not), to co-operate closely (or not), to stay with the programme (or not), to seek to extend the programme (or not), to learn lessons (or not), to retain lessons (or not) and to apply lessons (or not). All programmes work though the volition of their subjects and somewhere in this capacity to provide continual support for positive choices lies the secret of lifelong prisoner education. It is time for the Prison Service to think again about programmes that are de-coupled from the hubris-ridden notions of 'experts' who insist that they know what is best for others. It is time for another look, through new lenses, at *all* of those standard, old-fashioned education and training programmes

There is of course a postscript to this conclusion. Although the history of research-led policy-making is hardly glittering and although evaluation research on penal initiatives is thin on the ground, I have on the whole been upbeat about the prospects for using research to develop prisoner education. But please note, dear reader, that the programme upon which I have concentrated here was closed by the Canadian Correctional Service in 1994, and the miniature British version, which I briefly mentioned above, was curtailed at HMP Full Sutton in 1998. I will not enter into the financial and political dramas that led to the demise of two of the great successes of prison programming. Suffice to say, in the last analysis, *it is more than research that is needed.*

BIBLIOGRAPHY for *Chapter 4*

Campbell D. (1969), 'Reforms As Experiments', *American Psychologist*, Vol. 24, pp. 409-429

Cormier R. (1997), 'Yes SIR! A Stable Risk-prediction Tool', *Forum on Corrections Research*, Vol 9 pp. 3-7, Ottawa: Correctional Services Canada

Cohen S. and Taylor. L. (1977), 'Talking About the Prison Blues' in C. Bell and H. Newby (eds.), *Doing Social Research*, London: George, Allan and Unwin

Duguid S. and Pawson R. (1998), 'Education, Transformation and Change', *Evaluation Review*, Vol. 22, pp. 470-495

Duguid. S. *et al* (1998), *British Columbia Prison Education Project: Final Report*, Institute of Humanities, Simon Fraser University

Finckenauer J. O. (1982), *Scared Straight! and the Panacea Phenomenon*. New Jersey: Prentice-Hall

Martinson R. (1974), 'What Works? Questions and Answers About Prison Reform', *Public Interest*, Vol. 35, pp. 22-45

Pawson R. and Tilley N. (1997), *Realistic Evaluation*, London: Sage

Reuss A. (1997), *Higher Education and Personal Change in Prisoners*, PhD Thesis, University of Leeds.

CHAPTER 5

Dealing With Time: Factors that Influence Prisoners to Participate in Prison Education Programmes

Petra MacGuinness

This chapter explains the findings of a research project in prison education within the context of a maximum security prison. As a practitioner in prison education in the fields of Basic Skills and Key Skills and with an interest in adults' participation in post compulsory education, I recognised that many of the learners in prison would have been classed as traditional non-participants, had they not been imprisoned. Research suggests that the majority of prisoners come from the section of population that has the lowest initial educational attainment and the lowest participation rate in formal learning episodes after leaving compulsory education (*National Prison Survey, 1991*). Yet, as Stephen Duguid claims and most practitioners in this field will have experienced, many prisoners are successful learners (Duguid, 1987: 329).

INTRODUCTION

The research was undertaken at the Education Department of HMP Whitemoor which was then one of the five prisons of the Dispersal Estate, where a large proportion of prisoners have very long sentences, including that of natural life, and high security categories.

HMP Whitemoor is effectively divided into two prisons; one half—two wings—houses rule 45 prisoners and the other two wings accommodate the remainder. A full-time education programme is delivered to both sides with a programme ranging from Basic Skills to Open University studies. Inmates' educational levels are assessed on arrival at Whitemoor by the ALBSU Screening test. Participation in the education programme is voluntary and inmates have to apply to the labour board if they want to attend.

The primary data for this research was drawn from students studying full-time at the Education Department. To provide some basis for empirical generalization, a survey in the form of a questionnaire was administered to every group of the Education Department. Those studied in more detail came from the two groups I worked with on a regular basis. Group One consisted of a mixture of A-level and Open

University students, studying mainly independently, Goup Two was an Access group. Academically these students are placed between Basic Skills and GCSE level. Although this research does not claim to be representative of the entire prisoner population it covers the academic range of prisoner education.

LEARNING IN EXTREMIS

Most people, at some stage, have to deal with extreme or shattering events that disturb the normal routine of their life. A long-term prison sentence also falls into this category, regardless of whether it is served as a prisoner of war, hostage or as a result of criminal activity. One marked difference, between the long-term prisoner and other people is 'that the prison sentence is all encompassing for the prisoner as he or she is unable to compensate with other domains of life' (Cohen and Taylor, 1981: 53).

Events such as death or environmental catastrophe tend to occur in part of one's life, in one domain, other domains can then be called into service to provide reassurance and to re-establish credibility. When, for example, having to contend with the sudden loss of a close relative, then it is possible to 'keep going' by 'losing oneself in one's job'. However, 'The long-term prisoner cannot play one domain off against another in this way and must learn to live with it if incarceration is to be survived' (Cohen and Taylor, 1981: 53). Gresham Sykes (1958) categorised the experience of imprisonment into five pains i.e. isolation from the larger community, lack of material possessions, blocked access to heterosexual relationships, reduced personal autonomy and reduced personal security. These foster alienation from prison staff and management and from the larger community.

For many people who have had to endure such a prison sentence, keeping their mind active by learning has played an important part in maintaining their ability to live within extreme situations, and to survive all kind of deprivations. In his article 'Learning in Extremis' Williamson considers a class of human experiences which are characterised as extreme and which perplex those who believe that learning requires freedom (Williamson, 1998: 23).

Furthermore, a model of motivation is put forward by Boshier who believes that humans aim for the state of homeostasis. An imbalance in our personal stability motivates us to learn because we aim to overcome the difference between the ideal state and the actual state of affairs. 'This tension state 'motivates' the learner to participate in adult education which hopefully 'satisfies' the need by restoring balance. Homeostasis can be attained by adjusting the 'ideal' sought, so it becomes more congruent with the 'actual' state of the learner, or by acquiring the knowledge, attitudes and skills embodied in the 'ideal' state' (Boshier, 1986:18).

Life in a maximum security prison is far from anyone's ideal state. Learning and academic achievement can not only be valuable tools in overcoming the psychological instability of imprisonment but also raise the prisoner's self-esteem. Worth confirmed this theory by reporting 'some [Open University] students saw degree studies as status— conferring and enhancing self-esteem. And for a few, the OU provided a way of separating themselves entirely from the experience of imprisonment' (Worth, 1991: 38).

According to Primo Levi, who survived life in a concentration camp, prisoners also have to learn not to think and to wipe out both the past and the future (Williamson, 1998: 23). A cogent illustration of this concept can be found in Cohen and Taylor's observations and descriptions of the long-term prisoners in Durham jail's high security wing. 'It is just not possible for many prisoners to believe that wives or friends will wait for 20 years. There may almost be some fatalistic relief in reducing the emotional reliance upon outsiders (Cohen and Taylor, 1981: 78). Terry Waite, hostage in Beirut for nearly five years, remarked

Remembering can be painful, and for much of my captivity I hardly allowed myself to think about my family and friends in order to protect myself from emotions which might have got the better of me. (Waite, 1995: 15)

This statement is re-inforced by inmate autobiographies. Boyle for example writes:

The only way to pass the time was to do exercises and reading and thinking thoughts of hatred. My former life was far in the distance and I would try not to think of my family as it hurt too much. (Boyle, 1977:179)

A further kind of learning often found in prisons, is that of learning in order to maintain sanity, to mark time and to stave off the hopelessness. Some of the most recent publicised examples of this type of learning are those of the hostages of Lebanon '... Survival under those conditions was achieved through a great effort of will, of memory, of an active mental engagement during which Keenan interrogated the resources of his own mind to retain a hope of survival' (Williamson, 1998: 25). But 'learning in extremis' needs to be contextualised against the broader framework that characterises education in prisons.

THE PROVISION OF FORMAL EDUCATION PROGRAMMES IN PRISONS

Prisoner education in Britain—in its present organized form—did not become topical until the eighteenth century when 'the modern concept of the prison was emerging in England inspired by the work of reformers such as John Howard, whose *State of the Prisons* was published in 1777' (Forster, 1998: 59). The first formal provision of education for prisoners in England was introduced by Robert Peel's 1823 Parliamentary Gaol Act which required instruction in reading and writing in all English prisons by appointed schoolmasters. Forster (1998) describes how post war years facilitated a return to the more liberal regime of reform, and prison education in England and Wales became the responsibility of the Local Education Authorities (LEAs), who would supply teachers from local colleges to prison education departments.

The discourse of prison education is not value free and is vulnerable to changes 'in public policy as government responds to public feelings about crime, safety and correction' (Duguid, 1998: 20). The post-war approach of the Medical Model saw criminal behaviour as an illness. It was briefly accepted in Britain but the May Committee of Enquiry report in 1979 argued that '. . . the rhetoric of treatment and training has had its day and should be replaced' (Malin, Kell, Rust, 1994: 7). This model was superseded by the Cognitive Behavioural approach which considered that cognitive deficits are learnt rather than inherent. It teaches the offenders in behavioural programmes to face up to what they have done, to understand the processes that led to the criminal behaviour and to develop strategies of controlling behaviour. Whilst the 1966 Mountbatten report had resulted in more education in prisons, national economical difficulties and a reduction in public spending led to pressure on the prison system. Similar to the effects caused by the market forces that govern provision at Further and Higher Education Colleges, prison education staff and students today experience a considerable amount of insecurity raised by individual prison budget problems, changes in governorship and the possible five yearly change of provider, introduced as part of the Further and Higher Education Act 1992.

THE CONCEPT OF TIME

One aspect that influences participation in prison education is the concept of time. For most of us, time is a resource and people complain of not having enough time. McGivney elaborates that time is the 'obstacle most frequently stated by adults in American and British surveys to participation in education' (McGivney, 1990a: 17).

Long-term prisoners experience time differently as they have been given time as a punishment. 'But they have been given someone else's time. Their own time has been abstracted by the courts like a monetary fine and in its place they have been given prison time. This is no longer a resource but a controller' (Cohen and Taylor, 1981: 100).

Reporting on a research project with Open University tutors teaching in prisons, Worth remarks that 'Education also functions as an "activity" like work, to fill time, to contribute to "a busy and purposeful life" and a way of coming to terms with, making sense of a long/life sentence by being able to set determinate markers and running a kind of parallel time-track' (Worth, 1991: 34/38).

Boyle describes how he organized his time by following a strict routine every single day. He split his day into physical exercises, '.... sculpting, doing a psychology course with the Open University and writing. Prison is all about freedom or the lack of it and the definition of this as far as I'm concerned isn't purely physical, it is also a state of mind' (Boyle, 1977: 254). But what 'type' of person, in these circumstances (of imprisonment) turns to education as a 'time-marker'?

NON-PARTICIPANT TYPOLOGIES

The background to an adult's participation and non-participation in educational activities has been well researched and documented. A range of British surveys invariably came to the conclusion that 'Mature students do not represent a cross-section of the adult population ... Participants in adult educational activities frequently come from 'those of working age; those in non-manual occupations; and those with more than minimal educational success' (Woodley *et al*, 1987: 13).

Woodley concludes that adult education is largely the preserve of the middle classes. He is not alone with these conclusions. Most surveys identified age, previous educational attainment and class as factors influencing participation in post compulsory education (NIACE, 1996; ACECE, 1982; NIACE, 1997).

Further evidence can be found in several theories which explain how this phenomenon repeats itself through the actions of working class people themselves. Paul Willis (1977) believes that 'failure' to continue participating in education and training is a working class response to capitalism whilst Westwood, who researched working class women argues that there is 'a relationship between the association of education with childhood and work with adulthood'. This results in a counter-culture which reinforces the non-participation of working class people in education and training. (Westwood, 1985: 57)

McGivney argues that peer groups have a cumulative effect in shaping people's attitudes and behaviour; this, she believes, creates and reinforces a culture (McGivney, 1990a: 20). Examples of these effects are described by Sewell (1997) and Macan Ghaill (1994) who worked with African Caribbean youths. Examples of peer groups' positive influences are the Nubian Link, an after school black history group where initially 'at risk' participants all left school without experiencing permanent exclusion, some of them unexpectedly with formal qualifications (Runnymede Trust, 1998).

NON-PARTICIPANTS AND IMPRISONMENT— THE LINK

The relevance of the influence of social class on participation in adult education to prison education has been recognised on a wide basis. Several national and international surveys and reports suggest an indisputable link between social class and those who are committed to prison. The Home Office research study 'Reducing Offending, An Assessment of Research Evidence on Ways of Dealing with Offending Behaviour' states: 'Offenders serving custodial and community sentences are considerably more likely than the general population to be *poorly educated* (author's italics) with low levels of literacy, have few qualifications and skills, and to be unemployed (Crow *et al*, 1989).

McGivney believes that 'Low school achievement often goes together with truanting, school exclusion and offending behaviour'. Similar findings were reported by J. Duprey-Kennedy in France (1998), Mednis in Latvia (1998) and Crossroads, a partnership between organizations in Belgium, England and The Netherlands, who devise model training programmes for prisons in the three countries (NACRO, 1998).

In England and Wales, the most relevant background information to adult learners in prison comes from the 1991 *National Prison Survey*. It was commissioned by the Home Office Research and Planning Unit and confirms the above findings in other countries.

REASONS INMATES GIVE FOR PARTICIPATING IN PRISON EDUCATION PROGRAMMES

The strongest contribution to the discussion of factors influencing participation in prison education must ultimately come from inmates themselves. Only they will be able to relate their experience of imprisonment and the effects this had on them but little is known about the reasons prisoners give themselves for participating in educational programmes.

'The pioneer in quantitative efforts to delineate reasons for participation is Roger Boshier' (Parsons and Langenbach, 1993) who developed an instrument that claims to reveal reasons for participation in prison education programmes, known as the Prison Educational Participation Scale (PEPS). After administering a 60 item scale to 102 inmates, Boshier arrived at five factors that motivated prisoners to participate in education: Personal control, Self-assertion, Outside contact, Self-preservation, Cognitive interest (Boshier, 1971). It is against this brief background 'sketch' of education in prisons that I conducted my research project on factors that influence prisoners to participate in prisoner education programmes.

METHODOLOGY

One aspect of this research was to apply methods that would not only be suitable to study the field of learners in prison, but also effective in establishing the required data. As the area studied is complex and involves aspects such as students' individual cultural backgrounds, current and past paradigms and policies of formal prisoner education, also the effects imprisonment has on the individual prisoner, it seemed prudent to employ a range of suitable methods. 'Methodological triangulation or using different complementary methods to study the same events, can improve both the validity of the data, and its interpretation, as the imperfections of each method are compensated for by the particular strengths of others' (Liebling, 1992: 108).

Based on the philosophies of positivism and naturalism, the diversity of strategies that can be used to conduct educational research can broadly be divided into qualitative and quantitative methods. 'Quantitative research typically employs what are usually referred to as structured forms of data, consisting of frequency counts or measurements of other kinds. By contrast the data that qualitative researchers typically deal with are verbal descriptions in natural language, produced by them or by informants' (Hammersley, 1994: 25). As the studied area is so diverse and concerned primarily with people and the environment that influenced their development and because inmates' perspectives, feelings and experiences were actively sought, I decided on employing the principally holistic approach of naturalism in order to discover the influencing phenomena and to build theory.

Semi-structured interviews and group discussions with inmates of the two groups I worked with on a regular basis, and questionnaires to all students studying at the Education Department, established the required primary data. Using questionnaires was an attempt to increase the validity of the research findings by means of technique triangulation. 'As a diversity of techniques involves different validity threats, they provide a basis for checking interpretation' (Hammersley and Atkinson, 1994: 231).

For analysis the method of grounded theory (Glaser and Strauss, 1967) was employed as this allowed coding of the largely qualitative responses for statistical analysis. Classifying the given reasons for starting education into four different groups was an attempt to conceptionalize the data. As students were expressing their feelings and reasons in a variety of ways—using a range of words that mean the same or describe a similar occurrence—but also describing a variety of aspects of the same concepts this process appeared fair. Strauss and Corbin call this process 'conceptional ordering' 'the organization of data according to their properties and dimensions and then using description to elucidate those data' (Strauss and Corbin, 1998: 19).

As a further step in reducing the interplay between the researcher and the data, categories identified in the literature review were taken into account. As Strauss and Corbin mention, 'Interplay by its very nature means that a researcher is actively reacting to and working with data' (Strauss and Corbin, 1998:58).

RESULTS

The questionnaires
In total 64 per cent of the distributed questionnaires were returned. Inmates had been invited to give as many reasons as they liked for first enrolling in the formal prison education programme and the replies were classified into 19 different reasons/phenomena according to their significance. Out of these I constructed four categories which, although sharing common characteristics, represented discrete elements of their own.

1. Starting education to catch up.
2. Starting education to keep occupied.
3. Starting education to improve employment prospects.
4. Starting education to survive prison and to manage the given time.

Most of the reasons (53.6 per cent) given for first starting a full time education programme fell into this category. Many subjects chose their time in prison to catch up on the academic qualifications they had not achieved during their initial education. At Whitemoor, the percentage of those who had no qualification when they left initial education is very much higher than in the general population (34 per cent) but also much higher than indicated in the 1992 *National Prison Survey* (43 per cent). Joining formal prison education for wanting to catch up was also spread equally over all age groups.

The majority of students at Whitemoor were between 26 and 45 years of age—this is a reflection of the total Whitemoor population. Whilst the general population shows a slow but steady decline of participation with age the Whitemoor population is fairly stable across all age groups. Starting education to keep occupied was also distributed fairly evenly across all age groups, 21 per cent of the answers were connected with occupying time. Thirteen per cent of responding inmates felt that qualifications might help them to gain a job after release, and some inmates saw learning a particular skill as a means to 'go straight'. The highest response to this category came from inmates aged 25—34 years of age. Twelve given reasons were concerned with keeping the brain active/stimulated and making sense of the given time (sentence). Survival by managing to retain an element of control over their own lives by choosing the daily activities was important to some inmates. Most responses were found in the 25-34 year age group, whilst no replies were given by inmates aged 20-24 years of age.

The semi-structured interviews
Altogether nine students participated in the semi-structured interviews. The extreme parameters of initial educational experiences ranged from fairly successful, protected by parental support, to perceiving school as a retreat.

> I did not have a happy childhood but enjoyed the protection the school offered as a non-violent environment for certain hours of the day'. (Harold)

Only two students had experienced a relatively settled initial education, four had spent education time in borstal or children's homes and two had endured frequent interruptions caused by family moves. Two of the nine interviewed students had achieved qualifications by school leaving age; this translates into 78 per cent non-achievement, confirming the higher than *National Prison Survey* results of the questionnaire.

During the interviews concepts in three of the categories developed from the questionnaire returns emerged. Inmates had initially joined education programmes to catch up, to keep occupied and to manage dealing with the given time. The dimensions of the categories were stretched, and extremes, such as a deeply seated fear of developing a mental illness, induced by the prison environment and an inability to realise the dimension of the given time, emerged. None of the inmates mentioned that gaining academic qualifications might help in gaining a job after release. The question was dismissed by comments like, 'Who is going to give me a job with my record?' 'I am not going to get a job at my age'.

One possible explanation for this phenomenon is that out of the nine students who participated in the semi-structured interviews, seven were serving a life sentence, to whom employment problems present no immediate concerns.

Discussion

Starting education to catch up
This category of issues was concerned with awareness, acceptance and low self-esteem, demonstrating a very realistic perception of the significance our society places on a successful initial education. On reflection students claim to have realised that they have missed out and that this lack of education contributes to their low self-esteem. Owing to its long tradition as a provider of education, the prison environment is deemed acceptable for 'catching up' on this deficit thereby overcoming institutional barriers. As many in the peer group come from a similar background prisoners feel more comfortable attempting formal learning.

Reasons in this category are inferring that education is a measurable quantity that has yet to be achieved:

I wanted to achieve certificates and exams.

I need to read and write to get through life.

These statements, made on questionnaires and during interviews, are a clear indication that many inmates are in no doubt about the value society places on achievement in education. The very high incidence of prisoners who admitted in the questionnaires to not having achieved any qualifications during their initial education confirms the 1991 *National Prison Survey's* intimation of a strong link between low or non-achievement in initial education and crime.

Initial non-achievers tend not to participate in further formal learning in between leaving school and coming to prison, in this sample, 61 per cent out of the 69 per cent of the students who had no qualifications. According to Williams, 'Many of the teenagers who leave school without qualifications persist in their failure (1997). A disproportionally large amount of these non-achievers end up in prison. McGivney (1999), Crow *et al* (1998) and Mednis (1998) argue that low social class is the key to this phenomenon.

I joined education to learn what I should have learnt at school.

I joined education to catch up on the things I should have done when I was outside.

These statements, made during a group discussion on the subject of reasons why inmates present had not achieved at the end of their initial education, strongly demonstrate an acceptance of a need to 'catch up'. Situational barriers, such as time and cost are often stated as reasons for non-participation in adult education and might explain why 'free' education in prison is perceived as an acceptable opportunity. Boshier also arrived at the conclusion that education is accessed by prisoners in order to overcome past failures. He linked this factor with the attempt to get personal control of life. It could be argued that the decision to improve one's prospects by catching up on missed opportunities is synonymous to taking control of life. However, being in control of life acquires an extra dimension in the prison environment when this environment is perceived as a total institution. There is very little room for individuality within such an institution and being in control of one's own learning can become more significant under such restraints.

As previously stated, one explanation for voluntary learning in prison is likely to be the long established tradition of provision of prison education. As provision is part of the institution, situational and institutional barriers such as' ... perception of inappropriateness, hostility towards school ...' (McGivney, 1990a: 21) that often account for non-participation 'on the out', are removed.

As a 'side effect' of this provision, the power of peer group pressure, that prevented participation in formal learning before coming to prison, is also lessened. Just as the 'peer groups have a cumulative effect in shaping peoples' attitudes and behaviour, creating and re-enforcing the anti—school culture' (McGivney, 1990a: 20), the prison culture makes participation in education acceptable. An explanation for this phenomenon was put forward by a Whitemoor student, during a discussion on this subject:

> One of the reasons why prisoners who attend prison education programmes—prisoners who wouldn't think to join an education programme in the community—is because they are in the company of peers—with similar backgrounds and educational and emotional stages and standards. (Peter)

It is important to remember that all received answers on the questionnaires are of a reflexive nature. All students are referring to a point in the past, meaning that sometimes inmates have the benefit of the secure knowledge of progression or a perceived, changed self. This factor might be contributory in the high incidence of reference to a low self-esteem being the reason for initially joining the education programme. Fourteen references were made to the concept of self-esteem in the questionnaires, some answers to this question were straight forward:

> ... to boost my self-esteem.

Others were of a more descriptive nature:

> ... to feel better about myself.

One might theorise that the already low self-esteem of the initial non-achiever receives such a severe battering by being sent to prison, that the celebratory mood of the school-counter culture (Willis, 1977: 56) is questioned or abandoned. This theory is supported by Boshier's model of motivation, as in this state of tension—created by the gulf between the extreme environment of the dispersal prison and his personal ideal—the prisoner tries to restore the balance (homeostasis) by addressing the apparent deficit, evident by a lack of certificates or maybe suggested by a person in authority during his initial education. 'Homeostasis can be attained ... by acquiring the knowledge, attitude and skills embodied in the ideal state' (Boshier, 1986: 18). As the education programme necessary to achieve this is acceptable and accessible, the prisoner addresses the imbalance by adjusting his ideal.

Starting education to keep occupied
Concepts of attitude, challenge and avoidance construct this category of factors that under prison conditions can lead inmates to access a formal education programme. A prisoner, encouraged by the removal of various barriers to learning, might accept a challenge to prove to himself or others that he can in fact achieve. The consequence of this action would be the application to join the education programme. This category is perhaps the only category where the interests of the prisoner and the Prison Service merge or at least run parallel to each other. Keeping occupied is in everybody's interest.

Every prisoner will have come across the concept of boredom during his or her sentence. Boredom in an environment that constricts movement and does not offer many distractions or comforts becomes enforced boredom, and must be particularly problematic.

> Probably the greatest factors that affect an inmate who stops behind his door, are paranoia or boredom. Both breed frustration and some sort of displacement is needed, if only to satisfy psychological needs. (Ged)

However, only two returns admitted to boredom as a reason for accessing the formal education programme. The decision to join the education programme in order to keep occupied was often triggered by the concept of challenge. Challenge creates excitement by itself and the concept was cited in both the questionnaires and the interviews.

The challenge to disprove someone's prophecy was invariably linked to teachers' expectations or remarks during initial education. Angela Devlin (1995) observed 'Such comments could have a devastating effect as too often these labels become a self-fulfilling prophecy'. In an interview Tom illustrated one of these consequences:

> When it came to the multiplication tables everyone had to stand and recite from memory. I had difficulty in doing this and as a consequence had to

suffer this teacher's anger and bullying, which made me feel ashamed and inadequate. Since then I have never been confident in working with the multiplication tables

Tom took up the challenge and is now studying Mathematics with the Open University.

Harold remembers how teachers mis-reading his behaviour added to his already overwhelming problems by inducing guilt:

I was not disruptive but was pulled up for dreaming. Actually, I was traumatised by [the violence of] my mentally disturbed father. I was made to feel guilty and was always told that I could do better, but I was busy trying to keep alive.

These comments clearly illustrate that these incidents from early years in education are not forgotten but harboured. Sometimes, years later, students try to prove that the teacher was wrong.

Students also mentioned that they had joined the education programme to find out whether they could achieve. Students reported that they had enrolled to prove to themselves that they could complete the task set, as a self challenge and development, and because they found the challenge stimulating.

A third strand of challenge was gaining access to the education programme because the inmate wanted to 'get what I want'. In these cases students had a particular interest and needed the assistance of the education department in order to pursue this interest. In each case, before accessing the education programme, the student had partaken in a lot of reading about the subject, increased his interest and was inspired to gain a qualification in this subject.

Andy remembered:

I mainly joined education because I wanted to get my own thing off the ground. I was told by the Education Co-ordinator here 'You prove to us what you can do and then we will help you.

In the third concept of this category students reported a general interest in learning. They said that they had joined education because they had a general interest in educational activities, some said that they found learning interesting and another claimed to 'simply like education'. Several students also mentioned that they liked reading and that they had participated in informal learning before joining the education programme.

I have always read, especially about mythology, folklore and subjects that were connected to people's cultures. I used to go to the library and teach myself. I have always done that. (Andy)

As the emphasis of the above answer is clearly on learning—not on education—the bias of the perception that learning is solely an academic activity was removed during analysis. This added a new dimension to the answers given during the interviews. All students were asked about their learning history and eight out of nine interviewees had a long and/or frequent history of learning episodes. As not all of these had led to formal or academic qualifications, they were not recognised as learning.

From this stance it is fair to question the value society places on compulsory education certificates at the expense of other less formal ways of learning. The assumption too easily leads to the dismissal of other valuable skills.

Starting education to improve employment prospects
This apparently straightforward category with its pragmatic features, can in some cases be based on intricate processes of sublimation. Inmates decide that the time spent in prison is worthwhile if qualifications, that help to secure future employment are gained, thereby using the time of their sentence to address the gap between the ideal sought and the present reality. Students whose answers fell into this category studied predominantly GCSE subjects, Information Technology and Business Studies. Inmates' answers demonstrated their belief that 'having an education' can assist in avoiding recidivism.

> I joined education to get prepared for the outside world without resorting to crime.

> I wanted to become confident enough to go straight.

The above statements re-enforce what students said in the category 'Joining education to catch up', indicating awareness of their initial non/underachievement, recognising the value society places on these achievements, adopting these values in an attempt to amend the deficit.

Linking 'going straight' to confidence demonstrates that students related low self esteem caused by low/under achievement to offending.

Some students focused on learning particular skills:

> I want to gain qualifications to become an accountant.

> I want to gain internationally recognised qualifications to enable me to make full use of my experience and previous knowledge ... so that I can have the best chance of employment after release.

These straightforward, future oriented statements imply that students are seeking the stability of a particular occupation. Students could also be searching for a new identity e.g. by saying 'I am a (occupation)' rather than 'I am an ex offender'.

There are also strong links to some of the properties of category four, surviving prison, where in one of the interviews Ged described his attempt to deal with the effects a total institution can have on the individual '... I needed to create my identity and give myself new avenues. I joined education'.

Starting education to survive prison and to manage the given time
Two major issues constructed this category—survival and time management. Inmates' responses strongly indicated that they accessed education programmes in prison to help to survive the prison environment and the given time. In many cases the properties and dimensions of these issues overlapped to such an extent that it was difficult to define their parameters.

Two dimensions of life in a prison are the physical environment and the psychological environment. Jimmy Boyle explains 'Prison is all about freedom or the lack of it and the definition of this as far as I'm concerned isn't purely physical, it is also a state of mind' (Boyle, 1977: 254). Human beings have the ability to adjust to life in extreme environments, and all prisoners will have to learn to come to terms with the physical environment of the prison.

The psychological environment of prison is concerned with features of the total institution as defined by Goffman 'batch living, binary management, the inmate role and the institutional perspective' (Goffman, 1961: 70) Inmates have to perform most of their daily activities in the immediate company of others (chosen by an outside agency) e.g. queuing up for food and walking to the workshops/visits/education. All inmates get subjected to the same treatment and have to perform the same daily routine at precisely the same time. Darren observed:

> Some people don't notice that they are vegetating through routine. They plod along and don't know what day it is because they don't keep track of time. Sometimes they ask 'is it dinner time?' when it is night time. This is a slow process, at first you are bored, then you become lethargic.

Gresham Sykes describes aspects of the 'total institution' in his 'Pains of Imprisonment'. Apart from where he agrees with Goffman, Sykes identified lack of material possessions, blocked access to heterosexual relationships and reduced personal security as the features of imprisonment each inmate will have to learn to live with. The following excerpts from the interviews suggest how onerous adjustment to life in a dispersal prison can be and that it takes some time to come to terms with the role of prisoner.

Ged described how prison affected him at first:

> I spent the first few months behind doors and then I worked in the prison kitchen for six months, then I felt it was time to change.

Asked what he meant by 'change' he explained

> I thought 'there's got to be a purpose to this. Is this who I am? I asked myself lots of questions like: 'What is the point?' 'Who am I' 'Do I belong?' and I decided that I want to be something rather than just be.

Asked to explain how he went about changing he elaborated

> Prison is like a conveyor belt, you can stay on or you can get off. I decided that it was time to get off, to do this I had to raise my self-esteem and I needed to create my identity and give myself new avenues. I joined education.

In this attempt at dealing with the effects a total institution can have on the individual, the student recognised that he could be passive and succumb to the institution or actively participate in his life. He utilised the opportunities the Education Department could offer to 'get off the conveyor belt', took charge and with this overcame some of the psychological influences and effects of the institution. In her study 'Identity and the Experience of Dispersal Conditions', Waller came to similar conclusions: 'All of the subjects agreed that the experience of a long sentence under dispersal conditions is arduous, and puts pressure on personal identity, tending to cause disjunction'. (Waller, 1999)

Darren also struggled with accepting the 'conveyor belt 'and decided to 'get off'.

> After conviction I spent six months not doing a lot. Then I spent some time in the workshops painting plastic soldiers and going dulally. It was my idea to apply to go on part-time education.

Some references regarding the prison environment were also made on the questionnaire. One inmate said that he had 'joined education to achieve an enlightened environment away from the prison culture' another stated that he 'wanted to be in a better, more adult environment.'

However, in order to be de-categorised, an inmate will have to show that he has addressed his offending behaviour. Within the current paradigm of crime and the role of prison, progression can be demonstrated by participation in offending related behaviour courses e.g. Sex Offender Treatment Programme (SOTP) and Enhanced Thinking Skills (ETS).

A student explained his response to this requirement on his questionnaire:

> I have always wanted to attend education, though at the beginning of my sentence I was looked upon as a disruptive element and was refused. Since coming out of the Seg after three years it was pointed out that I was way behind in the courses I needed to do to progress through the system.

This student's response illustrates how the system can influence prisoners to participate in adult education programmes.

HMP Whitemoor has a very high proportion of long-term and life sentence prisoners (83 per cent of prisoners served sentences of more than ten years in August 1999) and many of these study at the education department. Every inmate will have to deal with his sentence and consequently deal with the concept of time, as stated earlier in this chapter.

Tom described the two ways he managed his time.

> On my first sentence I followed every minute of my sentence, how many days, hours and minutes. I used to write it down. When it started to get near the end I counted backwards, because it is important to count back, I got gate happy. By the time I got out it had really got to me.

Tom clearly illustrates Cohen and Taylor's (1981) concept of someone else's time. He had been given prison time to serve—this was not his time. He counted the minutes of it and then, after his release, went back to his own time. Tom continues:

> So, on my second sentence I didn't do it. I told them, 'Now I do my time my way'. I often don't know what day or month it is because I don't think about time anymore. Every day is the same and it does not matter what day it is.

Tom is now studying Maths with the OU. At the time of the interview he stated that the OU had made a difference to his perception of time because now he has to work to strict time limits. Tom thought that this might become a problem as he did not want to be rushed. Since then, he has often complained that he has not got enough time to work on his course. Jimmy Boyle adopted a similar strategy:

> Being in prison usually means that one is left with the enormous problem of having to cope with time, so in may ways I was reversing the process which meant that instead of too much time on my hands I found too few hours in a day to allow me to get all the work done that I wanted. (Boyle, 1977:254)

Managing time in prison can, as Tom clearly demonstrates, be achieved by structuring time into set periods with intermediate time limits such as those given by Tutor Marked Assignments (TMA) with the OU and by working towards an exam. Worth explains this phenomenon by the findings of his research project with OU tutors who teach in prisons. He observed 'Education ... constituted a way of coming to terms with, making sense of a long/life sentence by being able to set determinate markers and running a kind of parallel time-track' (Worth, 1991:34/38).

Darren, another long term prisoner studying with the OU made the following observations about managing prison time, by opting for education:

Education in prison serves a purpose. When I spent six months in the shop it was tedious. The OU is challenging, having to organize time to meet deadlines. It measures out the year from February to October. Studying compacts time because you don't have time to think, it keeps your brain ticking over. You can usefully fill your time.

Trying 'not to think' is one of the main activators of 'learning in extremis'. The experience of prison is all pervading and keeping the mind busy, so that there is no time left for other thoughts, seems to help in maintaining the determination to survive this experience. Learning not to think is applicable to all types of prisoners. Primo Levi described how concentration camp prisoners had to 'learn not to think and to wipe out both past and future' (Williamson, 1998: 23).

Ged wrote down his reflections on thinking whilst he was 'behind doors':

> I also spent a lot of time thinking. I was depressed and had even attempted suicide. The thinking was becoming dangerous. ... the world beyond my cell started to become what I thought it would be, rather than what it was. I pondered on past events, and was forever anguishing about my future. Reality, my reality, was narrowing down to fit in a space of seven foot by 12 foot!

The perception, that time is a commodity that can be used, made the most of, done or wasted is re-enforced by the answers given in the questionnaires. Students said that they joined the education programme because: 'I wanted to use my time in prison constructively.' Another student also took ownership of the time in prison: 'I don't want to waste my time pushing broom.'

These reasons demonstrate inmates' struggle to make sense of the given time by doing something constructive; assembling light switches etc. is perceived to be a mindless and useless way to spend time.

Uche came to the conclusion that participation and success in such a prison training programme can be influenced by the way inmates perceive the primary motive of such a scheme (Uche, 1994: 55). This conclusion could explain the above motives for joining education. Shop work is often repetitive, of little training value and prisoners cannot see the benefit of it. Education and training on the contrary, have some relevance to the prisoners and are therefore perceived of value to the future.

Dennis said:

> Education is the only thing in prison I can do for myself. Workshops just help them to keep me in prison.

Well documented examples of accessing learning in order to aid psychological survival during captivity are to be found in the accounts of hostages who were held in Lebanon. McCarthy, Keenan and Waite respectively, describe how they managed the time of their imprisonment by devising projects with the help of encyclopaedias, reading any book they were given or learning foreign languages from each other.

The similarities between Whitemoor prisoners and Lebanon hostages lie in the conscious act of learning, of exercising the brain in order to survive the psychological aspects of imprisonment.

CONCLUSIONS

This research identified a range of factors that directly or indirectly influenced inmates of prisons to participate in a prison education programme. It reaffirms the international claim that a disproportionate number of prisoners failed to successfully complete their compulsory education.

A large number of students (54 per cent) indicated that they had joined the education programme in order to catch up on their education. Prisoners indicated their awareness of the lack of certificated achievement at the end of their initial education and that as a result they had a low level of self-esteem. Further, inmates had a realistic perception of the significance society places on this success, some students indicated that they had adopted these values or at least accepted that it was important for their own children to achieve.

The development of opportunities in adult education (Tuijnman, 1996: 36) based on the belief that a successful economy depends on a flexible educated workforce with transferable skills does not appear to have reached those sections of the community that tend not to engage in formal learning after school. This research established that many prisoners had not taken advantage of the above opportunities before they came to prison.

One factor that facilitated inmates to overcome these constraints whilst in prison appears to be the long established tradition of provision of education in prison. The literature claims that '... there is substantial evidence that many people from working-class communities are acutely conscious of the fact that attending classes renders them conspicuous and an oddity among their neighbour' (McGivney, 1990a: 20). Prison removes this feeling of disjunction to a large extent. The notion of inappropriateness and lack of relevance of adult education is lessened by the requirement to participate in purposeful activity. One inevitable effect of provision of education under these conditions appears to be the reduction of peer pressure. Students indicated that it is easier to enrol in an education programme in prison because they feel more at ease 'in the company of peers—with similar backgrounds and educational and emotional stages and standards'.

It was also established in this research that prisoners had joined formal education in prison to keep themselves occupied recognising that boredom can lead to frustration. These prisoners demonstrated some insight into the effects boredom can have on the mental health of the inmate of a total institution. In this case enrolment in the education programme was used as an aid to maintain sanity and mental health.

Some students at Whitemoor kept busy by accepting challenges placed by people in authority during their initial education. They joined the formal prison education programme to achieve either in a particular subject—such as Mathematics—or to generally achieve the targets of compulsory education, e.g. GCSEs. Cohen and Taylor believe that this setting of targets allows—especially long-term prisoners—to achieve goals in an otherwise undifferentiated future (Cohen and Taylor, 1981: 84).

Although they had not achieved the targets of compulsory education, some students indicated that they had always enjoyed learning. Informal learning and achievements tend not to be recognised as much as academic or vocational achievement and are therefore often undervalued. These students found that prison education provided the opportunity to study their interests. The influencing factor here appears to be that prison removes institutional and situational barriers, such as the middle class character of mainstream adult education, and time and cost.

Some inmates declared that they had joined the prison education programme in order to improve their future employment prospects, but doing so also removes the element of 'doing time' enabling the prisoner to 'do something' whilst serving a sentence. The literature might see this reaction as an attempt to gain homeostasis; the tension state created by the huge imbalance between the actual state (imprisonment) and the ideal state (freedom) that motivates the prisoner to learn in the hope to acquire the knowledge, attitudes and skills embodied in the ideal state (Boshier, 1986: 18). It is also feasible that the student sublimates the time in prison as a 'payment' for future gains, i.e. gaining skills, confidence and the ability to lead a life without crime.

Prisoners also claimed that they had started a formal prison education programme in order to survive prison and to manage the given time. Some students felt that the atmosphere in the Education Department was better and that they would receive better treatment there than on the wings and in the workshops. Other students stated that they had identified some of the effects a total institution can have on an individual's mind and decided to actively combat these effects. Formal learning and academic rigour are employed as a vehicle to keep the brain active and the mind alive. The literature confirms this procedure by the accounts of hostages, prisoners of war and in biographies of long-term prisoners (McCarthy, 1993; Waite, 1995; Williamson, 1998; Boyle, 1977).

One factor that influenced prisoners' enrolment in the education programme was the prison's requirement to show evidence of addressing offending behaviour. Regular participation in an academic course and/ or addressing educational needs indicated in the sentence plan are thought to address offending behaviour. This is a cogent example of how the current paradigm of crime can be an indirect factor in influencing prisoners to join the education programme.

Students indicated that participation in academic courses helped with the management of the given time. They described how long-term imprisonment had affected them and other prisoners by losing track of time and how they feared for their mental health. The literature describes how life-sentenced prisoners in particular, find it difficult to understand the nature of their predicament. Students utilise the structure of courses that offer a 'parallel time track' (Worth, 1991: 38) in order to structure the time of their sentence and with this pass the time.

Few of the above factors that influence prisoners to participate in a formal education programme will work in isolation. Each inmate will experience different needs governed by his or her own background, the length of sentence and other variables. An awareness of these identified factors however, could be instrumental in sentence planning, communication between internal prison agencies and the issues of recidivism.

BIBLIOGRAPHY for *Chapter 5*

Boshier R. (1986), 'Proaction for a Change: Some Guidelines for the Future,' *International Journal of Lifelong Education,* 5(1) pp. 15-31
Boyle J. (1977), *A Sense of Freedom,* London: Pan Books
Cohen S. and Taylor L. (1981), *Psychological Survival: The Experience of Long-Term Imprisonment,* Harmondsworth: Penquin
Duguid S. (1987), 'What Works in Prison Education?', *Adult Education,* Vol 58, No 4
Forster W. (1998), 'The Prison Service and Education in England and Wales,' in *Education Behind Bars: International Comparisons,* Leicester: NIACE
Glasser B. and Strauss A. (1967), *Discovery of Grounded Theory,* Chicago: Aldine
Goffman E. (1961), *Asylums,* Harmondsworth: Penguin
Hammersley, M. and Atkinson P (1997), *Ethnography: Principles in Practice,* London: Routledge
Liebling A. (1992), *Suicides in Prison,* London: Routledge
Macan Ghaill (1994), quoted in 'Improving Practice: A Whole School Approach to Raising the Achievement of African Caribbean Youths,' The Runnymede Trust (1998)

Mallin S., Kell I. and Rust J. (1994), *Inside Perspectives: Ex-Prisoners' Views on Prison Education*, London: Goldsmith's College

McGivney V. (1990), 'Participation, Non-participation and Access—A Review of the Literature' in *Adult Learners, Education and Training*, London: Routledge

NACRO (1998), *Crossroads: Prisoners into Employment—Enhancing the Role of Prison Education*, London: NACRO

Parsons M. Longenbach, M. (1993), 'The Reasons Inmates Indicate they Participate in Prison Education Programs—Another Look at Bushier's PEPS,' *Journal of Correctional Education*, Vol 44, Issue 1

Sewell J. (1997), quoted in 'Improving Practice: A Whole School Approach to Raising the Achievement of African Caribbean Youths,' The Runnymede Trust (1998)

Strauss A. and Corbin J. (1998), *Basics of Qualitative Research*, London: Sage

Waite T. (1995), *Footfalls in My Memory: Reflections from Solitude*, London: Hodder and Stoughton

Williamson B. (1998), 'Learning in Extremis,' *Adult Learning*, Vol 10, No. 2

Willis P. (1977), *Learning to Labour*, Adershot: Gower

Worth V. (1994), 'The Same Difference: Tutoring for the Open University in Prison,' *Open Learning*, Vol 19, No 1, pp. 34-41.

CHAPTER 6

Disjunction and Integration in Prison Education

Elizabeth Waller

My research was conducted at the High Security Prison HMP Whitemoor to examine the extent of disjunction and integration in ethnic minority inmates in the Education Department.

INTRODUCTION

It was the intention to examine the impact of racism on ethnic minority prisoners as a contribution to a sense of disjunction, bearing in mind the fact that ' ... education in prisons should respond to a range of needs of prisoners as individuals, paying regard to a range of deficits, including emotional and behavioural difficulties, learning difficulties, and criminogenic factors' (Prison Policy Paper, 1998). Questions were constructed and drawn from an extensive review of the current literature, focusing on the impact of racial difference. Areas investigated throughout my research included Schooling, the Criminal Justice System, and the Dispersal Prison.

The resultant data was analysed using a modified form of Grounded Theory, showing in the analysis that the impact of racism was almost certainly a significant cause of disjunction in ethnic minority prisoners. However, education in prison was shown to contribute towards personal integration in a number of ways, and to have an ameliorating effect on the pain of disjunction.

Many inmates attending education classes experience disjunction. This refers 'to a sense of feeling at odds with oneself, as a learner in a particular set of circumstances' (Weil, 1989 in Thorpe, Edwards and Hanson, 1993: 161). According to Weil, this sense is associated with personal and social identity, and how present learning experiences relate to 'previous or concurrent experiences within and outside the formal learning context' (*ibid*). Disjunction sets up 'the potential for education or miseducation' (Dewey, 1938, in Thorpe Edwards and Hanson, 1993: 161) depending on the educator's response. Integration may be defined, in this context, as a consideration that 'one's sense of personal and social identity does not feel itself to be fundamentally at issue, or at risk, in a particular learning environment'. It is '. . . associated with a sense of equilibrium, or an "all of a piece feeling"' (Weil, in Thorpe, Edwards and Hanson, 1993: 163).

In the prison as a whole, research showed that 74.5 per cent of prisoners were classified as white. The remaining 25.5 per cent were from ethnic minority groups, and out of this group 16.1 per cent were black.

The first section of this chapter will examine broad theoretical approaches to racism in order to provide a framework against which to analyse the findings. The second section will discuss my methodological approach with the third and final section offering an analysis and discussion of the results.

SOCIAL THEORIES OF RACISM

There are various meanings ascribed to racism in sociological discourse. Because of the complexities of the subject, the analytical framework used drew on insights from a range of interpretations—from Stuart Hall's 'Cultural Theory' (1988), through to the Feminist Perspective of Abbott and Wallace (1996).

According to Stuart Hall (Donald and Rattansi, 1992: 254) the 'category black' is no longer to be perceived in essentially monolithic terms, as if all black people, and presumably prisoners amongst them, shared an identical cultural inheritance. Rather, 'black' is to be understood as a 'politically and culturally constructed category which cannot be grounded in a set of fixed transcultural or transcendental racial categories, and which therefore has no guarantees in Nature'. In contrast, racism, and the inevitable disjunction which flows from its effects, relies for its implementation as an ideology on the 'constructing of impassable symbolic boundaries between racially constituted categories'. These categories are of necessity understood as static and unchanging in their definition. Hall offers as an example of this the recent understanding of 'Englishness' in the dominant discourse as being inseparable from 'nationalism, imperialism, racism and the state'. 'Black' has been defined, in the terms of this discourse, as inherently excluded from the definition of Englishness. It is to be understood as 'other'. So insidious is this process, that it contains within itself the possibility of 'the internalisation of the self-as-other' for black people (*ibid:* 255-257).

Hall claims that this concept of 'Englishness', as understood in the dominant discourse, 'will have to be transcoded, to include the idea of ethnic diversity. 'Ethnicity' acknowledges the contribution of history, language and culture to personal and group identities, as well as the fact that all knowledge is contextual. This process is already under way, as the dominant discourse of the West comes into collision with the newly written non-European histories.' (*ibid:* 257)

Abbott and Wallace (1996: 43), supporting Hall's view of racism causing disjunction by the social construction of impasssable symbolic boundaries, claim that racism is a 'specific form of exclusion' from the seat of power. It seems to legitimise the idea that certain groups have been 'racialised—they have been constituted as inferior, subordinated groups', by the majority culture, and therefore deserve a lower allocation of that society's goods. Like many other writers Abbott and Wallace (1997) trace back the origins of racial discrimination in Britain to the historical legacy of Colonialism.

Following Troyna, (Gill *et al*, 1992), many writers concede that, although racism is of significance in black peoples' lives, it is not the only influence. Other factors, such as physical location, social class, and gender, have to be taken into account. Kushnick (1998), in a somewhat controversial structural Marxist analysis, supports the importance of historical context, and argues that racism is a powerful ingredient in the emergence of western capitalistic societies. As a consequence of globalisation it was necessary for western capitalist societies to undergo restructuring. This meant that from the late 1970s onwards wealth has been redistributed from the working classes as a whole, to the professional and ruling elites. He claims that right wing political parties have 'played the race card' in order to divide the working class, and remain in power.

If Kushnick's claims were true, it would support Stuart Hall's argument that racism is socially constructed and these forces would have helped to shape the social world in which many prisoners in this study grew to maturity. They would have contributed to the fact that immigrant workers and their British born families 'were expected to occupy the dirtiest, lowest paid, lowest status and most dangerous jobs— a pattern still found to be prevalent in the 1990s by the Policy Studies Institute' (*ibid:* 174). Apart from disadvantages in the labour market, these people have also been subject to levels of racial violence in Britain during the last decade, which have 'been the worst in the European community'.

Ratcliffe (1994: 95) claims that a crucial component of racism 'is the existence of deterministic belief systems' based on racial superiority, related to a misapplication of Darwinian science. As these are now unacceptable, new forms of racism labelled 'differentialist racism' are now in evidence. These appeal, Ratcliffe claims, 'only' to the harmfulness of abolishing frontiers, the incompatibility of life-styles and traditions'. In Britain, a 'certain coyness' is observed in that 'the language of ethnicity and ethnic imagery' is often used to represent race. Ratcliffe considers that the main significance of the term ethnicity 'lies in its salience for group consciousness and collective action'. Its meaning includes 'common ancestry', memories of a shared history, family ties, shared religion, linguistic origins, geographic origins, common nationality or physical features. These issues have always, Ratcliffe maintains, been those around which human societies have organized and struggled. For the black prisoners in Whitemoor, they are clearly tied up with personal identity, and consequently disjunction or integration.

However, there are certain problems with this definition of ethnicity, for as Ratcliffe maintains, it might be 'too broad.' It is also, in Hall's terms, fixed and static, and too homogeneous. Ethnicity as it is experienced is subject to change over time, even within the life-time of the individual. Shifts in international events also subtly impinge on local understandings. This is particularly relevant in a dispersal prison like Whitemoor, where prisoners from ethnic minority groups who are British born mix with others from all over the world. Finally, Ratcliffe claims that ethnic identity is elusive. It is in some sense mythological, an 'imagined' creation invested with meaning and affected by both internal and external forces (Ratcliffe, 1994: 7). These differing theoretical approaches need to be considered when assessing the relationship between the criminal justice system and prisoners from ethnic minority backgrounds.

THE CRIMINAL JUSTICE SYSTEM AND ETHNIC MINORITIES

According to Blagg (1989: 63), 'a . . . prison population is the product of a conscious policy choice'. Just as it appears very likely that racism is endemic in British society, so it is almost certain that in some respects its effects can be seen within the criminal justice system itself. Statistics do show that a higher proportion of people from ethnic minorities are in prison in England and Wales than would be expected (Wilson and Ashton, 1998: 23). According to the Home Office, ethnic minorities accounted for 18 per cent of the male prison population, of whom 12 per cent were black (Home Office, Section 95 Report, 1998). In the British population as a whole, 5.5 per cent of the British population were members of minority ethnic groups (Penal Affairs Consortium, 1996: 2). However, various reasons have been put forward to explain the apparent discrepancy in these figures. 'Although criminologists and other social scientists have long noticed the existence of ethnic (variations) there is considerable lack of consensus as to how these disparities should be interpreted and explained' (Baker, 1994).

Marian Fitzgerald, in her report to the Royal Commission on Criminal Justice (HMSO, 1993: 4) admits that the figures, taken at face value, appear to indicate that crime rates, especially amongst British people of Afro-Caribbean descent, are higher than those for whites. This view is not supported by all the research evidence. According to a Home Office study by Graham and Bowling (1995), Afro-Caribbean and White young people both admitted in 40 per cent of cases to criminal offending in confidential interviews to ascertain self-reported crimes. Fitzgerald (HMSO, 1993: 4) also points out that other evidence, apart from the raw statistics indicating high rates of offending for ethnic minority groups must be taken into account.

Firstly, Black people are over-represented in the peak offending age group of 14-25 years. Secondly, 'as a group, Afro-Caribbean males, in particular, are also strongly characterized by socio-economic factors associated with higher offending rates.' Fitzgerald also claims that certain aspects of the criminal justice process appear to compound the 'targeting effect' of criminal conviction of ethnic minority groups. (HMSO, 1993: 10)

This is supported by Home Office statistics. In 1998, 'overall, black people were five times more likely to be stopped (and searched) than whites' (Section 95 report: 13). According to the Macpherson Report, in the Metropolitan police force this is attributable to institutional racism where, 'Discretion operates at all stages of the criminal justice process', and this provides occasions for racial discrimination to be compounded, increasing the alienation and disjunction of ethnic minority group prisoners, and the outcomes, which are more severe than those for white prisoners. 'There is widespread evidence that the criminal justice system is now one of the key mechanisms by which ideas about racial differences in British society are reproduced' (Solomos, 1993 in May, 1997: 73). For example, according to the Home Office Section 95 Report (1998), 'black offenders were five or six times more likely than white offenders to be received into prison'. Even when 15 key variables were taken into account, Hood (1992) found that there was an overall 5-8 per cent greater probability of custody for Afro-Caribbean males in the West Midlands Crown Courts. However, this percentage was variable, and in Dudley it was 23 per cent. 'Comparing the outcomes at Dudley with those at Birmingham, there was a 29 per cent greater probability of a black offender being sentenced to custody . . . at Dudley' (Hood, 1992: 29). This experience of perceived unfairness is highly likely to lead to feelings of disjunction in ethnic minority prisoners at Whitemoor; those experience now need to be considered.

THE BLACK PRISON EXPERIENCE

The experience of long-term imprisonment in high security establishments has traditionally not been considered a beneficial one for prisoners. One prisoner has described it as 'boring, hostile, overall unchanging, but always isolational' (NIACE, 1998). According to Flanagan (1992: 4) 'The mythology . . . of long-term incarceration . . . held that prisoners suffered inevitable deterioration of physical and mental health'.

Whatever the mythology, there is no doubt that prisoners suffer. Nils Christie considers that the deprivation of liberty in modern societies, where there is a high premium on individual freedom and autonomy, may be more costly than in those societies where such values are not so highly developed. (Nils Christie, 1968 in Cohen and Taylor, 1981: 205). However, whilst researchers readily admit that for many prisoners the experience is not one of well-being, i.e. disjunction rather than integration, recent research suggests that '. . . no systematic or predictable effect of long-term imprisonment exists' (Flanagan, 1992: 4).

Even so, it is certain that if black inmates have to cope with the effects of racism, imprisonment will cause even more disjunction. According to the former Director General of Prisons, Richard Tilt, much hard work has been done within the Prison Service to combat the issue of racism. However, 'still more work was needed to foster good race relations, to · provide equality of opportunity and treatment, and to combat racism' (Simmons, 1998: 6).

For everyone in the prison setting life can be uncomfortable at times. This is made more difficult for ethnic minority prisoners because of the existence of racial harassment. This is a fact of life throughout society, and is not confined to prisons. For example *The British Crime Survey* of 1996 estimated that there are around 140,000 racially motivated incidents in Britain each year '. . . In 1993, the Minister of State at the Home Office told a Home Affairs Select Committee . . . That the "true figures" could be 330,000 a year.' (Browne, 1998: 139). At the same time, only around 9,700 were officially recorded annually. According to Simmons (1998) the number of racially motivated incidents in prison reported by researchers is 'extremely low'. Prisoners themselves suggest, according to Simmons, that the 'problem is concealed rather than non-existent'. (*ibid:* 6)

In a report commissioned by the Home Office Research and Planning Unit (1994) 'Reported and Unreported Racial Incidents in Prisons', by the Oxford Centre for Criminological Research, almost half of black prisoners claimed to have been 'racially victimised by prison staff'. According to the Institute of Race Relations, between 1991 and 1995, ten black people died in custody in incidents where excessive force appears to have been used' (Leonard Woodley QC, 1999). Certainly, reports of racially motivated incidents in prisons, must tend to increase the experience of disjunction felt by ethnic minority inmates, and it is at this point that education can be considered as having a role in counteracting that disjunction. This may not, however, be the case in the education system as a whole and beyond the prison walls.

RACISM AND EDUCATION

Recent research indicates that the problems of racism in the education system of England and Wales are not being effectively addressed. Prisoners from ethnic minority groups have been subjected to this system from early childhood, and all through their formative years. However, many educators 'get over the issue of racism by presenting it as just not an issue'. (*Times Education Supplement*, 1999: 1). This dichotomy must be a potent source of disjunction for some inmates.

The Macpherson report states, 'There is evidence that there are difficulties in getting some schools to acknowledge and tackle racism, even where local authorities have sought to persuade them to do so' (*Times Education Supplement*, 1999: 1). Researchers claim that the reasons for black underperformance in school include teacher expectations and labelling, school exclusion, linguistic diversity, cultural deficit, a failure to provide black role models, and, according to Williams (Troyna, 1990: 46), 'discrimination within an unequal structure of opportunities'. It would also appear that there is a clear link between disjunction caused by failure at school and subsequent criminal outcomes:

> The vast majority of serious violent offenders had some school problem—91 per cent for males. There is a clear indication of overlap between school problems and serious delinquency'. (Loeber and Farrington, 1998 : 59).

Supporting Williams, Troyna (1990: 20) identifies the radical cause of black underachievement as 'the power relationship between black and white citizens'. Black powerlessness leads to 'differential access to experiences in, and outcomes from, the education system. Troyna's analysis falls within the definition of empowerment theory. 'These educators concentrate on the sociological and political analysis of structures' (Cassara, 1990: 149). They claim that pupils develop within social and cultural contexts defined by the power relationships within societies. The logic and interests of dominant groups define the parameters of what constitutes legitimate knowledge. This powerlessness of ethnic minority groups contributes to differential outcomes in educational achievement. In 1996, 45 per cent of white pupils gained five or more GCSE grades A-C, compared to 38 per cent of Asian, and 23 per cent of black pupils, according to the Office of National Statistics. In addition, Afro-Caribbean boys are the most likely group to leave school with no formal qualifications. (Weekes and Wright, 1998: 2).

In addition, there is much support in the literature for the decisive impact of teachers' attitudes towards their pupils providing a further factor for investigation in my study. According to Troyna (1990: 51), teachers' tenacious commitment to universalism, 'we treat them all the same', and child centred individualism, are incompatible with 'the needs and interests of an entire group of pupils'. Often teachers' false perceptions about black pupils informs their decision-making, Troyna claims. This may affect their streaming, and the allocation of resources, leading to their being placed in 'ability bands and academic sets' well below their actual academic ability.

Afro-Caribbean pupils are often placed in lower 'sets' for behavioural reasons, rather than for their measured academic performance. 'Black pupils are seen to exhibit more challenging behaviour' (Gillborn, 1990 in Weekes, 1998: 2). 'Black male pupils in particular are seen as more confrontational and less likely to obey school rules—the causes of which are often perceived to stem from particular aspects of peer group and youth culture' (Sewell, 1997, Macan Ghaill, 1994, in Weekes, 1998: 2)

Consistently over a long time scale, Afro-Caribbean children have been excluded disproportionately from school. As long ago as 1985, the Council for Racial Equality reported that black pupils in England and Wales were four times more likely to be excluded from school for the same offence (Skellington, 1996: 193). By 1997, black pupils were up to six times more likely than white pupils to be excluded. According to Parsons (1995) only one in five of those pupils excluded from secondary school ever returned to mainstream schooling. This has very serious consequences for some pupils.

One method that educators employ as a means of reducing racial conflict, and black pupils disaffection, is the teaching of Multi-Cultural Studies. However Troyna claims that its emphasis on pluralist values is insufficient to promote the 'enhancement of life chances for black pupils' (Troyna, 1990: 2). According to Willey (1984: 101) a further factor implicated in disjunction in ethnic minority pupils is the failure to address the problem of linguistic diversity. The needs of Afro-Caribbean children were ignored. Black pupils underachievement is not helped by the failure of the education system to offer them a wide experience of positive black adult role models. All these factors could possibly be a further cause of disjunction and failure to maximise school achievement in ethnic minority prisoners, together with the widespread experience of racial harassment in childhood. Serious disjunction is often the result. Children 'described feelings of self-hatred and rejection.' One boy stated 'I hate my dad. He made me black'. (*Times Educational Supplement*, 26 February 1999) This situation is one of long standing. In 1988, the national report 'Learning in Terror', found racial harassment in schools and colleges to be pervasive (Skellington, 1996: 87). According to Willey, if education is to be constructive, and not result in mis-education (the focus of my research problem), educators must enter into a constructive dialogue with their black students. 'The debate about . . . race and equality . . . must be consistently informed by a black perspective' (Willey, 1984: 126). Out of this debate, new positive responses will emerge, on the educational experiences of ethnic minority groups and especially of black ethnic minority groups. It is to their experiences that I now turn.

THE PURPOSES OF PRISON EDUCATION AND ITS IMPACT ON INTEGRATION

Traditionally, prison education has been associated with the process of integration, the attempt to 'repair damaged lives through the healing balm of learning' (Williamson, 1998). This in turn has a significant impact on prisoners 'normalisation', by reducing the impact of prison culture and by 'nurturing pro-social norms' (Harer, 1995). Education for the integration of the individual is always associated with empowerment, with finding one's own voice. Paulo Freire, the Brazilian Educationalist, describes people without a voice, such as prisoners, as 'submerged in reality'. According to Braithwaite (1989: 14), utilising the 'Reward—Cost Model' of crime, some criminologists claim that 'there are quite rational reasons for the lowest strata in society to engage in crime'. The 'legitimate employment opportunities, particularly for young black men, may be low paid, vulnerable to lay-off, and relatively demeaning and unattractive. In contrast, Letkemann's research shows that 'rewards of crime are not only relatively high economically, but also comparatively high in terms of job satisfaction'. Clearly, no-one would claim that this criminal outlook was the product of an integrated personality, and consequently, one aim of prison education must be to attempt to 'lower the reward-cost ratio for crime for prison releasees'. In order for this to be facilitated, the 'Principle of Greater Eligibility' must be applied. Generally, prisoners and particularly ethnic minority prisoners, represent a disadvantaged section of the population in terms of the goods and services, including previous educational services, they have received prior to sentencing. Justice and equity suggest that this deficit be addressed.

As early as 1939, Wallack suggested that the aim of prison education in the USA must be 'to bring about a gradual transfer of allegiance from anti-social groups and methods to socially desirable ways of achieving desired goals, and to enable the individual to live a worthwhile and yet an interesting life'. Clearly, in a dispersal prison with a major emphasis on security and control this may be difficult to achieve. However, as Blagg (1989: 75) claims:

a prison regime which is viewed simply as a means of storing people . . . leaves (us) with a moral vacuum—and a prison system which could almost have been designed to increase the criminal potential of its inhabitants.

The recent history of prison education in the North American context has a direct bearing on events in England and Wales. Following the impact of the Swatsky Report, in 1985, a rising Canadian national debt, the removal of prison education policy decisions from educators, and a growing fear of violent crimes, a 'New Medical Model', was introduced. This was based on psychological expertise and claimed to be 'directly rehabilitative' through the delivery of Cognitive Learning Skills. By 1993 all university level programmes in Canada were cancelled. Similarly, in the USA, whilst there was a growth in literacy education, 'prison higher education programmes offered by approximately 300 colleges and universities . . . are being dismantled' (Davidson, 1995: xiii).

In Britain according to a Home Office Research Study (No. 171, 1997) there is a similar shift towards a paradigm of 'The New Medical Model'. The report claims certain forms of rehabilitative intervention can be effective in reducing recidivism, particularly 'cognitive behavioural' methods. Their effectiveness is enhanced by using 'active, participatory, problem-solving methods of working' (viii), and 'matching the intensity and duration of intervention to likely future risk of offending' (viii). Canadian research so far does not support this contention (Robinson, 1995 in Duguid). In Britain, the adoption of the 'New Medical Model' is supplemented, as in the USA and Canada with an increase in emphasis on basic skills in education. Whilst a grasp of basic literacy and numeracy must be associated with empowerment of the individual, and consequently integration, 'each individual wins back the right to say his or her own word, to name the world' (Friere, 1995: 15). It can also be based on a functional model of education designed to address criminal deficits of the individual as the primary intention.

There appears to be an intermediate position adopted, at least in dispersal prisons in the UK. Directly taught higher education programmes, as in the prison education project provided by Leeds University, in a maximum security dispersal prison, from 1988 to 1998, have been cancelled, although there is support for Open University degree courses. In the Canadian Study, 'Education, Change and Transformation' (1998), Stephen Duguid claims that the higher education, humanities centred, model of delivery 'clearly works' (Duguid, 1998: 491) although 'the degree of its effectiveness differed widely across the various groups that together composed the group of 654 men included in this research'. Duguid claims that how such programmes work depends on a multiplicity of individual choices made by prisoners, in their own particular contexts. 'It is the sum total of a myriad such decisions that adds up to the big choice: Should I quit crime?' He is unsure if Canadians have the patience to allow 'Non-directive' programmes, such as education, time to work. The importance of his study for the research at Whitemoor is that he helps to demonstrate that integration for the individual prisoner is not achieved by programmes themselves, 'but their capacity to offer resources that allow participants the choice of making them work'.

Black issues in prison education

The seminal report on ethnic minority prisoners appears to be *Black People in Prison: The Role of the Education Service*, produced by NACRO, following a seminar held in 1987. In this report, Margaret Clayton, Director of Prison Regimes comments on the 'particularly positive' relationship between prisoners and education staff. As the opportunity for discrimination in prisons is very great, one of the responsibilities of prison educators is to counter racist attitudes which, if effective, would clearly assist in black prisoners' integration. Although it is recognised that black people have a wide variety of educational needs, the prison education service, the report claims, 'is well known for its conspicuous success in raising the level of basic education. In this area it can make a special contribution to black people without in any way singling them out.' Obviously, this would contribute to the integration and wholeness of black prisoners, always providing they were not abandoned educationally at the level of basic skills.

The report emphasises 'the necessity of prison education departments using their students rich cultural backgrounds and wide range of experience as a resource in creating learning materials'. Gus John, the education officer from ILEA points out the 'need for progression and continuity concerning the work done within prison education departments'. This is particularly relevant in dispersal prisons like Whitemoor, where prisoners often move on to other establishments where there is much less educational provision. He suggests that because of the 'powerful experience for black prisoners' gained by being taught by skilled black staff, not readily available in rural areas, the Home Office should make funds available for travelling expenses for black teachers from cities.

Finally, the report recommends that racial issues should be built into all staff training programmes. Education staff should receive specialist training on black history and achievements. Integration in the black prisoner is more likely to be achieved if staff are 'able to inform both black and white prisoners about the positive contributions black people have made to society over centuries to counteract the more negative images normally presented'. Integration through the amelioration of the corrosive effects of racism, and the search for an authentic voice, is the subject of a further report 'Nuff Respect'. This describes a project devised by the Unit for the Arts and Offenders, which aims to address 'the creative and rehabilitative needs of black offenders'.

Stuart Hall's understanding of ethnicity and racial identity is applied in a profound and penetrative study by Roxy Harris (1996). Harris points out that the majority of prisoners in the East Anglian Region from ethnic minorities are the children and grandchildren of the migrants of the 1950s and 1960s. Following Hall, and Hewitt (1991: 8-9) he suggests 'a new more useful pedagogic model'. This must acknowledge 'the fluidity, and interpenetration of black and white language and culture, which is the primary medium of communication in the young adult peer group in multi-ethnic areas'. Black inmates, are generally to be understood contextually, as situated within the black diaspora, young black men, born and raised in London or Birmingham 'retain both real and imaginary global African, Asian and Caribbean diasporic affiliations.' This means that they are comfortable and attached to South London, or the language and culture of Birmingham, for example, as well as 'to varying degrees', Caribbean Creole language and Caribbean culture. Conversely, the average white prisoner at Whitemoor, or other prisons in the East Anglian region, is unlikely to be completely unfamiliar with Jamaican Creole language and culture. 'The degree of overlap is abundantly clear'. The key to teaching style is therefore, Harris suggests, to move from the general—the shared culture and language—to particular examples reflecting the nature and history of the distinctive approaches to 'art and music associated with particular peoples'.

For the purposes of personal integration of black prisoners, this seems particularly apt and significantly appropriate. It is both 'inclusive', delivering material which is shared by most prisoners and teachers, and 'particular', acknowledging and respecting difference. (It avoids what Harris calls 'misguided multiculturalism', Troyna's 'saris, samosas and steel bands').

RESEARCH METHODOLOGY

The chosen methodology for the study aims to construct a dynamic interaction between the research material and relevant social theories. The intention is that each will inform, moderate and amplify the other. Taking account of 'process' should facilitate the 'sharpening of our insights into the practice and place of social research in contemporary society' (May, 1997: 28). In addition, because social theories are abstracted from everyday life, exposure to this interplay of theory and research should produce an increase in coherence, and a more unified perspective. Total coherence however is not possible in practice, because, as Habermas claims 'At best . . . all social theories can do . . . is make us more sensitive to the ambivalence of development'. This ambivalence is mediated by the fractured nature of social life itself which is 'characterised by divisions, and is not a unified phenomena'.

The interview as the chosen method of primary research

In this study, the interview is considered to be an effective research tool for investigating this complexity, for a number of reasons. Firstly, it becomes possible to transcend to some extent the 'Pervasive dichotomy of objectivism and subjectivism in Western thought' (Kvale, 1996: 66) Secondly, the interview can accommodate the fact that subjects already have ways of attributing meaning to their social milieu. 'The Sociologist has as a field of study phenomena which are already constituted as meaningful. This is an expression of what I call the "double hermeneutic"'. Giddens (1984: 284).

Philosophical approach and interpretation of meaning

In the interview situation attempts are made not to interrupt the flow of meaning produced by the subjects so as to make it their story. 'In current thought, there is a shift from modern formalised knowledge systems to the narrative knowledge embodied in storytelling' (Lyotard, 1984 in Kvale, 1996: 43)

This postmodern emphasis, where meaning is constructed 'intersubjectively' through the vehicle of the relationship between researcher and subject, contains a certain ambiguity. Their trust and mutual respect, based to a degree on a shared understanding of life in a dispersal prison holds within itself a difference of perspective and a differential in power. In the analysis of the data produced in the interview, the researcher's perspective becomes dialogical, between situation, text, and published literature. Interpretation of meaning is then characterised by Radnitzky's hermeneutical circle so that 'Interpretation of a text is not pre-suppositionless.' (Kvale, 1996: 47-49).

The sample

Given the statistical composition of ethnicity at HMP Whitemoor, and also in the Whitemoor Education Department, it was decided to focus on black prisoners as the subjects of this research project. The reason for this was that they appeared to be disproportionately over-represented. It was hoped that something discovered in this study might contribute towards understanding this phenomena.

Following the Chicago School, 'the chronological method' of interviewing was employed, focusing on the concept 'of a person's "career"', and 'the transformations people undergo in adopting particular roles as the result of new experiences' (May, 1997: 120). For this reason, the subjects selected were all black and British, so that their early school experiences could be studied, as well as their later experiences in the criminal justice system, and in the education department.

Because the research method employed had a post-modern emphasis on relationship and inter-subjectivity, it was decided to select subjects who had been my students in class groupings for at least 100 hours of teaching time. The age of the subjects was within the range of 30-34 years, and their sentences were within the range of 13 years to life imprisonment.

Analytical method
The interviews were tape-recorded, and the resulting data transcribed. The data produced was a response to the same questions posed from the interview guide. However, because of the use of the phenomenological approach, a fair range of answers were produced, as the questions were somewhat open-ended. The interviews fell between being semi--structured and focused, posing complex problems of analysis.

For this reason the data was coded, using line-by-line analysis. It was subjected to a degree of Socratic induction, and the meaning was condensed. 'Meaning condensation' was effected using a phenomenological method, which involved interrogating the text with the principal questions asked in this study (Kvale, 1996: 194). Patterns and themes were noted, and the text subjected to conceptualising, 'the conceptual name or label should be suggested by the context in which the event is located'. (Strauss and Corbin, 1998: 106). These concepts were then examined and grouped into categories. 'Certain concepts can be grouped under a more abstract, higher order concept, based on its ability to explain what is going on'. (Strauss and Corbin, 1998: 113). From these categories, a theory is constructed, which aims to offer a generalizable explanation, in the context of this research, of the extent of disjunction, and how integration is effected.

RESULTS AND DISCUSSION

Section one

Childhood identity
Disjunction and integration are bound up with the relationship between ethnicity and the forging of personal identity, 'our ethnic identities are crucial to our subjective sense of who we are' (Hall in Donald and Rattsani, 1992: 258).

Cultural location
All the subjects interviewed for this study were born in England, and define themselves as black and British. They have all spent their

childhoods in an urban environment, either inner-city London, or in Manchester. In contrast to the relatively homogeneous nature of the white population, they have diverse cultural 'roots', being situated simultaneously in British urban life, and also being part of the African diaspora. As Hall claims:

> the black experience is a diaspora experience, and the consequences which this carries for the process of unsettling, recombination hybridisation . . . the process of cultural diasporaisation. ' (*ibid:* 258)

For example, most of the immigrant parents made great efforts to maintain these cultural links. Two of the subjects had travelled to the Caribbean as children. Antonio explained:

> My parents tried to show me my culture, where I came from. Took me back to their place of origin (Jamaica). If I was inquisitive and asked them questions, they would answer me to the best of their knowledge.

Jonathon's family sent him to learn about his background whilst he was a primary school pupil, although he didn't altogether appreciate the experience at the time.

> This was before Secondary School . . . I stopped going, I used to go to Sunday School to learn Black History. I doubt if I did enjoy it. It was on a Sunday, a time when I should be out playing.

Clearly here the dominant culture proved too powerful an attraction!

Only one subject claimed that his family hadn't taught him about black culture. He had found out 'only a little bit from books, and talking to people and TV'. One reason for this appears to be the pressure on members of immigrant communities to establish themselves in a new country. According to Horatio:

> My parents have always . . . you know how you are now Liz . . . you're working and studying . . . that's what my Mum's like. Always (chuckles) always working and since I was about nine or eight years old. My mum has always been working and.. at the office . . . studying, and my Dad's the same thing . . . so I haven't had plenty of time with them.

In contrast to the efforts of most of the families themselves, the schools attended by the subjects, in both London and Manchester, failed to teach anyone either Black History or Multi-Cultural Studies. Horatio's response carries overtones that the school disapproved. 'They wouldn't let us do it'. This dichotomy may have contributed to a sense of disjunction.

Language is a significant component of cultural identity, and according to Willey (1984) failure to express the Afro-Caribbean experience of linguistic diversity can have a profound effect on attitude and achievement. Three of the four subjects in this study spoke Patois at home as small children. However, contrary to some of the findings in the research literature, they all claim to have also been fluent in standard English from a very young age. For example, Antonio states that 'my mum and daddy speak Pidgin English at home', but says that he has always spoken English as well at home. Jonathon also confirms Hall's model of fluency in two cultures. As far back as he can remember he was able to move as appropriate between English and Patois.

> As you grow up, and you go out to play, and you've got a lot of friends out there . . . a lot of white people and black people. I come from London. You talk about the (black) Londoner—different language is spoken at home . . . But when you go outside, you speak (English).

Therefore, it would appear that for the subjects in this study, linguistic diversity is not a significant cause of disjunction.

External societal pressure
The social world that the subjects inhabited as children appears to have had a decidedly unfriendly face. As Hall claims, in the past 'black' has been excluded from the 'definition of Englishness' and even small black children appear to have been defined as 'other'. Whilst out on the street, or walking to school, all the subjects report that they have been the target of verbal racist abuse. Two of the subjects report that they were in frequent danger of being chased by skinheads.

Jonathon says 'I came from a community that is predominantly black. We used to get chased by skinheads a lot'. Antonio recalls that when he was 'quite small', in the late 1960s he was attacked in the street. He was in the company of his brother, and on a legitimate family journey, 'walking home from my sister's house'. The two were 'attacked by about 50 skinheads and teddy boys, and so we had to run for our lives'. In the reporting, he conveyed a sense of remembering being overwhelmed and outnumbered, although there was also a degree of hardiness shown. The two coped with this situation.

Jerome, who lived in a predominantly white area of Manchester, wasn't so troubled 'a couple of times, when I was on the way to school, I experienced a bit of racism'. But Horatio, from a racially mixed area of urban London experienced racist taunts in the street, and in shops where he experienced 'Just peculiar looks—you just sense it, you feel it. Just how you are spoken to, and how you are dealt with'.

The most disturbing description of the experience of racism in this research project comes from Antonio. Again speaking of life in urban London in the late 1960s he says:

I can remember when we were not allowed to live in our front rooms because they would see that blacks were living in that house, and you would get targeted. So we had to live in the back of the house or upstairs.

Now imprisoned in intense custody for serious offences as an adult—as a child, he and his family had the space that it was possible for them to inhabit defined by fear of racial attack. This space was 'hidden from view', 'at the back of the house', 'upstairs'. This conforms to Abbott and Wallace's (1997) concept of exclusion, although from habitable space, as well as power. 'Certain groups have been constituted as inferior, subordinated groups', by the majority culture. Antonio, himself, perceived this experience as not particularly serious in the context of the area where he lived. He states, 'The racism I encountered was very limited'. Hall claims (1998) 'So insidious is this process that it contains within itself the possibility of internalisation'. Although adopting generally a phenomenological perspective of bracketing out my responses in the interview situation, I felt obliged to challenge Antonio's description of his experience 'That doesn't sound very limited to me'. Antonio's response was 'No—to me—I have met other people who have had worse. They have literally got battle scars'.

It appears that when there is such a dichotomy between a person's experience of living in society, involving a defensive retreat expressed in use of domestic space, and that society's public ideology of support for family life, there must be a level of disjunction produced. This is not an extreme reaction, but one widely supported in the research literature (Wright, 1988; Skellington, 1996).

Family relationships
All of the subjects mention aspects of family life in the interviews, although this was not a focus of this research project. It may be significant that subjects generally make much more mention of their mothers than their fathers when discussing important aspects of their childhood. Antonio's parents are mentioned frequently, being considered caring and responsible by their son. 'My parents have done the best they can do for me, I've never gone without because of their fault'. Antonio mentions his father with pride. He is 'a very well qualified tradesman—an electrician', and he 'knows everything to do with re-wiring—everything'. It is possible that in some of the subjects there is a dichotomy between the strong matriarchal influences in Afro-Caribbean culture, and the essentially patriarchal nature of British society. This could be a source of disjunction. As Hall claims, the 'category black' is no longer to be perceived in essentially monolithic terms.

Failure of communication and self-perception
The subjects themselves show considerable understanding as to the causes of disjunction in their lives. . For example, Antonio reports that as he moved into his later childhood, the clash of cultures and the generation gap led, he claims, to an attitude of rebellion. He began to feel that his home life was unreasonably restrictive, and discovered that he could move out of reach of parental control. He started to engage in illicit activities:

> Easily led by peer pressure and that's . . . what caused some of the initial . . . you know . . . plus the rebellion. A little rebellion. too strict at home . . . Not being allowed to do certain things. So once I got to a certain age, and I found out I could test the waters, then I started to . . . branch out a little bit.

Horatio explained that as a child he wasn't as communicative with his family, particularly his mother, as he would have liked to have been. This was because everyone was always working. His material needs were always met, but there always seemed to be a shortage of time. Today this must be true of many families in Britain:

> I didn't talk a lot when I was a kid . . . I didn't have long conversations or anything like that. Even when I was a kid I remember being either frustrated or trying to please someone.

Identity and experience at school
The link between disjunction caused by failure at school, and subsequent criminal outcomes, as reported by Loeber and Farrington (1998), is all too obvious in the results of this research project. By the early years of secondary school, social interaction—one of the basic building blocks of society according to Habermas (Urmson and Ree, 1989: 123), between all the subjects and the school as the agent of society, had clearly broken down.

Whilst some problems do begin to be identified at the late primary school age, secondary schooling appears to be disastrous. All of the subjects failed to complete school, and all left for various reasons between the ages of 13 and 15 with no qualifications. This is not unusual, as even in 1996 only 23 per cent of black pupils gained five or more GCSEs, and Afro-Caribbean boys were the most likely group to leave school with no passes.

Pupil behaviour
The subjects all reported few initial problems in the primary school years. Horatio very much enjoyed school, and at first 'didn't play truant a lot'. The school was ethnically mixed, and in the early years there was little problem within the actual school itself with racism. Jonathon's experience was similar, although in his inner city school it was

'predominantly black people there anyway'. Jerome found early nursery schooling unproblematic. He entered primary school in an accepting group where he was known. The school was in a white inner city area, and there were only three black children in the school. He says he did fight at school occasionally, but these fights were not perceived to be racially motivated. 'I can remember going with all my friends to the junior school when I was five. So I knew quite a few people in the class. I got on fine at junior school, up to about eleven'. Antonio also enjoyed primary school. 'But I found school was fun, because of the area where I lived. It was very multi-racial. You didn't really see racism, or know what it was at the time'.

All the subjects are consistent in their enjoyment of the early experience of schooling. To a certain extent, the literature indicates that racism is pervasive in schools, and this research does not therefore always support this view (Skellington, 1996: 20). In the later primary school years and in early secondary schooling it is apparent that things started to go seriously awry for all the subjects. For example Horatio claims, 'when I was nine or ten, I started being disruptive'. He also began to be subjected to racist taunts in school, but developed a counter-strategy. 'If anyone ever said (anything racially abusive), unless they were too big for me, I'd go and punch them in the face (chuckles) . . . and it quickly stopped'. Jonathon's behaviour pattern closely followed Horatio's, both in disruption ('I was a pain . . . I used to joke about') and in his response to racial abuse. Although black boys were a minority in his secondary school 'We were all kind of big . . . Even though we were in the minority we were loud, and people were more afraid of us than we were of them'. According to the literature black pupils are frequently identified as exhibiting aggressive and challenging behaviour (Weekes, 1998: 18). It is possible that a contributory factor to this disjunction may be a learned response to racial abuse.

Teacher attitude

All of the subjects discuss the importance of teachers in their developing attitude to learning. There is a degree of admission that black male pupils can appear very badly behaved in class. Antonio explains 'Teachers can misinterpret the fact that sometimes we can appear to be a disruptive element . . . it's just part of our psyche . . . naturally loud . . . Naturally boisterous'. The subjects do not appear to respond well to didactic styles of delivery, although failure to engage with the learning process is definitely exacerbated by their bad behaviour. Jonathon reports:

> Teachers have to captivate someone to make them work. Even at primary school, the teachers failed to capture my imagination. One teacher was effective—strict but fair. She made the lessons exciting and you wanted to start writing.

Teacher stereotyping does seem a contributory factor in pupil disjunction, contributing to black childrens' under-performance (Williams in Troyna, 1990: 15-17). None of the subjects report that they were streamed below their actual ability.

Jonathon claims he was left in the top set when he did no work, and was behaving very badly. However, they do report a lack of encouragement. Antonio says that only sports enthusiasts gained extra praise 'they were given extra little perks'. There does however appear to be a serious underestimation of the subjects' potential ability. According to Jonathon 'My mother used to say now I was smarter than the teachers, and they didn't try and stretch me'. Horatio claims that he was clever at primary school 'but not one teacher ever said "oh you're bright, or you are fast"'. In an ironic, self-reflective and depreciating manner conveying his sense of racial difference, he explains. 'The teacher must have felt "you're naughty, oh it's this black kid . . . they're all like that . . . what can I do?"'. At secondary school, one English teacher tried to help. 'He would sit me down, and come over to my table, and say "I know you can do better", but by this time I was really going down the pan'.

Horatio had already entered on his criminal career. There is conveyed in tone of voice a sense of loss, of being valueless, an infinite wistful sadness. At 15 he left school with no qualifications.

Section two

Identity and the criminal justice system
An investigation into disjunction and integration, and the relationship between the subjects and the police, courts, and prison service is somewhat fraught with contradictions. At a more profound level, if deviant behaviour might be considered an expression of disjunction, then, in one sense the subjects' apprehension by the police, and subsequent sentencing, might ultimately be considered a contribution towards personal integration. The outcome—disjunction or integration, would depend on the appropriateness of the sentence, and the subject's admission of its legitimacy. In fact, although not a direct part of this investigation three of the four subjects admitted, either tacitly or overtly, that there was a degree of legitimacy in their prison sentence. Jonathon explained 'I realise where I am, and I realise I've done something wrong to be here, and I deserve to be here'. Antonio claims:

> At the end of the day, I was not found in possession of any drug. Irrespective of whether I was guilty of the crime or not. Say I am guilty . . . of conspiring. That means I colluded with others to conspire to distribute a Class A drug.

and Horatio admits—'I know I'm getting sentenced for what I've done'. However, this sense of legitimacy felt by the subjects is tempered somewhat by a belief that the criminal justice system is biased against black people.

Identity and experience of policing

All of the subjects believe that racism exists in the police force, particularly the Metropolitan Police. For example, Jonathon considers that he was stopped and searched more than white people. 'Sometimes police picked on me I reckon because I am black, and stopped me in the street now. . . Right' Research shows that police stop and search powers are still exercised more in relation to black people. Two of the subjects recall the 'sus' laws of the early 1980s with reference to feelings of racial discrimination by the police. Jonathon recalls:

> But the thing about it is now . . . this was back in the early eighties when they had the sus Law, and there was a big debate that black people used to get stopped more than anyone else. They never stopped me, I think I was a bit too young . . . but my brother was older than me. He had never been in trouble with the police, but he used to get stopped all the time.

Jerome also recalls that time, 'in the early eighties', when 'getting a slap or a punch' when being stopped and searched 'was no big deal'. Under the sus laws he remembers, at the age of 16 coming home from work in the evening, about six o'clock:

> I got stopped in the snow . . . the street lights were on . . . and I was stripped down . . . and my trousers had to come down and everything, and I had my top off and I was standing in the snow by the police car.

There appears to be a developing understanding of the relationship between ethnicity and racism in society in all the subjects. This supports Hall's (1998) findings, rather than Ratcliffe's (1994) more static definition of racism. 'Ethnicity as it is experienced is subject to change over time'. However this does not necessarily lead to disjunction, if experience corresponds to reality. For example concerning getting arrested, and stopped and searched in the snow, Jerome explains: 'I didn't look at it with outrage . . . as I would today. Things like that . . . Certainly didn't warm me . . . to the police'. Antonio also shows a developing understanding of personal identity and racism. 'I've encountered more (racism) since growing up, because now I understand it'.

Police attitude

Two of the subjects mention that they experienced verbal abuse from the police in the 1980s. A contemptuous attitude by those in authority may lead to disjunction. Jerome claims 'They would just say "oh, so and so" and give you a clip'. However, there does appear to be a perception that police actions, though not necessarily attitudes, have improved in the 1990s. For example, Jonathon admits—'But when it comes to actually getting arrested, for something I've done . . . I can't really have any complaints'. Jerome, after referring to being 'pushed around' by the police in the 1980s explains that, 'back in those days there was more of that'. Horatio's analysis of the situation is subtle, and meaning is forged in the actual interview situation:

> I think it must have been around ninety-ninety-one, I noticed a big difference [in police behaviour]. Every time I got nicked they were on their best . . . serious, this was everywhere, Met, out in the country, they were on their best behaviour.

His description carries the impression that some policemen still didn't like black people, but they didn't let it affect their overt behaviour. 'Trying to be professional about their job I suppose, but it still . . . you know . . . It's hard to say'.

Attitude to the legal authorities
The subjects show a mixed response in their attitude to agents of the court—solicitors, barristers and judges. On the one hand there is a tacit acknowledgement of the forbearance of the authorities in the face of their persistent offending behaviour. On the other, a widespread belief that the court process, based on the judgements made by those in authority, is biased against black people because of the cumulative effects of racism. This ambivalence conforms to Habermas' claims about the fractured nature of social life. For example, Jonathon identifies societal pressure on black solicitors. He doesn't feel that being dealt with by black people in authority is particularly helpful to black people. This is because they 'come down double hard on you', in his opinion for fear of being seen to be discriminating in favour of people of their own colour. In this study, this concept would support Abbott and Wallace's contention, that racism is a 'specific' form of exclusion 'from the seat of power'. Jonathon explains that an example of this was an African black solicitor, who represented him whilst he was attending a youth treatment centre, aged 14. He 'had to go to court', but fortunately for Jonathon, articulate and socialised, he had previously been selected to show the judge around the treatment centre, where she had seen that he was making good progress. The solicitor insisted on asking for a lenient custodial sentence, 'He was an African man . . . and he was trying to send me to prison . . . I was trying to tell him I wasn't; I know the judge'. Eventually 'we had to sack him and get someone else'.

Attitudes to sentencing

The results of this study show that whereas all the subjects are convinced that sentencing policy in English courts is often biased against black people in individual cases this is not always so. Attitudes towards the appropriateness of the subjects' sentencing varies, and so does the extent of the disjunction experienced, Jonathon feels that he has been treated reasonably by the courts: from his early teens, he had many convictions, but he wasn't given a custodial sentence until he was 17:

> I think . . . a lot more black people get sent to jail, just because they are coloured. The judge sees a black face, and sends them to jail. But me personally, I can't really say that.

Horatio believes it is hard to judge racial bias from a sentencing point of view, 'some people get badly stitched up, others don't'. In fact, the current research literature tends to support this view, in for example Hood's study showing the variation of sentencing policy between Dudley and Birmingham Crown Courts. In his case he has always received quite severe sentences, 'but you can't really say it's because I'm black'. Antonio is convinced that in his case, the courts handed out a very severe penalty. 'If I could see that it was a one-off occurrence, or that these occurrences were few, and far between I would put it down as each case. But this goes across the board'. To a certain extent, this view is supported by Wilson and Ashton (1998) and Hood (1992) and the 'cumulative' effect is likely to cause disjunction.

Identity and the experience of dispersal prison conditions

All of the subjects agree that the experience of a long sentence under dispersal conditions is arduous and puts pressure on personal identity, tending to cause disjunction. Horatio explains 'In this environment . . . nothing at all, just brick and officers and men'. The human interaction that occurs is highly visible and the effect concentrated, intense. Antonio, wrestling with the construction of meaning in the interview, describes it as 'a fine line that you have to thread in these places'. The subjects describe the cumulative effect of the regime as a psychological 'weight', 'the searches, the pat downs, the arguments, the constant surveillance'. Small domestic details become problematic in a high security prison. Jerome gives examples—'Where's that knife? In the kitchen, in the kitchen and where's the iron?—and where are you?' The focus for the subjects is to 'do their time', to 'just get through this, and get out the other side with all my faculties', as one person explained it.

Attitudes towards other prisoners

Three of the four subjects reported difficulties in their relationships with some white prisoners. With some of the subjects there is a reluctance to discuss this issue. This reluctance was also found by Simmons (1988). One subject reported 'Sometimes white prisoners are extremely racially prejudiced. One prisoner had to move spurs because of the language white prisoners used in front of him'. It would appear that where there are sufficient numbers of black prisoners on an accommodation spur there is no problem because 'no white prisoner is going to use verbal abuse against black prisoners, because he would be threatened with physical violence'. On those spurs where there are few black prisoners, physical threat is not an option, so white prisoners 'get away with' verbal racial abuse. The atmosphere that this produces contributes towards disjunction. However all the subjects report that the problem is 'containable'.

Relationship with the prison authorities
There were no reports of physical violence against black prisoners by prison staff at Whitemoor in this study. This means that prisoner/staff relations are not a source of extreme disjunction. This contradicts the experience at such prisons as Blakenhurst (Wilson and Ashton, 1998). However, there was a feeling amongst the subjects that some prison officers felt more comfortable when dealing with white prisoners, an attitude which may produce some disjunction. Horatio explains:

> The problem is one of dislike, and lack of interest, not hatred. Probably they have had one or two bad experiences with black people, and they had no context, to put them into perspective.

The context, Horatio explains is that black people are not a homogeneous group, 'there are many different cultural faces'. Some are loud and 'talk Patois', 'some are quiet', depending on where they come from. If all these faces 'are distorted into one', then 'every black person is seen as having the potential to act in all these different ways' generating fear and bewilderment. This understanding of ethnicity as 'no longer to be perceived in monolithic terms' conforms to Stuart Hall's definition. This view, that there may be some lack of understanding, is confirmed in this study by one of the governor grades:

> Geography is a big problem. I've come here with a lot of knowledge, but most staff here don't have that knowledge. The bulk of staff here have not lived with ethnic minorities. They don't understand how they speak, or many aspects of their culture.

Antonio points out that there are few black prison officers. Some white officers go by the 'Old Boy Network' which puts black prisoners at a disadvantage and causes some feelings of disjunction:

> "Oh, I knew your Dad, yes, he was a right Jack-the-Lad. You are a right gangster. I'll treat you with respect . . . Some of these officers look on some

of these inmates as their sons, so they more take to them than they would us
. . . because I don't remind any on them . . . of their sons. So . . . (grins).

There is a feeling amongst some of the subjects that they don't always
get acknowledgement from the authorities when they behave well. One
subject explains that you can alter your pattern of behaviour, adopt a low
profile, but still be treated in the same way. The prison, he claims, uses
the incentive scheme to control prisoners. However, some people who
are well behaved 'are not on "enhanced standard", and they are black
guys'. He claims that 'Feeling that equal treatment doesn't happen
because of colour is very frustrating'. This feeling might cause
disjunction.

Section three

Prison education—Reforging identity
Prison education affects personal integration through a number of
means. The results of this study show that the main categories are
Normalisation, Change in Self-Perception, Socialisation, Increased
Understanding of the World, and Personal Fulfilment.

Normalisation
Three of the four subjects reported that prison education created a more
normal environment. This contributed to personal integration by the
amelioration of the pains of imprisonment under dispersal conditions.
This result is supported by Williamson (1998) and Harer (1995). Jerome
explained that there is a different type of professional relationship
between prisoners and teachers, rather than custody staff. This alters the
environmental referent. 'It is a release in some way . . . from the more
intense custody environment of the main prison'. A greater sense of
normality is achieved, he claims, because all prisoners have experience of
school or college, so it is familiar, and they can more easily adapt to it.
'Not away from prison, but it isn't impinging on you. You are not
conscious of it all the time. You feel in a more—student mode . . . than
I'm a prisoner mode'. Jonathon contrasts the environment of an
education class, which challenges the mind, with that of the workshops:

> If there wasn't education, I'd be pretty bored, because the last thing I want to
> do is go and work in that shop. The alternative to studying is just to become
> mentally dead

and worryingly he adds:

> physically dead as well. It's a great opportunity for me to be allowed to do
> my education, rather than just let your mind get dead, and be dead in a
> package, or something like that.

Change in self-perception

Results of this study show, in all four subjects, that participation in prison education brings about a process of integration achieved over a considerable length of time, possibly years. One of its main components is an increase in the depth of self-knowledge. For example, Jonathon now regrets his failure to gain qualifications at school. He is aware that in prison he must take responsibility for his own learning. 'It's more relaxed [than at school] . . . I know now, if I don't get on with it, no one is really going to push me'. Attending prison education has, he claims, altered his sense of self. When he first came into jail he 'didn't feel too good about myself', but gaining high marks 'made me feel better about myself'. Education has altered his expectation, and given him a realistic understanding of his own ability, which is much higher than he had previously believed. He explains:

> Teachers in the GCSE class said 'I'm definitely getting top marks', but I didn't think that. The marks then kind of surprised me . . . I didn't know I was that good.

This integrative self-discovery now has a general application. 'To become fully human it is necessary to become 'self-aware" (Friere in Kirkwood, 1989). 'This made me feel good about myself, and that helps with everything. Liking yourself now makes you feel good about certain other things'. Antonio also acknowledged that attending prison education had an integrative and transformative effect. The manner in which this change is effected, he explained as an increase in self-knowledge:

> 'Don't get me wrong . . . Liz . . . a degree in humanities is nice . . . it does alter . . . teach you about . . . who you are. Makes me look at the world in a more precise manner. It allows me to make a more structured analysis of whatever it is I am doing.

This view is supported by the work of (Duguid, 1998) in his Canadian study where he claims that the humanities centred model of delivery 'clearly works'. Another component in this change of perception is the concept of delayed gratification. Dewey describes this as 'the crucial educational problem, that of procuring the postponement of immediate action upon desire until observation and judgement have intervened' (Dewey, 1938: 69 in Thorpe, 1993: 140)

Horatio describes this integrative effect as a transformation which involves a radical reassessment of how you achieve your desired goals, a process which takes many years. 'It takes a year to get your GCSEs, it takes this many years to get your 'A' levels, and this many to get your degree'. He explains, 'you used to think about something and then say 'well—I'll go and get it'; you get into a new way of looking at things. You get fulfilment and satisfaction from struggling for a while to achieve something'. This process supports Wallack's (1939) view that the aim of prison education is to effect a transfer of allegiance to socially acceptable 'ways of achieving desired goals'.

Socialisation
Three of the four subjects mentioned the positive integrative impact of relationships in the professional and ordered environment of the education department. This view, that the relationship between prisoners and teachers is 'particularly positive' is supported by Clayton already alluded to above. This importance of right relationships between staff and inmates was also confirmed by Liebling and Price (1998: 89) in their study based at HMP Whitemoor. Although this refers to correctional staff, its main findings are relevant to teachers. 'Right relationships . . . which include fairness, respect, and dialogue become instruments of legitimacy', and again, quoting from the Control Review Committee Report (Home Office 1984: 90):

> Nothing else that we can say will be as important as the general proposition that relations between staff and prisoners are at the heart of the whole prison system.

Integration is effected, not only through the subjects' engagement with teaching staff, but also with their relationships, built up in group work, with other prisoners in the class. Antonio mentions the importance of 'interaction with others (both teachers and students) in debate and argument', and Horatio the importance of 'interacting with other students'.

Increased knowledge about the world
In this study, three of the four subjects reported that one of the important things they gained from studying in the Whitemoor Education Department was an increased knowledge about the world: 'To exist humanly, is to name the world' (Friere, 1993: 69). Apart from the intrinsic value of learning for its own sake, access to a wider knowledge contributed to integration, the subjects claimed, in two different ways. Firstly, it increased understanding, and secondly, it assisted in more effective decision-making. If this is the case, then education programmes appear to meet the criteria outlined in the paradigm of the 'New Medical Model' namely 'active, participatory, problem solving methods of working', and 'matching the intensity and duration of intervention to likely future risk of offending'. For example, Antonio describes the effect of an increased understanding of the world. He has always, he claims, had 'what you would call 'street knowledge'', gained through life experience:

If you let me out this week wearing just my trousers, and a pair of trainers, I would get home in luxury (laughter). I know how to manipulate circumstances, so that, without hurting people, I can just get by.

However, he now understands that meaning is multi-layered:

But education is universal . . . you get to see the reasons . . . to test your own parameters . . . to test society's parameters . . . You get involved in debate . . . argument . . . and you can understand what is going on in the world. For me . . . that's what education has given me.

Antonio then illustrated the application of this knowledge in narrative form:

But even if I go on holiday . . . I went for instance to Tenerife. Without the education, I go there, and I look at it and I say, it's a nice little sunny place. I can get some Timeshare here, and go and have some drinks and whatever. But with an education now, when I look back on the holiday . . . I look at it differently. When I look at the volcanic landscape, I look at the mountain, and I see exactly what it entailed. I can see the culture of the place. You see . . it's a totally different holiday now. Then I could see . . . which influences are in Tenerife. It's different. And it's in a million ways I suspect education is going to help me. I just can't wait to get out there and start using it.

Jerome explained how the process of education, and the wider understanding it provides, increases the effectiveness of decision-making:

Once you do start getting into learning and study . . . you can gain the mental tools . . . you know . . . to be able to analyse anything, and reflect— you've got better mental tools to reflect with, about your situation, what's happened to you—where you are going, and how you know your place in the world.

Antonio also described this process: 'It allows me to make a more structured analysis of what I am doing'.

Personal fulfilment
The results of this study show that all four of the subjects found the experience of learning to be personally enriching, a contrast to the somewhat bleak environment of a dispersal prison.

To learn involves the integrated functioning of the total organism—thinking, feeling, perceiving and behaving (Kolb, 1984 in Thorpe, 1993:148).

It appeared to be important to the subjects to go back to that point where they had failed in the past, and start again. Jonathon describes this as a second chance:

I left school with no qualifications whatsoever and this is a chance for me to do what I know I can do. You think of a GCSE, even an RSA exam now. It might not be very big, but it's big to that person. He's achieving something for the first time in his life. Even though he's doing it in prison, he's showing himself he can do it, that builds up his self-esteem.

Antonio describes the enrichment provided by education as a transformation of vision—the total way he looked at the world:

Gaining . . . some semblance of an education has let me, on reflection . . . see how blinkered my life really was, because it's alright, and fine attaining all these material things. Before . . . I'm going down this path. I'm going to have 100 thousand pounds, and I'm going to live a good life . . . But, when I got the hundred thousand pounds. It's just a wage packet at the end of the day.

He then describes 'the opening out' process of education:

What you have done now is open the basis of the argument, so I can take it [life experience] on different spheres. You know, take it on different levels, and before . . . I was tunnel visioned.

Horatio also describes the experience of learning as a transformative experience. Personal fulfilment is achieved through a process of reflection and action which involves wrestling and conflict. The result is an increase in stability. 'Ideas that evolve through integration tend to become highly stable parts of the person's conception of the world', in Piaget's terms (Kolb, 1984 in Thorpe, 1993: 146) Horatio explains:

When you are studying, your brain becomes like a basket. Enormous amounts of material are thrown into it. You are also interacting with other students, and being drawn into ideas that you would never have thought of.

The final word on this study of disjunction and integration rests with Horatio. He continues:

And that will change your perspective on things, and even if you didn't want it to. You steadfastly . . . I don't like this, I don't like that, and I hate those, you can't help it . . . you will meet things that you didn't know before, and take an interest in them. You never used to take an interest in that before, so you will change.

He describes this process of integration as 'acclimatisation'. 'You can't help it. You know . . . acclimatisation if you can say that'.

If the effects of racism in our society and more particularly its effects as experienced by black prisoners are to be negated, which my research shows is possible through prison education programmes, then those programmes must not be curtailed. According to Kekes (1985 in Hanfling, 1987: 244), 'To a considerable extent, our present moral confusions, and their destructive consequences, are due to having forgotten that liberal education (the teaching of humanities) is moral education'. As Hall explains, if we are to reduce the effects of racism in our society as a whole, and also its impact on offending behaviour, then our understanding of what constitutes 'Britishness' must be 'transcoded'. The content of a liberal education must include the 'idea of ethnic diversity'. 'Ethnicity' acknowledges the contribution of history, language and culture to personal and group identities, as well as the fact that all knowledge is contextual. This must be acknowledged and recognised in our prisons.

BIBLIOGRAPHY

Abbott P. and Wallace C. (1997); *An Introduction to Sociology—Feminist Perspectives*, second edition, London: Routledge

Alfred R. (1992), *Black Workers in the Prison Service*, Prison Reform Trust

Baker D. (ed.) (1994), *Reading, Racism and the Criminal Justice System*, Canadian Scholars Press Inc: Toronto

Bernstein, R. (1983), *Beyond Objectivism and Relativism* in Kvale S. (1996), *Interviews: An Introduction to Qualitative Research Interviewing*, California: Sage

Blagg H. and Smith D. (1989), *Crime, Penal Policy and Social Work*, Longman: London

Blumer H. (1972), *Society as Symbolic Interaction*, Routledge: London

Braithwaite J. (1989), *Prisons, Education and Work*, University of Queensland Press, Australian Institute of Criminology

Browne K. (1998), *An Introduction to Sociology*, second edition, Polity Press: Cambridge UK

Cashmore E. and McLaughlin E. (1991), *Out of Order. Policing Black People: A Comparative Analysis of the Policing of Blacks in both the UK and the USA*, London: Routledge

Cashmore E. (1994), *Dictionary of Race and Ethnic Relations*, London: Routledge

Cassara B. (1990), *Adult Education in a Multi-cultural Society*, New York: Routledge

Christie N. (1968), *Changes in Penal Values*, in Cohen S. and Taylor L. (1972), *Psychological Survival*, London: Pelican

Cohen S. and Taylor L. (1972), *Psychological Survival: The Experience of Long-term Imprisonment*, London: Pelican

Cunningham P. (1983), 'Education as a Social Agent', Review of Adult Education in *Adult Education Quarterly*, 33. Cited in Cassara (1990)

Davidson H. (1995), *Schooling in a 'Total Institution': Critical Perspectives on Prison Education*: London

Devlin A. (1995), *Criminal Classes: Offenders at School*, Waterside Press: Winchester

Dewey J. (1938), *Experience and Education*, in Thorpe M., Edwards R. and Hanson A (eds.) (1993), *Culture and Processes of Adult Learning*, London: Routledge

Donald J. and Rattansi A. (1992), *Race, Culture and Difference*, London: Sage Publications

Duguid, S. (1995), 'Policy, Praxis and Rehabilitation—Prison Education in Canada 1945–95', in Forster, W., *Education Behind Bars: International Comparisons*: NIACE—Leicester 1998

Duguid, S. and Pawson, R. (1998), 'Education, Change and Transformation: The Prison Experience' in *Evaluation Review*, Vol. 22, No 4: 470-495

Fitzgerald M. (1993), *The Royal Commission on Criminal Justice—Ethnic Minorities in the Criminal Justice System*, London: HMSO

Flanagan, T. (1992), *Forum for Corrections Research*, Vol 4, No 2 June 1992: 19-24, Correctional Service of Canada

Forster W, (1981), Cited in National Institute of Adult Education (London), *Prison Education in England and Wales*

Freire P. (1993), *Pedagogy of the Oppressed*, London: Penguin

Giddens A. (1984), *Constitution of Society: Outline of the Theory of Structuration*, Cambridge: Polity Press

Gill D., Mayor B. and Blair M. (1992), *Racism in Education*, London: Sage

Hall S. (1988), 'New Ethnicities', ICA London Lecture in Donald J. and Rattansi A. (1992), *Race Culture and Difference*, London: Sage

Hanfling, O. (1987), *Life and Meaning*, Blackwell: Oxford, Cited in Hanfling, O. (ed.) (1987), Kekes, J. (1985), 'Moral Tradition' from *Philosophical Investigations*: Blackwell

Harer, M. D. (1995), *Prison Education Programme Participation and Recidivism*: Federal Bureau of Prisons Office of Research and Evaluation Washington DC3

Harris R. (1996), Norwich City College Conference, Multi-Cultural Awareness, Report of the Third Annual Conference of the School of Continuing Education, 8 June 1996

Home Office (1998), Special Conferences Unit—Criminal Justice Conference Report: Race Issues in a Criminal Justice System (Swindon, March 1998)

Home Office (1998), Home Office *Section 95 (Report): Statistics on Race and the Criminal Justice System*, London: Home Office

Home Office (1997), Home Office Research Study No. 171, Vennard, J. *et al*, *Changing Offenders' Attitude and Behaviour: What Works?*, London: Home Office:

Home Office (1998), Section 95 (Report), Research Study No. 185, London: Home Office

Hood R. (1992), *A Question of Judgement: Summary of Race and Sentencing, A Study in the Crown Court*, CRE (Booklet)

Jepson N. A., *Education in Prison: The Relevance of Criminological Theory*

Kenny A. (1975), *Wittgenstein*, London: Penguin Books

Kirkwood G. and Kirkwood C. (1989), *Living Adult Education*, Milton Keynes: Open University Press

Kolb D. A. (1984), *Experiential Learning*, New Jersey: Prentice Hall

Kushnick L. (1998), *Essays on Racism and Inequality in Britian, the US and Western Europe*, London: Rivers Oram Press

Kvale S. (1996), *Interviews: An Introduction to Qualitative Research Interviewing*, California: Sage

Liebling A. and Price D. (1998), *An Exploration of Staff-Prisoner Relationships at HMP Whitemoor*, Cambridge: Institute of Criminology.

Loeber R. and Farrington D. (1998), *Serious and Violent Juvenile Offenders: Risk Factors and Successful Interventions*, London: Sage

Lyotard J. (1984), 'The Post-Modern Condition: A Report on Knowledge' in Kvale S. (1996), *Interviews: An Introduction to Qualitative Research Interviewing*, California: Sage

Malm S., Kell, I. and Rust, J. (1994), *Inside Perspectives*, Department of Continuing and Community Education, Goldsmiths College, University of London

May T. (1997), *Social Research: Issues, Methods and Process*, second edition, Buckingham: Open University Press

NACRO (1987), *Black People in Prison: The Role of the Education Service*, Seminar 2 November 1987

NIACE (1998), *Prison Education Diaries*

Penal Affairs Consortium (1996), *Race and Criminal Justice* (Report) Sept. 1996

Prison Reform Trust Extract, Home Office Research and Planning Unit 1994 (Extract), *Racial Incidents in Prison*, London: Prison Reform Trust

Prison Reform Trust (1991); *Prisoners and Offending*, London

Ratcliffe P. (1994), *Race, Ethnicity and Nation: International Perspectives on Social Conflict*, London: UCL Press

Runnymede Trust (July 1998), Briefing Paper No.1, *Race Policy and Education* Gilborn, D. and Gipps C., *Recent Research on the Achievement of Ethnic Minority Pupils* (Ofsted, 1996)

Simmons, M. (1998), 'A Long Way To Go: Report on Racism in Prison', *The Howard League Magazine*, Vol.16, No.4., Nov. 1998

Skellington, R. (1996), *Race in Britain Today*, London: Sage

Solomos, J. (1993), *Construction of Black Criminality: Racialisation and Criminalisation in Perspective* in May, T. (1997), *Social Research: Issues, Methods and Process*, second edition, Buckingham: Open University Press

Strauss and Corbin (1998), *Basics of Qualitative Research*, California: Sage

Thorpe M., Edwards R. and Hanson A. (1993), *Culture and Processes of Adult Learning*, London: Routledge

The Times, 25 February 1999

Times Educational Supplement, 26 February 1999

Troyna B. and Carrington B. (1990), *Education Racism and Reform*, London: Routledge

Urmson J. and Ree J. (1989), *Western Philosophy and Philosophers*, London: Unwin Hyman

Weil S. (1989), *Access and Institutional Change* in Thorpe M., Edwards R. and Hanson A. (eds.) (1993), *Culture and Processes of Adult Learning*, London: Routledge

Willey R. (1984), *Race Equality and Schools*, London: Menthuen

Wilson D. and Ashton J. (1998), *What Everyone in Britain Should Know About Crime and Punishment*, London: Blackstone Press

Williams J. (1986), 'Education and Race: The Racialisation of Class Inequalities' in *The British Journal of Sociology of Education*, 7(2), 135-54

Woodley L. (1999), *The Criminal Justice System*, Institute of Race Relations

Weekes D. and Wright D. (1998), *Improving Practice: A Whole School Approach to Raising the Achievement of Afro-Caribbean Youth*, Nottingham Trent University: Runnymede Trust

Williamson W. (1998), 'Learning in Extremis', *Adult Learning*, Volume 10, No 2, 24, Education in Prisons Policy Paper (1998); Home Office.

CHAPTER 7

An Inside View: Prisoners' Letters On Education

Emma Hughes

Efforts to determine the value of prison education have proved to be the source of considerable debate (cf: Duguid and Pawson, 1998; Reuss, 1997; Davidson, 1995; Linden, Perry, Ayers, and Parlett, 1987). Given the lack of universal consensus as to the actual purpose of prison education, this is not surprising. The result is one of competing ideas as to what should constitute the measure of prison education's 'success' or worth. Issues of appropriate evidence and correct methodology become central to the debate and questions as to the actual purpose of imprisonment are also raised.

INTRODUCTION

Rather than addressing re-offending rates of prisoner-students, or considering perception of change in prisoners, this study seeks to make an alternative contribution to prison education evaluation by focusing on the views of prisoners who are themselves engaged in education. The source for this work is a sample of letters written by prisoners to the Prisoners' Education Trust, a charity which funds distance-learning courses. In reading the prisoners' own reports of their experiences of education, we gain greater insight into what these courses mean to them, what role they play in their lives as prisoners, and ultimately what the value and the benefits of this education may be.

The Prisoners Education Trust ('the Trust') was established in 1989 with a view to providing prisoners with a wider choice of courses than those offered through their prison education departments. Given the budget cuts that have restricted the offerings of these departments, and the current focus of prison curricula on basic skills education, the Trust offers a valuable alternative for the prisoner interested in pursuing more advanced study or undertaking a particular course.

In order to receive a grant, a prisoner must first submit an application to the Trust for the specific course he or she wishes to take. The application must include a reference from a prison education officer and the prison must also agree to contribute ten per cent of the cost of the course. The Trust monitors the progress of the successful prisoners on a quarterly basis through questionnaires sent to the education department of each prison involved. The questionnaires are completed by the education staff who indicate the status of the students' progress. Apart from the actual application and the letter sent by the Trust to inform of the result of the application, there is no further contact required between the Trust and the student. In its notification letter, however, the Trust does express its hope that the students will write to keep the Trust informed of progress. Pre-paid envelopes are provided for this purpose.[1] It is these letters, written by prisoners to the Trust, which form the basis of this study.

The sample consists of the 71 letters written to the Trust during the six-month period of December 1998 to May 1999.[2] This interval was chosen for several reasons, most notably that it is a recent, convenient and coherent time period. Additionally, the Trust altered its filing system at the end of May 1999, making it less conducive to locating all of the prisoners' letters received within a given time frame.

The letters reviewed were written by a total of 62 inmates, consisting of 58 men and four women. The letters were sent from a total of 27 prisons, ranging from open institutions to those of maximum-security. Three of the prisoners in the sample have written to the Trust more than once during this six-month period, thus explaining the discrepancy between the number of inmates and number of letters.

In the first six months of 1999, a period which almost coincides with the time frame of the sample, the Trust awarded 310 grants. Eighty-eight of these were awarded for academic courses, 174 for vocational courses and 48 were grants to support creative work, predominantly in the form of funding for art supplies, but also including music lessons (Prisoners' Education Trust, 1999b).[3] Although only approximate calculations can be performed, the figure above suggests that during this period approximately one in five prisoners funded by the Trust wrote regarding their studies. The letters range from brief notes to lengthy and colourful descriptions of a prisoner's experiences, plans and hopes.

---

[1] A copy of the letter sent from the Trust to each successful applicant is included as *Appendix 1* to this chapter. Although the letter is altered occasionally, and varies slightly for those receiving grants for art supplies, the essence remains the same.

[2] The letters are held in the archive of the Prisoners Education Trust in a file entitled 'Letters from Prisoners.' The numbers assigned to the letters are my own, imposed chronologically from the starting date of the sample.

[3] Not all of the letters refer to which type of course the prisoner is engaged upon; therefore, from the sample alone, it is not possible to determine the breakdown of course type. Additionally, it is interesting to note that at the end of June 1999, the Trust reports that 188 of these courses were still in progress and 72 had been completed, accounting in total for 84 per cent of the courses funded. Of the remaining courses, 15 had not yet commenced, five were recorded as unknown, four prisoners had been released, and 26 had abandoned their courses (Prisoners Education Trust 1999b.)

The use of these letters as a source is not without its complications; there is a fundamental question as to whether documents written by prisoners are a valid criminological source (cf. Morgan, 1999). I would argue, however, that the potential value of these letters outweighs their methodological limitations.

The first problem, particular to this sample, is that the letters are in effect a 'thank you' for funding provided by the Trust, and are therefore less likely to be critical of the course or of the enterprise of prison education. However, this does not negate the value of the specific responses to the courses that are described by the prisoners. A second limitation is that it is not possible to determine if any 'pressure' was applied by education officers in encouraging prisoners to write. However, according to Ann Creighton, the director of the Trust, while some education departments do encourage prisoners to write, this does not explain all of the letters; many prisoners write 'simply because they want to' (personal communication). The number of prisons from which letters are received supports this conclusion that encouragement from staff is not the significant factor. A third issue that arises is that a portion of the letters are written upon the completion of the course, and are in part a request for funds for further courses. Nevertheless, the fact that the course has been completed and that another is desired is noteworthy in itself.

It also may be argued that the sample represents a prisoner 'elite', and is not reflective of the prison population in general. After all, the sample consists of prisoners who have opted to submit applications to the Trust, these applications have been successful, and they have subsequently chosen to write to the Trust about their progress. This does not, however, discount the value of that which is reported in the letters. Indeed, it also points to the existence of prisoners who wish to avail themselves of advanced educational opportunities. Additionally, the sample also includes individuals who report that prior to entering prison they had not received much education, suggesting that their interest in education developed whilst in prison.

The significant strength of this source is that the letters provide valuable, unfiltered, insight into the motivations and experiences of a prisoner involved in education. There was no interviewer asking potentially leading questions; the letters are spontaneous expressions of the prisoners' thoughts and ideas at the time of writing. Although each letter may describe only an aspect of a prisoner's experience of education, that which is written is revealing, thus providing a valid contribution to criminological understanding.[4]

---

[4] In his study of prisoner autobiographies, Morgan (1999) concludes that 'Prison autobiographies are not criminology in a formal sense as they do not adhere to any formal conventions of sociological method. They are, however, texts or documents of

The excerpts from prisoners' letters which are quoted in this chapter have been edited, when necessary, in terms of spelling and essential grammar. It was felt that the intention of these quotes was not to point out any inadequacies that may exist in written skills, but rather to let the prisoners' views be expressed without unnecessary distraction. Furthermore, these letters were written to the Trust without any anticipation of their being published, removing the possibility for the more careful attention which that may have entailed. Additionally, no names of prisoners or prisons have been included for reasons of confidentiality.

The following is a survey of the evidence with a view to discovering what issues and concerns emerge. The findings are grouped according to the major themes which arise. These topics can be categorised as follows: the prisoners' perception of opportunities brought about by education, particularly in regards to post-release; the effect of education on the life of a prisoner; the prisoner as 'student'; problems encountered and external connections developed through education.

THE POTENTIAL EFFECT OF EDUCATION POST-RELEASE

Of the 71 letters under analysis, 12 acknowledge the opportunity that the Trust's funding offers them, and in nine of these the word 'opportunity' is specifically used. For the prisoners, opportunity translates into a range of meanings. For some of the prisoners, this opportunity is directly related to the desire to further educational study, for others it means the chance of having their own art supplies for personal and independent use within their cells. In other cases, opportunity refers to improving their post-release prospects. In fact, in over 25 per cent of the letters, the prisoner-students express a hope that their educational pursuits in prison will have a beneficial effect on their lives post-release.

In many of these letters, the prisoners refer to the goal of gaining qualifications which may in turn open the door to further possibilities, such as an improved chance of gaining employment upon release. Of course a qualification in and of itself, especially to the holder of a criminal record, is hardly a guarantee of finding work, and this itself is acknowledged in several letters. In these cases the prisoners express their hope that a qualification, or indeed any other academic or vocational training received in prison, will at least help to improve their chances in

direct and critical understanding of the discourses and social practices of prison which can and should be analysed using formal methodology' (p. 337).

the job market, perhaps helping to offset the existence of their prison record.

As a prisoner taking an A-level course in Art explains: 'It makes it more possible for me to get the 'leg-up' in life I've needed for a long time, and although it might not get me a job, it does make the idea more feasible' (Letter 70). 'At least at long last, I am on the road to acquiring recognised qualifications' (Letter 52) explains another prisoner. A prisoner with at least three years left to serve adds: 'Who knows what the next three years may bring, but whatever happens, I will be better qualified to resume my life when the time eventually comes' (Letter 28).

A number of letters demonstrate how a more explicit link can be made between courses taken and future employment prospects. A prisoner pursuing a Sports course writes: 'This course will be a very important stepping stone towards my personal aim of using my skills to gain employment on my eventual release. Sport has always been my priority for many years, and this opportunity to enhance my knowledge is a breath of fresh air' (Letter 4). A prisoner studying a Computer course indicates that the '[course] contents will give me the knowledge that I need to improve my career in computers' (Letter 41). A prisoner who has completed numerous counselling courses, and who has the prospect of working for a Christian hostel upon his release, writes to the Trust: 'You have all helped me gain so much for my future job as a counsellor ' (Letters 53 and 27). Clearly, there is a connection in the minds of many students between qualifications earned in prison and improved career prospects.

In a further five letters the prisoners express their more general belief that pursuing education in prison will help them to redirect their lives in a more positive way after they are released. A prisoner enrolled on a Writing course explains: 'I am very grateful for you giving me the opportunity to begin a positive reconstruction of my life and the tools to head in a new direction. It means an enormous amount to me' (Letter 21). After receiving news that an application for an A-level course had been successful, a 'thrilled and extremely grateful' prisoner informs the Trust: 'I endeavour to prove worthy of the chance given to me to better myself through study' (Letter 19). A third prisoner who had already previously received funding from the Trust expressed his gratitude for yet 'another chance to rehabilitate and be qualified for foreseeable gainly employment' (Letter 17).

THE IMPACT OF EDUCATION ON THE LIFE OF A PRISONER

While over a quarter of the letters refer to the future benefits of pursuing education in prison, an almost equal number of letters point towards the important role that a distance-learning course can play in coping with the day-to-day reality of life in prison. For those serving particularly long sentences, such benefits as these may appear crucial—future benefits, such as improved employment prospects, may seem irrelevant or a long way off.[5] As the following examples from prisoners' letters will demonstrate, participation in education can provide mental stimulation, personal satisfaction, a boost to self-confidence, a sense of purpose and a way to spend one's time constructively—experiences not typically associated with the serving of a prison sentence. In fact, almost a third of the letters actively refer to the course or anticipated course as a positive experience. For those concerned that prison is actually 'a good way of making bad people worse' these letters offer hope that alternative outcomes exist. In addition, for those concerned that a prison sentence can lead to mental deterioration and a harmful loss of self-determination, these letters suggest how this may be alleviated.

A prisoner included in the sample summarises the situation when he describes how his positive experience of education contrasts with the remainder of his prison experience. He explains that: 'Prison is not a nice memory but always I have this course [which was] a positive thing from the time I was here in prison' (Letter 39). A prisoner who earned a university degree whilst serving time in a high security prison argues that the education department 'really is the only place you feel both human and confident' (Letter 47).

In an environment which severely restricts the independence and personal choice of its inmates, education can provide a forum in which some degree of autonomy and self decision-making is restored. Distance-learning, which by its very nature requires a choice of course, independent study and personal responsibility, can go some way towards achieving this aim. In so doing, it provides more realistic and appropriate preparation for prisoners to resume their lives upon release. A prisoner who received a grant for art supplies thanks the Trust for 'enabling me to pursue and manage my art work independently' (Letter 52). Reflecting his opportunity for choice, a prisoner explains: 'the

---

5 The records held by the Trust do not contain information regarding the length of the prisoners' sentences, or indeed the crime committed. This rules out the possibility of categorizing the prisoners' responses here accordingly. Instead, the letters provide an insight into general ways in which the courses are applied to the experience of being a prisoner.

module that I will be taking [next] is International Trade and Payments and once that is out of the way I will be looking to take one of the last two but I have not made up my mind which one yet. I will in due course write to you again with an application form for whichever one I decide to take' (Letter 28). Not dissimilar to this opportunity for autonomy and independence is the opportunity for self-expression. Two of the prisoners involved in creative pursuits acknowledge the value of this (Letters 66 and 67).

In approximately 15 per cent of the letters[6], the prisoners describe their courses with words such as 'interesting', 'stimulating', 'worthwhile' and 'meaningful'.[7] A trainee yoga instructor describes how his course is 'very enjoyable, very interesting and very worthwhile' (Letter 5). 'Thank you again for granting me the funding for the Creative Writing course. It really is an interesting and worthwhile course to do. For me anyway' (Letter 26). 'The first four [sections] are in the area Politics, Economics, and Globalisation. Should prove interesting!' (Letter 49).'The last two months of study have been very inspirational and interesting. It is amazing how the studying process helps me to feel satisfied and content that I am at last doing something useful and worthwhile with my time available during my sentence' (Letter 34).

This notion of use of time is one that surfaces in several letters. As one prisoner points out: 'This is not the best of times for me to study, but one thing is for sure is that I have plenty of time' (Letter 55). A prisoner close to finishing his course, and with only six weeks left before his release, reports of his course that 'all in all I've thoroughly enjoyed it and the 'time' has been put to good use so I'm happy about that' (Letter 22). What specifically constitutes meaningful use of time will undoubtedly vary between individuals. It may range, for example, from earning qualifications to learning something new and inspiring. The important point, however, is that prisoners are reporting feeling satisfaction with the way they have elected to pass their time.

According to research conducted by Cohen and Taylor (1972) in their study of long-term imprisonment, 'time' takes on even greater significance for those prisoners serving long sentences. Faced with the prospect of many years to serve, 'prisoners who have to sustain their lives in some way look around for ways of marking out the passage of the days, ways of differentiating and dividing time' (p. 93). Given that a prison sentence is not geared towards 'the notion of linear progress' (p.

---

[6] This figure also includes letters in which prisoners refer to *anticipated* courses.

[7] It is noteworthy that in the letter to the prisoners the Trust expresses a hope that they should find their course 'interesting': see *Appendix 1* to this chapter. While this may have had an influence on the prisoners' responses, enough prisoners use words of similar meaning for one to argue that their responses were the result of spontaneous expression rather than prompted by the original letter .

94), namely the measured development of an individual prisoner over a period of time, Cohen and Taylor argue that:

> The men tend to create stages themselves. They build their own subjective clock in order to protect themselves from the terror of 'the misty abyss'. There are a few achievements which can be used to mark the passage of time. One can engage in mind-building (reading or studying) and in body-building (usually weightlifting). Some of the men talk about an educational career, describing the passage from O-levels to A-levels to university with an enthusiasm which is rarely found in even those who have a chance of occupationally capitalising upon the restricted years of specialised study which constitute contemporary secondary education. (p. 95)

Similarly, Forster (1998), in a study of prison education in England and Wales, describes how the exams that form part of an academic programme provide useful 'milestones' with which to 'mark time' (p. 69).

In an eloquent explanation of what a distance-learning course can be worth, a self-reported long-term prisoner anticipating the arrival of his course materials makes the following observation:

> It is advents like this that give a focal point to my incarceration. Having a meaningful course to study is a great help in coping with prison life. In the long term it helps to quell 'today's' feelings of anxiety when it comes to the thought of job securing opportunities upon release. Having additional qualifications can only be a plus and these courses are giving me that opportunity and a feeling of hopefulness. (Letter 14)

In the following year the same prisoner wrote again to the Trust. Although this second letter falls outside of the time frame of this sample, I have chosen to include it here as an *addendum* for it further emphasises his earlier point, echoing a concern that long-term prisoners may have:

> At the beginning of the year I had a catastrophic set back when my appeal hearing was rejected, I had high hopes! However, I've now composed my self again and I'm looking for another educational challenge. I have a few things in mind, that will coincide with what I'm currently doing and my sailing interests. It needs to be 'long-term' and give even better job prospects upon release. This has led me to the thought of doing a degree in a related subject, as yet I'm still collating the relevant course prospectuses. Unfortunately the OU doesn't cover the fields that I'm interested in so it's turning out to be quite a hunt for a suitable course. (Letter A)

The activity of setting goals and personal challenges is evident in several of the letters from the sample. A prisoner who had recently begun a Level 2 Open University Psychology class, having completed Level 1 the previous year, set himself the following goal: 'My target is to achieve higher grades than I got last year in each essay—some challenge!' (Letter 46). A prisoner who received a grant for art supplies offers thanks 'For giving me the opportunity to pursue a goal whilst in jail' (Letter 24). Another artist writes 'I will keep in contact with you as my art improves (hopefully)' (Letter 63). For those engaged in structured distance-learning courses, the courses themselves provide targets and goals.

Success in achieving these goals may play a significant role in boosting the self-confidence of the prisoner-students in an environment where the opposite of this is more likely to occur. A prisoner who obtained a grant with which to purchase art materials 'so I could experiment in the five credit Art course' writes that: 'Thanks to the Trust I will succeed in these art accreditations, two I've passed already, and [I'm] starting another two' (Letter 58). A female prisoner who passed a course in Business Development and another in Basic Philosophy (and enclosed a copy of a certificate to illustrate her progress) wrote that: 'It was a great success for me' (Letter 59). Others refer to teachers noting 'big improvement' (Letter 63), and describe receiving 'very good scores' that served as 'encouragement' (Letter 56). 'Since the beginning of this course in February, I have received encouraging feedback on my assignments from my tutor. The final exams are in October and I am quite confident that I will get a pass' (Letter 45).

A total of 19 prisoners enclosed results, tutors' comments, or facsimiles of certificates that they had earned, although they were not requested specifically to do so. Ten prisoners reported earning certificates or passing their courses, and more than 15 prisoners indicated that their courses were going well, with a number of prisoners reporting marks in the ninetieth percentiles. Achievement is relative to each individual, as is their measure of 'success'.

Achievement for prisoners in the realm of education, be it academic or vocational, may be considered all the more significant when viewed against the backdrop of a prison population which has generally been linked with lower than average educational attainment (cf. Devlin 1995, Wilson and Ashton 1998). It is beyond the boundaries of this study to review the previous academic achievements of the individual members of the sample, and it is important to keep in mind the possibility that the sample may not be representative of the prison population as a whole. However, as the following examples indicate, the sample clearly includes individuals who had not gained any academic qualifications prior to arriving in prison.[8]

---

[8] Forster (1998) notes that one of the 'types' of offenders to whom academic education in prison appeals is the individual who previously did not achieve much academically, but who 'caught the bug' for learning in prison, is eager to make progress and make good use of time (p. 68).

The Trust received the following letter from a prisoner who had recently started on his course:

> I am really enjoying the course and the challenge, as I had very little schooling and have not actually done any lessons of any sort for 40 years prior to coming into prison.
>
> Forms and tests have always frightened me, so I find this new experience really beneficial to me. Hopefully as I work through the course it will all become a lot clearer and therefore somewhat easier to understand. (Letter 57)

A prisoner studying Principles of Law relating to Overseas Trade wrote to the Trust with the following report:

> The result is pleasing although I would have liked a slightly better grade. The pass mark is 65 per cent and I would assume from that a C grade should be between 65 per cent and perhaps 77 per cent. Whatever the mark I am pleased that I managed a pass, remembering as I mentioned in my last letter, the exam did take me the full time and although I have always expected that I had passed, it was my first proper examination since my eleven-plus some 35 years ago. (Letter 28)

As Forster (1998), points out, educational achievement in prison can act as an 'antidote to failure.' However, he also warns that there is a danger of 'further failure' (p. 69). A prisoner in this sample describes how 'this year has been quite difficult for me as I actually failed an exam last year which dented my enthusiasm a little, but after passing this module I feel confident to carry on' (Letter 66). This student now has plans to continue further with his studies and is 'making progress with obtaining the necessary books to do so.'

In addition to describing their courses as 'worthwhile' and 'meaningful', at least 17 per cent of the prisoners in the sample refer to the enjoyment and pleasure derived from pursuing a course or developing their artistic work.[9] Representative of these responses are the following: 'Well, I must say in all honesty that I am enjoying it very much, and hope that my enjoyment will continue' (Letter 20). 'I am really happy with the course' (Letter 41). 'I was able to get everything I wanted [art supplies]. I'll have loads of fun, relaxation and hopefully improve!' (Letter 68). 'I am really chuffed to bits and look forward to receiving my next module [of a Christian Communicator course] this week. I have

---

[9] This figure includes *anticipated* enjoyment for courses about to begin. It should also be noted that in its letter to prisoners, the Trust does express hope that the course will prove 'enjoyable'. As in the case of the word 'interesting' (see above), this may have provided guidance to prisoners' responses. However, enough prisoners use different, but similar, words or descriptions to suggest that the sentiment is genuine.

certainly got the learning bug and one day I will put it all to good use as a missionary in Sri Lanka' (Letter 13).

An interesting development that emerges from the sample is that several of the prisoner-students make use of their newly acquired skills by helping other inmates. This is in addition to those prisoners, such as in the quote above, who have plans to put their learning 'to good use' upon release from prison. This assistance and guidance offers actual benefits to other prisoners, and may be seen to contribute to the smooth running of the prison. Additionally, the experience of instructing or assisting others may serve to further improve confidence levels of the prisoner-students as well as provide an additional source of self-fulfilment and enjoyment. A student close to completing a Yoga Teacher Diploma Course, and receiving very high marks, informs the Trust that:

> I now teach yoga 'under supervision' here at HM Prison . . . once a week, so the benefits are already bearing fruit.
>
> I shall finish the course in the next few weeks and I would very much like to continue my studies after release. It really has helped me a great deal and I know of no better way of enjoying this experience than to be able to competently coach others in its benefits both physical and mental. (Letter 5)

In the same vein, a prisoner enrolled in a counselling module has also been able to make use of his skills within prison:

> I have been able to learn quite a lot more about the field of counselling. This extends the knowledge that I had from previous studies in this field. I have been able to use the skills learned in helping my peers with problematic issues.
>
> One member of staff in particular has been referring inmates to help, if I can. Of course, the main stay of counselling is listening, and I am very good at that. (Letter 33)

A third prisoner in the sample is also helping other prisoners through his education. As the Prisoners Education Trust's Annual Report (1999a) explains, his 'dedication to the piano has enabled him to progress from grade one to eight whilst in prison ... He has not only used his skills for himself but has set several others on the way to musical achievement. He hopes to make a living teaching the piano when he is released' (p. 7).[10]

---

[10] Although not a citation from the sample, this prisoner has written a letter that does constitute part of the sample. His letter, which in summary states: 'Thank you for the grant. I'm sure I'll enjoy grade eight piano studies as much as I did grade seven, I'll keep you informed' (Letter 10). This serves as a reminder that the letters in this sample only tell a portion of the story

THE PRISONER AS STUDENT

It is evident from the letters that many of the prisoner-students are very committed to their studies. Educational work appears to be a source of considerable enthusiasm as well as the source of a new identity, namely that of 'student'. Illustrative of this evolving identity is a prisoner who in one letter adds his prisoner identification number after his name (Letter 25), only to replace it with all of the many 'letters' he has recently earned in a subsequent letter to the Trust (Letter 62). A similar sentiment is echoed in the statement quoted earlier by the prisoner who considers his prison education department to be the only place in prison where he feels human (Letter 47). The following letters demonstrate how fully some members of this sample inhabit the role of 'student'. Given the negative connotations of the 'prisoner' identity, the assumption of the 'student' identity as an alternative suggests a basis for a more successful reconstruction of one's life. One letter, from a prisoner on a Practical Bookkeeping course, is illustrative of the considerable detail with which a number of the prisoners describe their academic progress and their approaches to their courses:

> To date I've completed four assignments obtaining marks of nine out of ten each one. My progress has been steady preferring to spend the time required to digest certain elements that are more difficult than others and appears to have been a good strategy reflected in my results. I've decided to delay sending the last assignment for marking as my situation could change soon with a decision expected concerning 'tagging.'
>
> Eventually I will sit the exam with a recognised examination board but before this the college advises the student to obtain a syllabus from the examination board and some past examination papers, the adage 'fail to prepare, prepare to fail' is the message I gather from their guidelines. (Letter 30)

Another student writes of his course:

> I'm waiting for a reply on lesson six. Lesson five, I've had to skip for the time being, a question on Italian water features is holding me back. The relevant information is on its way, and I hope to get lesson seven in the post this week. Its all a bit of a rush now as I've only got six weeks left until release date (hurrah) and I was hoping to get it completed, but realistically with Christmas post and holidays I expect to be left with one 'lesson' to do. There are ten in total each consisting of four questions, but it's far more in depth than I originally envisaged which has been brilliant. (Letter 22)

A student in an open prison, working diligently towards a May examination, writes to the Trust that he has been released home for the Christmas holiday period. 'I am using the break to try and master some topics that I found difficult' (Letter 3) he explains. Clearly the above examples indicate the extent to which many prisoners are deeply involved with, and sincerely committed to, their educational pursuits.

Some students plan 'educational careers' with the 'enthusiasm' described in the previous section by Cohen and Taylor (1972, p. 95). Fifteen of the prisoner-students in the sample mention a desire to pursue an additional course upon completion of their current one.[11] A prisoner who was the recipient of a grant for art supplies explains that he has sold some pictures and that he is saving for a course (Letter 24). Others indicate that they may be reapplying to the Trust for further funds. In terms of prior prison education it is important to bear in mind that the sample already includes prisoners who have previously completed courses funded by the Trust as well as others who have been involved in their prison's own education department.

A woman who has already completed three Open University courses writes that 'This year I am now half way through U206-Environment and I am receiving marks of 70-80 per cent. This year is a harder Level 2 course, but I am comfortable so far. I am hoping to gain a full degree eventually' (Letter 64). A counselling student engaged in two courses, and with plans to take further ones as soon as he passes these, enthuses that: 'I spend everyday working on my courses as my new job allows at least seven hours spare each day in the daytime' (Letter 25).

Another counselling student states:

> I have learned so much in the two months I have been studying and find the course very stimulating indeed. I don't think I'll have any problems passing the course and I will be looking forward to undertaking other associated courses with a hope of going on to the new GVNQ in Counselling and Advice. (Letter 12)

A student taking a course in Health and Social Care through the Open University explains: 'my ultimate aim is to acquire a degree in Social Science' (Letter 45).

A prisoner-student who earned an upper second class BA (Hons) degree through the Open University whilst in prison was continuing further with his studies:

> Essentially this course will close off and tie off loose ends for me, before I tackle the next challenge of obtaining a Masters Degree ... This year's course will then also allow me to add a Diploma in European Humanities to that Degree—provided I pass of course' (Letter 47).

---

[11] According to the combined records of the Trust from 1998 and 1999, almost one in ten applicants undertook more than one course funded by the Trust. It is important to keep in mind that these statistics do not present the complete picture of who decided to continue with education for they do not take into account the percentage of students released, nor those who found alternative sources of funding.

The examples above demonstrate that there is ample evidence from this sample to support Forster's (1998) conclusion regarding academic education in prison, that 'At it's best . . . [there is] an underlying sense of intellectual discovery and excitement' and the 'development of high quality work' (p. 69). In many of these examples, the educational commitment extends beyond the prison walls. Work is continued while on temporary release and plans are made to complete assignments or sits exams after release. Degrees will eventually be carried outside of the prison gates. It is beyond the means of this study to determine the role that the education actually plays in these individuals' lives post-release. However, the words of these prisoners certainly demonstrate a current commitment to the role of 'student' and their 'perception' of the value of this role.

THE PROBLEMS OF BEING A STUDENT IN PRISON

Some prisoners in the sample report difficulties that they have encountered specific to their being a student in prison. A common complaint made by prisoners in the sample is the delay in receiving post: 'My apologies for not replying to your letter before now, only I never received your letter until March 24. Which in turn shows part of the problems of being a prisoner' (Letter 44). For prisoner-students involved in correspondence courses this is of particular concern.

While many prisoners may find that they have plenty of time for study, others do not, especially if as independent distance-learners they are combining their study with prison jobs or are enrolled on other prison programmes. A prisoner who had recently completed a Computer studies course cites two difficulties that arose as a result of undertaking the course whilst in prison:

> One, I was given the opportunity to address my offending behaviour (SOTP), which I badly wanted to take up and the second, access to the reference books listed in the course. I was unable to obtain these through the prison library and hence had to do without. Although I don't feel that not having these books will effect the outcome, I did find it extremely frustrating, especially in conjunction with trying to find eight-nine hrs. a week, along with what the SOTP required and its effects on me. (Letter 61)

However, he goes on to add that he 'had good support from the IT lecturer here at the prison . . . who assisted me and encouraged me in many ways' (Letter 61).

Limited access to sources, as described above, is certainly a potential difficulty for prisoners. Another prisoner describes how friends and family send him newspaper and magazine articles that he may need, illustrating the restricted access that prisoners have to such materials (Letter 22). A GCSE Business Studies student explains 'I'm making good progress with [the course]. However, I no longer send off all the course/project work as it has proved too difficult to collect info etc. ... in my position. I am in touch with the NEAB who are very supportive and I am to enrol for the 1999 exam' (Letter 2). It should be noted, however, that many of the distance-learning courses do include necessary reference material.

Other prisoners point to difficulties in accessing necessary equipment. A computer student mentions that: 'I have some troubles to run the CD ROM and here we have not enough PCs for each student but I still have some days every week to work on it' (Letter 41). Another prisoner inquires about funding for typewriters, explaining that he previously used the education department computer in his own time one evening per week, but that this had since been 'stopped by security after someone misused the privilege' (Letter 52). A prisoner who writes poetry, and has submitted poems to the Trust, adds in a postscript to his letter: 'You will notice that there are no question marks in the poems. This is because it doesn't work on my typewriter' (Letter 67).

In a statement cited earlier, a prisoner indicated that he has plenty of 'time' for his studies, yet also remarks that 'this is not the best of times for me to study' (Letter 55). His statement serves as a reminder that the emotional strain of prison life may provide a difficult backdrop against which to study. The prisoner on the offending behaviour course who is quoted above points to a similar difficulty (Letter 61).[12]

EXTERNAL CONNECTIONS

In undertaking a course or artistic project funded by the Trust, the prisoners are establishing a relationship with an organization that is external to the prison and independent of HM Prison Service. A recurring theme that emerges from the letters is the desire of the prisoners to prove themselves worthy of the funding that has been invested in their course. Approximately 15 per cent of the prisoner-students write that they: 'endeavour to complete it successfully' (Letter 16), 'endeavour to prove worthy of the chance given to me' (Letter 19), 'will make every effort to complete it successfully' (Letter 40) and 'won't let [the Trust] down' (Letter 53). Submission of tutors' reports, copies of certificates, enclosure of artwork, essays and poems, all of which occur on a regular basis, can be read as further attempts by the prisoner-

---

12 Difficulties of this nature may go some way towards explaining why some prisoners abandon their courses (cf: Maguire and Honess, 1997).

students to demonstrate their commitment to their work. These efforts go beyond fulfilling the Trust's request to be kept informed of progress. The enclosure of creative work may also be seen by some as a token of appreciation.

Linked to this sense of commitment to working hard for the Trust is the gratitude expressed by several prisoners for the Trust's confidence in their abilities and the encouragement given. The Trust demonstrates its confidence through the granting of funds. From the prisoner's perspective, an organization with no former connection to himself or herself is willing to donate money that has been received from individuals and other organizations, purely for their benefit. The effect of this on the confidence levels of the prisoners may be considerable, particularly for those individuals who feel that they have rarely been supported in anything before.[13] A prisoner studying Exercise and Fitness writes: 'I appreciate your help and faith in me and promise to work to the best of my ability and give 100 per cent dedication to my work' (Letter 36). A prisoner awaiting an assessment for a course taken in an open prison thanks the Trust for 'moral and financial support' (Letter 35). An Open University student adds: 'I hope to continue the hard work but it should go without saying that without your support and confidence in my abilities it would have been almost impossible for me to study and enhance my knowledge' (Letter 9).

At the same time, this connection formed with an external organization goes a considerable distance towards achieving the community links that Woolf (1991) suggested are beneficial to the future reintegration of a prisoner into the outside world. This is not to suggest that all prisoner education ought to be funded by private donation as a means of achieving this objective, but rather to emphasise that external support, financial or otherwise, can be a very important part of the rehabilitation process.

The letters also point to other forms of external contact that are established or enhanced through education. Several of the prisoners describe how their studies have led to the involvement of family and friends. One prisoner describes assistance he receives in completing assignments through 'People ... saving articles from newspapers and magazines and also my girlfriend has sent me in some info. on various points' (Letter 22). A prisoner enrolled on a foreign language course believes that his course 'will help me in the future when I go live in the Philippines with my Filipino wife. She helps me also a lot, and likes it

---

13 In an interview featured in the Trust's 1999 Annual Report, John Gallacher, the Key Skills Co-ordinator at HMP Gartree explains that: 'Even if the Trust can only make a contribution to a course, I notice a change in attitude in the person. It's a confidence thing. Their self-esteem rockets as soon as they learn that someone else has confidence in them' (as quoted in Prisoners Education Trust 1999a, p. 8).

when I write some new sentences in my letters to her' (Letter 39). An Open University student informs the Trust that: 'I am receiving my degree (BA Hons (Open)) . . . in a ceremony [held in the prison] on the twenty-first . . . Obviously I have already received the necessary paperwork, transcript etc., but this is a nice occasion that enables my friends and my parents to feel a part of my studies' (Letter 47).

The significance of this involvement cannot be underestimated in light of the purportedly immense, and at times insurmountable, strain that a prison sentence can place on the relations between a prisoner and his or her family (cf. Light, 1993 and Matthews, 1983). The previous prisoners' experiences point to ways in which education can serve to strengthen these bonds at a time when they are placed under testing circumstances. The sample includes, for example, a prisoner who writes religious poetry. Although his wife has divorced him since he has been in prison, he is still in touch with his children to whom he sends poems (Letter 67). Additionally, education also affords prisoners the chance to demonstrate to loved ones their commitment to a positive enterprise. Ultimately there may be consequences for post-release behaviour, given that released prisoners with strong family ties have been found to be less likely to reoffend (cf. Light, 1993).

Other prisoners describe ways in which they have received outside recognition for their work, suggesting additional avenues through which prisoners may not only establish external links but also gain confidence for the work that they produce in prisons. For example, the prisoner who writes religious poetry reports that 12 of his poems have been published in anthologies produced 'by a press for budding poets' and that he has also submitted work to the Koestler competition[14] (Letters 26 and 67). An artist informs the Trust that he has won Koestler awards for his art, which has also been displayed in his prison (Letter 66). Another artist refers to exhibited work (Letter 54) and yet another mentions the sale of his artwork (Letter 24). Additionally, it must be remembered that through engaging in distance-learning, a prisoner becomes a student in a course that is external to the prison. Although not specifically referred to in the letters in this sample, it is worth considering the impact that involvement with external tutors in 'classes' that contain non-prisoner students may have in enabling the prisoners to feel part of the wider community. The fact of the course being external may also have implications for the prisoner's perception of marks received.[15]

---

[14] The Koestler Trust, established in 1961, awards prizes in their annual competition for art created in UK prisons. All entries are displayed in a public exhibition in London.

[15] Consider, for example, the possible effect for a prisoner described in the Trust's 1999 Annual Report. The Report states of this prisoner who earned an Open University degree in prison that: 'Not only did he get a first class honours degree, he came top of his year ...' (Prisoners Education Trust 1999a, p. 6).

CONCLUSION

As stated in the introduction, the letters in this sample are primarily 'thank you' letters; in almost all of them the Trust is thanked for its support. Many of the prisoners emphasise that without the Trust's help they would not have been able to pursue these courses. Typical of these expressions of gratitude are the following: 'Maybe one day I can repay your valuable support—even send works for you to exhibit and inspire others to help change their lives' (Letter 66). 'Many thanks for your help. I would have found it impossible with limited options because I don't have outside contact' (Letter 58). 'There is no way to return what you have done for me' (Letter 41). In analysing a 'thank you' letter it is important to keep in mind the motivations of the writer for stating what they do; however, there is no reason to believe that these writers have exaggerated their dependence on the Trust's support, given the circumstances of their imprisonment.

The combination of recent prison budget cuts in prison education, the tendering out of education contracts, the establishment of a core curriculum and the Prison Service's current focus on basic skills such as literacy and numeracy, have conspired to severely reduce the educational opportunities in many prisons.[16] Those who have already acquired basic skills, those who wish to study subjects outside of the core curriculum, as well as those who wish to follow extended programmes of study are particularly disadvantaged.[17] One of the prisoners in this study independently pursuing his artwork explains that there was 'no suitable Art class' (Letter 66) in his prison.

There are also implications for female prisoners who, it has been argued, 'are treated *differently* from men' (italics in original) with 'sewing, cooking and other domestic tasks predominat[ing] in prison labour for females' (Cavadino and Dignan, 1997: 285-286.) The following quote from a female prisoner in an open prison highlights the range of opportunity that distance learning courses, in this case an external practical course, can provide for all prisoners, regardless of their gender:

> I would like to thank you and the trustees for funding the fork lift truck driving course for me … It was very interesting and took a lot of hard work to reach the standard that they required for you to pass. Having passed, I

---

16 In 1999, the Trust issued grants to prisoners worth a total of £92,290. For the first time since its inception, the Trust received financial support from the Prison Service during the 1999 financial year to the sum total of £25,000 (Prisoners' Education Trust 1999a, p. 14).

17 In an interesting development, in 1999 the Open University waived fees for prisoners who had successfully completed an Open University module and who wished to continue with their studies. Funds for this purpose were made available through a 'widening access' scheme. It remains to be seen whether this practice will be continued.

hope this leads to further training on different trucks and possibly a job in the future. Thank you once again, if it wasn't for your funding, I would never have been able to attend the course. (Letter 23)

Of course no prison education department could be reasonably expected to offer an extensive curriculum, but access to distance learning alleviates the burden on the teachers in the individual prisons to provide wide-ranging courses at varied levels. Clearly, there are prisoners who are willing and eager to take advantage of broad educational opportunities made available to them. As the evidence presented indicates, these prisoners' appreciation of education goes well beyond the limited reach of basic skills.

What emerges from the study is the extent to which the prisoners' letters testify to the tremendous value of these educational programmes, whether it be in coping with the reality of life behind bars, improving one's future prospects, helping other prisoners, raising one's confidence levels, developing new interests, adopting a more positive identity or constructively and positively using one's time. The value may be different to each prisoner, but its existence is self-evident.

Furthermore, this study suggests ways in which the observations of prisoners may provide an important contribution to the evaluation and monitoring of prison education. I would encourage a commitment by the Prison Service to consider the evidence of those most directly involved, the prisoner-students themselves.

In conclusion, it seems appropriate that we consider once again the views expressed by a particular prisoner-student in his letter, excerpts from which we have already encountered:

I just wish more people were able to take education seriously in prison. It really is the only place you feel both human and confident. Achievement I believe is the best possible form of rehabilitation, in both a personal and inter-personal forum. I believe educated people are more able to understand their own problems and are in a better position to achieve improvement. Why then does the Prison Service make education so unattractive? Low wages, poor facilities, management indifference, and little support or encouragement for staff, all make inmates on education feel like shirkers or trouble makers.

It is therefore a godsend that trusts such as yours exist. It is comforting to know that, despite any obstacles we encounter, there are those who are prepared to (a) help and (b) support, what is essentially a vital area of a prisoners objective, to improve himself, and hence lessen his chances of returning to prison after release. Perhaps a far more important factor than the prison service is prepared to admit? (Letter 47)

BIBLIOGRAPHY for *Chapter 7*

Cavadino M. and Dignan J. (1997), *The Penal System: An Introduction*, (Rev. 2nd ed.), London: Sage Publications

Cohen S. and Taylor C. (1972), *Psychological Survival: The Experience of Long-Term Imprisonment*, Harmondsworth: Penguin Books Ltd.

Creighton A., Personal Communication, 5 May 2000

Davidson H. S. (ed.) (1995), *Schooling in a 'Total Institution': Critical Perspectives on Prison Education*, London: Bergin and Garvey

Devlin A. (1995), *Criminal Classes: Offenders at School*, Winchester: Waterside Press

Duguid S. and Pawson R. (1998), 'Education, Change, and Transformation: The Prison Experience', *Evaluation Review*, 22 (4): 470-495.

Forster W. (1998), 'The Prison Service and Education in England and Wales', in W. Forster (Ed.), *Education Behind Bars: International Comparisons*, Leicester: NIACE: 59-74.

Light, R. (1993), 'Why Support Prisoners' Family-Tie Groups?', *The Howard Journal*, 32 (4): 322-329

Linden R., Perry L., Ayers D. and Parlett T. A. A. (1987), 'An Evaluation of a Prison Education Program', *Canadian Journal of Criminology*, 26 (1): 65- 73

Maguire M. and Honess T. (1997), *Supported Distance Learning in Prisons*, London: Prisoners' Education Trust

Matthews J. (1983), *Forgotten Victims: How Prison Affects the Family*, London: NACRO

Morgan, S. (1999), 'Prison Lives: Critical Issues in Reading Prisoner Autobiography', *The Howard Journal*, 38 (3): 328-340

Prisoners' Education Trust (1999a), Annual Report and Accounts, London: Prisoners' Education Trust

Prisoners' Education Trust (1999b), *Summary of Progress (1 January 1999–30 June 1999)*, unpublished report

Reuss, A. (1997), *Higher Education and Personal Change in Prisoners*, unpublished Ph.D. dissertation, University of Leeds: School of Sociology and Social Policy

Wilson, D. and Ashton, J. (1998), *What Everyone in Britain Should Know About Crime and Punishment*, London: Blackstone Press Ltd.

Woolf, Lord Justice (1991), *Prison Disturbances April 1990: Report of an Inquiry* by the Rt. Hon Lord Justice Woolf (Parts I and II) and His Honour Judge Stephen Tumim (Part II). Cm. 1456, London: HMSO.

APPENDIX 1 to *Chapter 7*

I am pleased to let you know that the Trustees have accepted your application for a study course. We hope you find it both interesting and enjoyable. Although we cannot guarantee success, you are welcome to apply to the Trust again if you wish to take another course when you have successfully completed this one.

We would very much like to know how you get on. I enclose a pre-paid envelope. Also please drop us a line if you are released or transferred. If you are transferred then please let us know to which prison you are moving. There's no need to acknowledge this letter. Again good luck with your studies.

CHAPTER 8

Prison Education: One Inmate's Experience

Ross Gordon

When asked if I would like to submit a chapter for this book, my initial reaction was that I could not possibly condense my educational experiences into one chapter. Yet, by doing so, I have learned the rather humbling lesson that all the years of self-sacrifice and sweat do not really warrant much more than a single chapter. True, I could stretch it out and add a little padding here and there simply by making connections between events and analysing them in as great a depth as I wanted. I could bring in a lot of educational theory and make a thousand references to build up an impressive bibliography. However, I felt that would probably just make the chapter accessible to academics when I really want to reach my peers. It is hoped that by being anecdotal rather than academic, this chapter will encourage inmates to use their time inside to embark on an educational path, whilst at the same time allow prison education providers an insight into prisoners' perspective. No matter what the level of study and how bad their previous school experiences were, I believe that prison education can and will change prisoners lives for the better.

A BRIEF HISTORY

My education started before I went to school because my mother taught my brothers, sisters and I in a way which I now realise was not common. We were taught to read, write and do basic arithmetic before starting at junior school and had to earn privileges, such as a biscuit or sweets, by answering questions correctly. There was no middle ground and marks of 100 per cent were expected if we were not to receive a punishment. As a consequence I found school boring since I already knew what was being taught and felt a little put out that I was not being rewarded for answering questions correctly. I soon learned I could get away with a lot more at school before being punished than was allowed at home and even then the punishments were not too bad by comparison. I discovered that the more disruptive I was the better as far as making friends and receiving peer support in the playground was concerned. This took away the boredom and allowed me the chance to have what I considered to be fun. I continued to be as disruptive as possible which set a trend which was to continue for many years and throughout my prison life.

Despite such behaviour I must have learned something because, much to my surprise, I was selected to go to Salford Grammar School. I had hoped to attend the much tougher Clarendon School because it was considered to be less 'cissy'. I rebelled and 'wagged off', as much as possible and made sure my reports were always bad. I felt this compensated in some way for my earlier disappointment. However, I had a natural gift for mathematics and was able to sell answers to homework for cigarettes or dinner money. This was much more difficult than I first thought because I had to ensure the teacher did not find out what was happening. I never gave anyone a mark of 100 per cent and made sure that people used different methods and got different sums wrong. To further safeguard myself I never scored very well with my own homework and rarely gave the correct answer when asked by the teacher in front of the class.

The teaching methods were mainly chalk and talk. We were set work from textbooks and expected to learn. Many teachers believed that what was taught was what was learned and concentrated on the brighter students at the expense of the others. This suited me fine and enabled me to get away with as much as possible. In hindsight I can see how difficult it was for teachers because class sizes were between 20 and 30 students so it was almost impossible for them to adopt a more student-centred approach. Not surprisingly, and apparently much to my teachers' relief, I left school in 1975, aged 16, without sitting any examinations. I had been offered a job and did not see the point of gaining qualifications. I had always been able to make money which was all I felt was necessary. I hated school and I hated the way I was taught. My experiences taught me that while the 'swots' were passing exams and going on to sixth form and university, I would be drinking, smoking, taking drugs and courting girls. There was no choice as far as I could see and I felt sorry for the others.

Life quickly deteriorated as I learned that the lifestyle I wanted would cost a lot more than I was earning and I needed to find a way to supplement my income. I started stealing which helped a little but this meant I was getting into more and more trouble with the police. However, my life of relatively petty crime and spiralling drug and alcohol abuse did not prepare me for what was about to happen. On a tragic day in August 1977 I lost control of my emotions and ended up on a murder charge, for which I received the mandatory life sentence in December of the same year. I found myself locked up on a VP wing with years of prison life ahead of me. I was placed in the laundry but found the work boring. I needed something more to stimulate my mind and knew if I did not make changes I was going to turn into a cabbage. I was unsure what to do because my earlier experiences of school were enough to put me off education for life. I definitely did not want to return to studying in a classroom but I could think of no alternatives since the prison library had few academic books. So, in 1978 and against my better judgement I applied for a place on education. Thus I embarked on a road which was to change my life completely and give me a thirst for knowledge which still remains unquenched.

By this time I was in Walton prison where education was run on a full-time basis. I had the same teacher both mornings and afternoons and for the first time I experienced an individual learning programme. We still had a few chalk and talk lessons but mainly we did our own work at our own pace. The teacher monitored and marked our work and we were free to choose whether or not we wanted to work in our cells. I got stuck into as much studying as possible because I found it helped the time pass more quickly and allowed me to escape from prison into my own little world. I joined night classes and learned a little about computers but my main subject was mathematics. I found I could spend hours doing maths without a break and was often reluctant to go to sleep until I had solved a particular problem. Once the problem was solved I quickly looked for another one. Often my dreams involved working on an unsolved problem and I would wake up with the route to the answer.

I would have been quite happy to continue like this but the education department wanted me to take examinations. I obliged and between 1978 and 1980 I passed RSA I, II and III Maths, Arithmetic and English, RSA I and II Computing, CSE History, O-level Maths, English and Religious Studies and A-level Maths. By this time I was ready to move to Wakefield prison and my teacher at Walton suggested I start a degree course. I laughed at this but agreed to be registered on the Maths Foundation Course, thinking that it would at least be a challenge and help me settle down in my new prison: 'Mathematics Across the Curriculum' I started in 1987 and completed when I moved to the Verne prison later that year.

During my final few months at Grendon I met students with special educational needs for the first time. A teacher was employed to work in the psychiatric ward of the hospital and asked if I minded helping. I thought it would not be a problem and was shocked to discover just how difficult it was to teach at this level. Not only did I need to find ways of teaching things which I had never really thought about in an academic way, such as $1 + 1 = 2$, but I soon discovered I needed the patience of a saint and had to be prepared to go over and over the same ground with the same student many different times. It was an achievement for many of the students to learn to hold a pen and write their names. Despite all this I found I enjoyed this sort of teaching better than I enjoyed teaching more able students and looked forward to my sessions in the hospital. Unfortunately my transfer to The Verne meant it was to be some time before I could pursue this interest.

The Verne was a category C prison so the whole regime was much more relaxed. The education department was much larger than any of the previous prisons I had been in and for the first time I was responsible for finding my own work allocation. I headed straight for the education manager's office and sold myself. I was employed as an inmate tutor and allowed a few hours per week to complete my OU studies. I was learning jargon such as 'enabler, facilitator, student-centred, tutor-centred' etc., which gave meaning to my experiences and allowed me to improve my mathematics teaching and communicate more effectively with the properly trained teachers.

After I completed my studies, I was employed as the education orderly and allowed to teach part-time, which again allowed me to work on education statistics and get involved with the assessment of inductions. I taught students who were mainly at GCSE and A-level standard, but in the back of my mind I wanted to return to teaching basic skills which I considered to be much more rewarding and worthwhile. Most inmates, and some staff said I would be wasted on basic skills classes but I put this down to their ignorance. I had seen enough to make me realise that the teaching would be more challenging and the potential rewards in terms of rehabilitation of inmates was tremendous. Even so I had to wait until my move to another prison before I could pursue this interest because I also realised that to some it was more important to have a number of exam successes to report in the statistics and basic skills students did not represent a good return.

From The Verne I was transferred to Sudbury open prison which had an education department run along the lines of a college. It also had what was known as an 'Educational Centre of Excellence' which was a sort of campus two miles down the road at Foston Hall prison. This had the attraction of many students being released to local colleges and universities on a daily basis, even the kitchen workers were doing catering courses. Not surprisingly I enrolled on education at Sudbury with the intention of working my way to Foston Hall and eventual day release. I was allowed to study Hebrew as an Open Learning student which meant I basically studied in a room with other students who were all doing their own thing. I was responsible for what I learned and the pace at which I learned it. I was told that the fastest way to get to Foston Hall was to enrol for five BTEC Business Studies Modules to make up a CBA (Certificate in Business Administration) so I put my name down for the course and was selected to start it.

Foston Hall was probably the closest I have experienced to living on a university campus. It had the best computer department I have ever seen in a prison and 90 students lived in the hall. I sailed through the five modules in three months of full-time education and enjoyed being a more conventional student again. The teaching methods were mainly chalk and talk and I found myself mentally assessing the teachers' performances, though I was diplomatic enough not to criticise. Many students asked me for help with assignments in the evenings and at weekends and were prepared to pay. However, a sign of just how much I had changed since my school days was my refusal to give answers for pay. I realised I was not doing students any favours by allowing them to cheat. I said I was prepared to explain to them my understanding of what we had to do and how the lessons related to the assignments. Thus I was able to reflect on what I had learned by going through it on a one-to-one basis or with a group of my peers and help them at the same time without anybody cheating. This had the added advantage of my ideas being challenged from time to time and often good discussions would develop. This period proved invaluable to me because it demonstrated the importance of reflection and group discussion in learning. The concept was not new to me because I had read about it but my experiences at Foston Hall made it real.

After completing my CBA, the education manager called me in for a chat. He asked me if I had thought about a career in teaching and explained that, if I was prepared to upgrade my degree to honours, the education department would pay for me to go on day release to college to study both stages of the FAETC (City and Guilds 730 Stages I and II: The Further and Adult Education Teachers Certificate). I agreed with reservations because it involved me in studying two courses at third level in the same year and I was not confident I would be able to pass. However, the opportunity of gaining formal qualifications which would give me better employment prospects as well as day release from prison was too good an opportunity to miss (the prospect of meeting and studying with 'normal' students, some of whom would be female, had also crossed my mind).

I enrolled on two third level OU courses which I felt would enhance my teacher training (Adult Education; and Research Methodology in Education and the Social Sciences) and was duly enrolled at a local HE college to start my teacher training. I found the workload quite a strain especially as I had to force myself to set aside periods for studying in the evenings and at weekends. This was not quite as easy as when I was in bang-up prisons because I had more options open to me in the evenings and felt I was not making full use of the openness of the prison if I was voluntarily staying in my room (we had rooms at Foston Hall rather than cells). There was also the disadvantage of my peers being free and able to call round for a chat, etc. I eventually resorted to putting up a sign on my door saying that I was not to be disturbed but this did not always work.

In addition I had found myself a voluntary job teaching basic skills to the unemployed and ex-offenders at NACRO in Derby which allowed me to get in the necessary teaching practice and to be observed by my course tutors. I found all the travelling (an hour each way by bus) very tiring and often fell asleep in the evenings with my books open or in mid-sentence of an essay. I struggled through the year and wondered how some of my fellow students coped because most were married with children. At NACRO I was expected to teach Literacy as well as Numeracy which created a fresh challenge and I was learning as much from my students as I was teaching them. To my surprise, I passed all my courses and was awarded honours and my FAETC so decided I had definitely reached the end of my formal studies and would just concentrate on teaching.

One of my OU tutors worked in a local Tertiary College and contacted the prison to ask if I was interested in helping to set up and run Literacy and Numeracy drop-in workshops at the college. I agreed and left NACRO to start on the project. I was given a set of keys, was asked to attend staff meetings and made responsible for a small budget from which I was to buy resources. I found this very difficult since I had not had such responsibility before nor had I had to make decisions. I was constantly seeking reassurance and being told that whatever I felt was necessary would be all right. I was never completely comfortable with this and realised just how much I still had to learn about everyday decision-making. The prison courses had not prepared me at all for this yet I do not know how they could have done so because you have to be in the situations to learn. I was pleased that I was getting the opportunity on day release rather than just being released completely and being told to get on with it.

The workshops were a great success and I experienced my first taste of 'real' teaching. Every student had a personal learning programme and records were kept of everything. Students varied from those learning basic skills to those studying for their A-levels. The latter used to pop in for help with homework or advice about a part of their lessons they had not understood. Ages also ranged from 16 to 70 and students were free to come and go as they pleased. Fortunately, there were quiet periods where I could catch up on the paperwork but there were also times when as many as 30 students were in the room and I had to ask the more able students to help out until I could get round.

I worked with other teachers who were assigned to the workshops for about an hour at a time. This meant I was the only one in the workshops for the whole day and other teachers relied on me to keep things running. I kept them up to date on student progress, had a set of keys, a credit card for the photocopier and use of the telephone. It was difficult getting used to being trusted (I rarely went into the storeroom because I thought I would be the first suspect if anything went missing) and I never felt comfortable locking doors and cupboards behind me. Two A-level students who regularly came to me for help turned out to be the daughters of prison officers at Sudbury. I only found this out when I was being interviewed for parole and the member of staff said, 'My daughter tells me you are good at your job'. I was shocked and immediately thought of 'Big Brother'—but I was also a little relieved to find out I was not paranoid and the Home Office really did have eyes everywhere.

The workshops became very popular so, after a few months, we decided to take on special needs groups outside of basic skills. This meant we had physically and mentally handicapped students dropping in at all times but at least we had more volunteers and more money for special resources. We also took on deaf and blind students and the work became more and more challenging. I remember thinking if I could have my time over again I would not be as disruptive at school as I had been. The workshops became very rewarding and I actually looked forward to coming into work, despite being run off my feet all day.

Only the secretary, the principal, my former OU tutor and one teacher who I had done the FAETC with knew that I was on day release from prison. As far as everyone else was concerned I was a volunteer research student which meant I was continually lying to my colleagues when asked how my research was going. For this reason I avoided the staff room as much as possible and kept the workshop open. I constantly had to turn down invitations to social events outside of college hours and was being told to get a life and have a break from my research!

I also had a lot of social problems which I had not been prepared for. For instance, I was in the staff dining room sharing a table with about eight others. We were chatting and I was concentrating so much on listening and trying to respond in an intelligent way, being careful not to mention prison, that I reached out to the open container to grab a handful of salt for my chips. The conversation went dead and I knew I had done something wrong but did not have a clue what. I continued to chat as I put the salt on my chips but as I tasted the first one I realised I had used sugar rather than salt (in prison salt is usually in an open container and is used by the handful. It had not entered my head to look for a salt pot). Not knowing what to do I continued to eat my meal as if I enjoyed sugar on my chips, feeling it was easier to let them think I had eccentric tastes than to explain how I could have made such a mistake. Clearly it would have been much easier had I been able to tell the truth.

A second example which springs to mind worked out much better by accident. A colleague had driven me into town at lunch time because we both had a bit of shopping to do. I bought some tobacco which left me with just a few pence in my pocket. I expected we would go straight back but my colleague said, 'Come on. We have enough time for a coffee'. I tried to get out of it by saying we could get one back at the college but she said I was being silly and she would treat me to a Cappuccino. I relaxed a little and was grateful that I did not have to explain that I had no money. I assumed that Cappuccino was just a brand name of a trendy coffee so confidently asked the waitress, 'Two Cappuccino's please. One without milk'. My colleague and the waitress burst out laughing and the waitress playfully tapped me with her order book and walked off still laughing. I joined in and pretended it had been a deliberate joke because that was obviously what the others thought and it was not until the waitress arrived that I realised for the first time what Cappuccino was. Such experiences were common and had the effect of making me feel insecure and unconfident outside of my working environment and prison.

During all this I had taken an interest in the way people had an irrational fear of mathematics and wanted to learn more so I would be better placed to understand and help. An interview was arranged with the Adult Education Faculty at Nottingham University and I was given a place as a research student doing a part-time MSc. I could not believe my luck since I was prepared to research for my own interest and yet here I was with the chance of gaining a masters degree. I never felt I would achieve it but was prepared to document the research and see where it led. I attended Nottingham University one day per week and worked at the college three days a week. At least now I was not completely lying when I spoke of my research at the college.

I left Sudbury for Wormwood Scrubs Pre-Release Hostel in 1991 and, after some teething problems, found a job working for NACRO. Part of my responsibilities was to teach Numberpower and Wordpower to the unemployed and ex-offenders who were doing an NVQ in Nursery Nursing. I also helped with portfolio building and ran a two day 'job-finding skills' course for ex-offenders and prisoners coming to the end of their sentence who were eligible for day release.

However, I was still not coping very well outside of work and was using drugs and drinking heavily. Academic success and good work experience had done little to prepare me for a social life and I was not able to cope outside of the work or academic environment. I found it difficult to meet people who shared my interests and soon learned how easy it was to kill a conversation by mentioning my love of mathematics. I was struggling to meet the deadline for my MSc. and did not complete it, and after a few warnings and a spell in a Chemical Dependency Unit I was eventually returned to closed conditions. I gave up on myself, spending the next couple of years using drugs and just doing my bird. In 1995, realising I was going nowhere, I asked for help and was sent to Littlehey prison to work on my drug and alcohol problem, along with any underlying problems which may arise.

After arriving at Littlehey I joined education but with no real plans. Within three months, and after a period of detox in the hospital, I cleaned up and started to take some basic computer certificates and to study A-level maths just to get my brain working again. It had the desired effect and I have now been clean for almost five years. After much persuasion over many letters and visits from a very good friend, I decided to enrol for a taught MA in Education. I had time on my hands and knew I could discipline myself to do it in a bang-up jail. I asked the Basic Skills Co-ordinator if I could help on the class and was fortunate enough to have been allowed to assist.

The education department at Littlehey displays the Basic Skills Unit's Quality Mark which guarantees a good quality of teaching by properly qualified staff, maximum class sizes which allows for individual programmes for students, and proper initial and on-going assessments. Littlehey offers the opportunity for all its basic skills students to gain certificates for their achievements whatever the level of basic skills need (which was not available to my students at college, though this may well have changed by now). Hence, the standard of basic skills teaching at Littlehey is by far the highest I have seen inside or outside of prison (no doubt the standard of all the teaching is as high at Littlehey but I am not in a position to make such a judgement). I consider myself very fortunate to have ended up in a position to learn from such dedicated, experienced and well trained staff. I was able to use the students I worked with as part of my research which has hopefully also benefited them as I made changes to the way I help as a result of what I learned.

In keeping with the Quality Standards, Littlehey paid for me to take the City and Guilds Initial Certificate in Teaching Basic Skills: 9282 Literacy; 9283 Numeracy; and 9284 ESOL, In addition I have been allowed to take coaching and assessors awards, the CACDP Stage 1 (Basic) Certificate in British Sign Language, an Advanced Diploma in Mathematics Education and an Advanced Diploma in Adult and Continuing Education. This time I completed my masters specialising in prison Adult Basic Education numeracy and made up of the following modules: Adult Education and Training; Researching Mathematics Classrooms; and Educational Research in Action. On the way I was honoured to be nominated for a Library Learners Award and fortunate enough to make the finals. No one had ever nominated me for anything before and it rammed home to me that I really must have changed.

TENTATIVE COMPARISONS

I feel it is necessary here to point out that since I started on education in prison there have been many changes which have made direct comparisons difficult. Possibly the most significant change was the introduction of competitive tendering and the contracting out of prison education so it is now provided by outside colleges interested in making a profit. As far as I am aware many inmates have gained as a result of a better educational service but this is a very subjective view and based on the relatively few prisons I have been in. Also, I have often heard the argument that tremendous self-discipline is necessary to study in prison and a lot of people would not be able to do it. However, I disagree because there are just as many, if not more, pressures in the real world and self-discipline is still needed. Indeed, I doubt very much if I would have been able to study as effectively in the real world. With hindsight, I can see the tremendous self-confidence I have gained in the academic setting and hopefully this self-belief will spill over into my social life.

It has been my experience that students in prison education departments tend to be there because they either want to learn, avoid the boredom of prison workshops or be in an environment which allows contact with civilian females. Many who want to learn are put off because of the low wage structure with no opportunity to earn production bonuses as they would in the workshops. In contrast, adult students in the real world may be funded by their local education authorities and have the opportunity to, say, fill shelves in a supermarket to earn a bit of extra cash, or they are already working and studying in their spare time.

The stigma of prison education being a no go area seems to be diminishing and it is quite acceptable to admit to being a student. However, prison education providers are seen by the prison authorities as providing a place of work for a few inmates. In response to the question 'Where do you work?' a student will reply 'On education' whereas in the real world I believe the response is more likely to be 'I do not work, I am a student'.

In academic terms I think the main differences between my compulsory education and my prison education have been the teaching methods used, the availability of open learning material and the study options open to me, in terms of courses, methods and timing. The prison education system has definitely helped to increase my self-confidence and motivation to learn, though I did have more time and less day-to-day pressures than someone on the 'out'. For example, I never had to worry about paying the rent, buying food or clothes, etc. In Maslow's terms, my basic needs had been taken care of.

Another difference has been the support available to me in prison which was not as good in my school days. At least if it was available it was not signposted and I did not know where to look. However, when I say support, I mean by education staff and some of my peers. Prison staff in the early days often commented that it was not right for prisoners to have more than a basic education provided free when they had to pay for their children's books and stationery, etc. I must admit to having some sympathy with this view but I always argued that in the long-term it paid for itself because inmates with a higher education were less likely to return to a life of crime and more likely to become productive members of the workforce and help boost the economy. This argument had absolutely no validity but it sounded good at the time and allowed me to make some sort of response (in those days it was a sin to agree with a prison officer under such circumstances). Nowadays I do not hear any negative comments from staff and education is certainly seen as a positive step forward which is included in most inmates' sentence plans.

Support in monetary terms has been very good. I am uncertain but I have probably found it a little easier to find funds in prison than I would have done if I had been on the 'out'. The funds for my initial degree came from a special Home Office budget which prisons are allocated specifically for OU studies. My teacher training and other professional development courses were paid for by the education department I was in at the time. Foston Hall paid from their general education budget whilst Littlehey claimed the money from the college contracted to the prison, who accepted it was covered by their staff development budget. My masters degree was jointly funded by educational charities and trusts, and Littlehey provided my set books. I could not have afforded to take out a student loan as is the current trend and realise how lucky I am not to have to start work with an outstanding debt to take care of.

In terms of rehabilitation I believe prison education departments should be more involved in providing and running courses. Not only will this allow a better quality of course run by properly qualified staff to a consistent timetable but it will also allow prison staff to be free to do many of the day-to-day jobs and paperwork, etc., which are often neglected.

CHANGE

Earlier I stated that I believe prison education can change prisoners lives for the better. This statement merits clarification but first it must be stressed that, as far as I know, my opinion is not backed up by research and has not been subjected to academic scrutiny. However, it is an opinion based on 23 years imprisonment, 22 years of which have been spent on education, with the latter 13 years being spent teaching and researching my peers. This, I believe, allows me the right to share such an opinion, though, of course, it does not make the opinion right. I will also cheat a little by defining the term 're-offending' as the act of committing the same or a more serious offence as before. So, for instance, in my case I have not re-offended since my return to closed conditions was a result of my inability to cope socially—which is not as serious as my index offence of murder. Relatively speaking, my return to society was more successful than my social interaction was prior to my index offence and hopefully my next attempt will be even more successful than the last one. It has been my experience that prison acts as a sort of timewarp which puts the maturing process on hold. Thus, if someone is sent to prison aged 18 years and leaves, say, ten years later that person will still behave like an 18-year-old. I believe that prison education allows an inmate the opportunity to start maturing again in a more normal way. There are many possible reasons for this but I strongly suspect that the self-discipline, commitment, responsibility and interaction with civilians involved are the major factors which aid the maturation process.

In my case, prison education has given me tremendous self-confidence and the belief that I have something worthwhile to offer society. Certainly, I have begun to think of the long term benefits and no longer look for a 'quick fix'. I have problem solving strategies, similar to those I use in mathematics, which may be applied to real life situations. I accept that the real world of emotions and social interactions does not fit neatly into a mathematical model, even if the model takes into account grey areas. However, just by using such strategies, this means I have stopped to think things through. I try to consider all the variables and factors and love 'brainstorming' because it allows me to be childish. Very often such thoughts lead me to ask for help and seek advice, something I was always reluctant to do before. I also take into account such things as ethics and morality, often questioning my integrity. Whatever the outcome, I am able to accept that I made the best decision I was able to make at the time and not feel a failure if I get it wrong. I have lost the need for a macho image and find doors opening for me which would previously have been slammed shut in my face. I am more aware of how my actions affect those around me and hence less selfish. It may be argued that such changes have come about as the result of natural maturity but I strongly disagree with such a view and give much more credit to the education I have done in prison.

Maturity level on →	1	2	3	4	5	6	7	8	9	10
entering prison	↑ ■		↑ ■							↑ ■
	Maximum Maturity level on leaving prison without doing prison education		Minimum maturity level on leaving prison after doing prison education							Potential maturity level on leaving prison after doing prison education

Figure 1

Not every prisoner has my skills and level of education but I believe that I am at one end of the scale such as the one shown in *Figure 1* above. Clearly, it is not quite as simplistic as shown in *Figure 1* but it gives the general idea and takes into account every level of prison education.

Much of what applies to me is also true for many of the students I have taught, who are rightly very proud of any certificates they gain in prison. Prison education has allowed prisoners the opportunity to see how hard work and patience pays off in the long-term. Many stop acting on impulse and start to think situations through, especially basic skills students who potentially stand to gain the most simply by learning to read/recognise everyday signs and sign their own names.

A CLOSING NOTE

Those who find out about my academic history (I never volunteer such information) seem a little surprised but I am quick to point out that common-sense has little to do with intelligence. If it did then there would be a book written on the subject which I would have studied, thus ensuring I had my fair quota. Such views have often generated interesting discussions and it is through such discussion that I have been able to learn a little about the reality of life on the 'out' and just exactly how far I can expect my qualifications to take me in terms of future employment. I am after little more than my CV redressing the negative impression given by spending so much of my life in prison and hopefully this will make the playing field a little more even when I attend job interviews.

As for the future I have been asked to do a PhD but, as usual, I feel I may well have reached my limit. However, I have learned enough to keep an open mind and would be lying if I said I do not want to attempt a doctorate. For now I will wait until I am in an open prison because access to a university library will be essential if I am to undertake such work. I have lots of ideas floating around in my head and already have a doctorate proposal ready since I had to do one to complete my masters. I would love to see better co-ordination and consistency of standards between prisons but realise how difficult this is given the restrictions and different limitations of the various categories of prisons and prisoners. Also, the introduction of competitive tendering means that market place forces come into operation so why should competing providers share information or resources.

Regardless of what happens in the future I have achieved more than I set out to achieve when I first applied to go on education in 1978. I often feel I have betrayed my working class roots but also realise that the education system was/is set up in such a way as to discourage the working class from becoming too well educated. We were there to be trained for work not educated but I have demonstrated that almost anyone with the time and motivation can become an academic if they want to. I realise this is a bit of a sweeping generalisation which many will disagree with. However, this is not the forum to go into greater detail or argue my case more thoroughly. In a nutshell, I still see myself as a working class lad from Salford because that is important to me but that does not mean I am not proud to also be able to write on my CV

Mr. Ross. Gordon MA (Ed.), BA.(Hons.), Adv. Dip. Ed. (Open), FAETC, CBA.

CHAPTER 9

The Way Forward

Anne Reuss and David Wilson

> The first step to improving the quality of life [of a prisoner] is to improve today, and although it cannot be proven that a prisoner who is engaged in learning will gain long-term benefit from doing so, he or she is gaining benefits during the hour or two during which they are learning. The immediate benefits are communicating effectively with a teacher and with fellow learners, focusing attention, learning a skill, not being disruptive, not offending, not being anti-social. These benefits cannot be denied. (West, 1997, 141).

The above observations on education in prisons serve as a useful starting point to anyone wanting to look closely at the role of education in our prisons today. Whilst West does not engage with the very complex issues relating to the 'linkage' between education, rehabilitation and recidivism, she clearly implies that there is a relationship as, presumably, the offender who lacked communication skills, suffered attention deficits, had no skills, and was anti-social has a means of re-gaining 'something' via education. This final chapter will look at some of the thorny issues concerning prison education, issues that have characterized it since 'educating' prisoners first became 'fashionable' in the nineteenth century. It will also offer views on education in prisons as a form of empowerment for the individual prisoner which may open up the debate on whether it is more appropriate to 'correct' or 'educate' in prisons, thus asking what is the way forward for prison education? The chapter suggests there are three stages or steps forward, which could be taken for those practitioners and policy-makers concerned with 'educating' prisoners.

Firstly, however, it is worth making one small but significant point. Most penal practitioners, policy-makers and academics interested in the area of penology talk about *prison* education. Germanotta (Davidson; 1995; 106), invites us to think about *prisoner* education and it seems that the implications are quite profound if applied both in theory and practice (Reuss, 1999). Prisoner education is about *people* learning in a particular setting—a prison setting—and once that distinction is made, education programmes in prisons can be seen as something that may offer benefits and opportunities to individual prisoners—*as people*. Alternatively, if we begin to talk about 'prisoner' education, does this *encourage* the view that prisoners really do suffer from some kind of cognitive deficits?

Analysing educational programmes and activities, or assessing their 'effectiveness' according to a particular criteria (and there are many) with this in mind *personalises* the process and shifts it to the domain of the individual prisoner rather than focusing on the demands of the prison or the policy-makers. The planning of prisoner education, its implementation and evaluation therefore need careful consideration for no other reason than that it is people who are on the receiving end of any policy decisions which are made—this becomes more than obvious if, as has happened in the past, traditional courses in a prison education department are cut and there is 'nothing else' for the prisoners to do, or 'nothing else' that they *want* to do.

THE ROLE OF EDUCATION IN PRISONS

Why do we have educational courses in prisons? What is their purpose and whose interests do they serve? These seem to be the most obvious questions to ask about prisoner education and yet they are amongst some of the most difficult and complex to answer, allied as they are to much broader questions about imprisonment as a form of punishment, and allied to whichever theories about crime and criminals seem to be most popular at any one time. Attitudes and ideologies pertaining to imprisonment in general impinge upon the provision of education in prisons shaping expectations and assumptions about whether or not the prisoner will be able to lead a 'good and useful life' on release. Where does prisoner education 'fit' into this scheme of things? Is it meant to be part of a programme of 'reform' or 'treatment', is it 'correctional' or is it something to be appreciated by 'the lucky ones' as the Woolf Report pointed out? (1990; 382).

The functions of education in prison mean different things to different people. The penal reformer may see it as a means of 'softening' a harsh regime; Prison Service staff may see it as a means of keeping prisoners occupied; security staff may see it as a 'risk'; education staff may see it as a vocation; whilst, for some prisoners, it simply passes the time. For the most part, these functions can be seen in a positive light with positive outcomes to be gained (with the exception of concerns of security), for all. There is little doubt that if education provides *all* the above, then it is indeed integral to prison life and educational opportunities should be extended wherever and whenever possible as opposed to being curtailed.

Following Williford (1994), in questioning precisely what the role of education in prison has been for the last 200 years, it is possible to identify that role as having been perceived as mainly correctional. Describing education programmes as initially vehicles for rehabilitation and/or reformation, Williford (1994, viii) goes on to cite the so-called medical models where education had a potential role in 'curing' the offender and the cognitive-deficits model, where education would 'correct deficiencies in problem-solving, interpersonal and social skills'. The use of words such as, 'treatment', 'intervention', and phrases such as, 'referring appropriate candidates for training' characterize the literature on these kinds of 'education' programmes. Williford further points out that following discussions with 'educators, prison officials and prisoners', such models do more harm than good, particularly as programmes which fall under the umbrella of 'cognitive skills' rarely seem to have attained the goal of reducing (re-)offending behaviour.

In developing Williford's point, it does seem to be somewhat artificial to attempt, through cognitive skills programmes '... to assist offenders in rehearsing both new behaviour and new thinking skills' in 35 sessions over eight to 12 weeks, six to eight in a group (specified in training for cognitive skills staff) using overheads, pictures, role-play and scenarios. Whilst well-meaning enough and not disputing the fact that these courses too may 'work' for some prisoners some of the time in some circumstances, the practice and delivery of the courses seems to ignore the *life-history* and *personal identity* of the prisoner. It is therefore hardly surprising that such courses do not achieve the goal of reducing offending behaviour, particularly in the light of comments from educational practitioners and prisoners (Reuss, 1997).

From suggestions that prison education is no more than a 'symbolic prop in the drama of rehabilitative services' (Thomas, 1995, 39), to the more personalised 'I knew right there in prison that reading had changed forever the course of my life' (Malcolm X quoted in Germanotta, 1995, 109), the range of differing views, agendas and ideologies in place in prisons render the correctional model and its desire to promote 'positive changes in the direction of more pro-social thinking' more than just a little unworkable. The promotion of such 'positive changes' *takes time* because people do not always accept the 'new' as easily or as readily as others may wish them to—the process is long, slow and sometimes very painful, especially if you are a prisoner serving a long sentence.

Thus, in research assessing the 'effectiveness' of a course in higher education within a prison setting (Reuss, 1997), it became apparent that analysing the role of education with a view to its capacity for 'changing' the prisoner's offending behaviour was essentially problematic because there are different views as to the merits of attending educational courses whilst in prison. On the one hand there is the prevailing view that education is a 'lifeline for people serving long sentences' (Wilce, 1996), whilst the opposing view suggests that it is a privilege and not a right for the undeserved, paid for by taxpayers whose money should be better spent. It does seem to be the case that most people feel that any education programme delivered to those imprisoned should be of benefit to the prisoners; but what the general public do *not* always appreciate or understand are the 'inherent difficulties' in doing just that (Flynn and Price, 1995, 3). Providers of such a service are also, as Flynn and Price indicate, working within institutions whose 'function' is to '... deprive offenders of freedom and to facilitate order and control', so the 'aims' of education and the 'aims' of imprisonment stand in direct opposition to each other.

This is the paradox that characterizes the provision of education in prisons where the conflicting interests and ideologies of the penal system and the education system, instead of reaching some kind of compromise through what Jones and d'Errico call 'accommodation' (1994, 13), lose sight of the individual prisoner who wants to learn something for personal benefit. This confusion makes any attempt at offering a 'way forward' problematic. It seems therefore that existing attitudes have to be assessed and understood with regards to the demands upon the 'providers' because there are in place long-standing views about prison and prisoners and if, for example, the general public have any views at all on the matter, they are likely to be grounded in what is culturally and ideologically acceptable as pertaining to the 'treatment' (in its widest sense) of offenders. This can be evidenced when those who have received 'schooling' in prison, re-offend on release. The courses in question would be deemed to have 'failed' because they did not rehabilitate. Learning for learning's sake seems not to be an option that is welcomed or encouraged for those imprisoned. How then can the public's appetite for a combination of punishment, deterrence, retribution and rehabilitation be satisfied? What is the contribution that education in prisons can make?

LISTENING TO PRISONERS

Educational programmes are often 'measured' against rates of recidivism to determine their effectiveness or 'success' rate, as opposed to a more radical interpretation of education as empowerment. The question that has to be asked is whether measuring the 'success' of a course of education in prison according to the rates of recidivism is any longer appropriate because, if prisoners views are to be listened to, then the very fact that some of them are faced with having to do specific courses whilst in prison to address offending behaviour, is in itself sufficiently 'de-motivating'. In other words, they will not attend such courses if they have no choice in the matter and in some cases attendance on such courses is akin to admitting guilt (cf Wilson, 1999). This is problematic for those prisoners awaiting or on appeal. Prisoners themselves are well placed to comment on the actuality, and the *first step forward* is to encourage other people to *listen* to them:

F: Look at in here; you might come down to education, to this class and find the teacher's talking crap all the time; you leave 'cos you can't handle it, so you've lost out on something ...

B: No it's not like that—you choose. It's about self-fulfilment. You don't know if the teacher's going to be crap until you've been on the course, you don't know that beforehand ...

F: ... but how many of us in here would choose to go on, say, the Anger Management course? That's like Sociology and the guy's a prat, so nobody goes ...

B: That's totally different, it's part of the system. If you want a cat. C, you go on his course, if you want fulfilment for yourself, you come here. (Reuss, 1999, 123).

These comments are about educational provision in prisons—*as perceived by prisoners*, and more importantly, *as experienced* by them. It seems to us that any assessment of the role of education in our prisons should not be undertaken without taking their views into account in the sense that any *future* plans or policies for the provision of education could be made whilst listening to prisoners about what kinds of education they have had in the past and what kind of education they themselves need for the future. A further dimension to the 'problem' of providing education in prisons is that the role of education in prison is often underestimated in terms of education's capacity or potential to empower the prisoner, as previously stated, and it is this concept of empowerment through education that can be most problematic for practitioners and policy-makers to 'see' as a legitimate and valid way of 'doing' time.

EMPOWERMENT

Empowering the prisoner is not about 'making smart cons smarter'. A basic dictionary definition claims that empowerment is not just about 'giving power or authority to', it is about 'giving ability to' and 'enabling'. It is with the process of 'enabling' that prisoner education can usefully be aligned and the *second step forward* is to ensure that practitioners do not misconstrue the meanings associated with 'empowering' prisoners.

The potential for 'traditional' education courses to empower the prisoner in terms of providing opportunities through education for 'individual attitude change' (Duguid, 1990, 113) is often overlooked. What seems to be important currently is to provide courses that satisfy prison management KPIs as indicated in the *Introduction* to this book (see *Chapter 1*). But again, it is worthwhile to think about 'what changes?' when looking at education's capacity to empower, as the question most asked of educational practitioners in prisons, closely followed by the questions 'How can you show it?' and 'How do you know if they've changed?' In thinking about the change-prisoner-education relationship we do the prisoner and ourselves a grave disservice in placing 'the change' beyond the prisoner's person or 'outside' of himself or herself. The key to our understanding of the processes at 'work' in education lies in our understanding of 'change' because 'What changes?' in prison education practice often metamorphoses into 'What works?' in penal policy.

For something to 'change', there is implicit a desire to 'make or become different' and in a prison classroom context, the making and becoming different refers, for the most part, to the prisoner. Is the prisoner-student who completes the course the 'same' as the one who started it? If practitioners can say 'No', then we do have to recognise that, something has occurred. Whether we call that something 'change' or not is a matter for some debate because use of the word 'change' seems inappropriate. It encourages prison educators and practitioners to have expectations which cannot always be met, thus adding to the belief that still, 'Nothing works' (Martinson; 1974).

Attending any course of education in any setting concerns personal growth and development as people acquire new knowledge through the *social* and interactive processes of learning. Prisoners are not immune from these processes, but in a prison education setting, people are all too anxious to seek changes in offending behaviour, as stated above, changes in personal attitudes, changes in lifestyle, changes in world views and so on. 'What changes' is all too often linked to issues of what should constitute a correctional programme of education that will stop offending behaviour. Now whilst this may be highly desirable, it is not always attainable for many complex reasons, so the 'way forward' in prisoner education is better served by considering the empowering potential of education *for the prisoners* in relation to personal development and growth through learning *from choice*.

It is possible, as research has shown (Reuss, 1997; Pawson and Duguid, 1998), to focus on learning outcomes of individual choice, responsibility and decision-making as parameters which underpin a variety of prisoner education programmes geared to the individual needs of the individual prisoner.

Prisoners are individual people and their motives for attending education whilst in prison are governed by the choices and decisions that anyone makes in a continually evolving social context involving other people. Prisons are not 'static' places, they may well be viewed as tragic places or even barbaric places, but within their walls are people whose sense of self, personality or identity is embedded in who they 'were' before entering the prison. If those imprisoned are to retain and/or regain a sense of personal worth and integrity in a world where exclusion and marginalisation of offenders are the 'cultural norm', then educational practitioners in prisons will have to refocus their aims on issues of self-actualisation and empowerment.

The biggest problem that HM Prison Service seems to have with this, is that of resourcing coupled with the very practical issues of providing suitable courses for those on remand or those within the dispersal system. If a prisoner is only going to be in a particular prison for a 'short' period of time, how can this be reconciled with the demands of any standard educational course, for example, planning and structuring a course over a number of 'terms' or 'semesters' where examinations may have to be taken at a specified time of the year? This is a very real problem both for the provider of the course, for the prisoner-student taking it, and for the prison. However, if it is acknowledged that short courses can also leave something of an impact upon those taking them by virtue of the fact that there is something to do beyond the walls of a cell, then surely the co-ordinating and designing of such courses is worthwhile—as long as the prisoner does not feel coerced into taking a course simply to satisfy bureaucracy.

Taking account of the prisoners' own views on education helps to delineate more clearly the role of prison education in terms of empowerment in relation to the manner in which education is currently practised. Just as Cook and Hoskison, Havel and Mandela (see the *Introduction* in *Chapter 1*) intimated at the capacity for education and education staff to 'get things done'—either for the prisoner on a 'transformative' level or as a means of instigating change at a more practical level within a prison system—the men in Reuss's study had a wealth of experience of prison education programmes because they were in the dispersal system serving long sentences, and many had attended a wide variety of courses in a wide variety of prisons as 'strategies for survival' (Cohen and Taylor, 1972).

CHOICE AND CONTROL

What the following comments show is that for some prisoners, being involved with educational provision—at any level—helps them retain a degree of *choice and control* in what they do whilst in prison. This is important from their point of view because it gives them a feeling of responsibility and autonomy in decision-making in respect of their own futures—provided that the course or courses on offer are not thought to be serving the interests of prison management. Choice and control also form the basis of the *third step forward* in prisoner education:

Tim: From a personal viewpoint it [education] helps to pass the time constructively and to remain mentally active. Generally speaking it depends on the particular inmate, whether they are taking part to learn a new skill or just filling in the time as an alternative to the menial labour on offer.

Trevor: It gives you hope for the future.

Kenny: Education offers the chance to catch up on subjects that were missed 'on the out'. I want to broaden my thinking on subjects I did not even know existed. To me education is prison is good, it stops me turning into a recluse and becoming institutionalised; this is the only prison I've been in that gives a choice of education programmes, other prisons have basics—maths, English, writing skills.

These kinds of comments again lead to questions raised earlier: What does the prisoner want from education? What does the prison want from education? What does the wider community want from education in this environment? Sadly, many prisoners believe that current provision does not serve their needs or interests at all, serving *only* those of the prison:

Allan: It's to do with the philosophy of dispersal. Dispersals are for the garbage of society as far as officers are concerned; that's all you are and the garbage of society should not get a degree course. It's that simple—they think it's too good for us, but if the course was called Reasoning and Rehabilitation or Anger Management, then the status quo is maintained. They don't like us to do education, in my opinion, they'd rather have us in the workshops ...

Matt: I won't go. You wouldn't get me in them, working for them. I'd rather do something for me. It's smart cons they don't want. The screws hate it you see, if they think you know more than them.

Allan: I reckon if they could shut all education down, they would. It's a threat you see.

The 'rewards' which prisoners obtain from attending courses range from providing an opportunity to 'blank off' prison life, as we can see from what prisoners themselves have to say, to idealistic pursuit of education for education's sake. It is this kind of attainment in educational terms that can seriously transform the prisoner's sense of self to the extent that 'success' in this area of prison experience counterbalances the felt experience of a sense of personal failure and loss of self-respect. This is where empowerment lies, in acknowledging that the outcomes of learning for each prisoner-student are *unique* and occur as a result of the way in which he or she has *synthesised* what has been learned into personal life experience. If post-release behaviour is to be affected or 'changed' in any way then it seems to follow that it will be determined by the prisoner's engagement with what has been learned and by the circumstances and situations which arose at the time of learning. In short, practitioners need to think carefully about the *context* of learning before being desirous of specific outcomes relating to reducing offending behaviour. *Learning* to 'think differently' does not have the same implications for prisoner education as having been *taught* to 'think differently'.

The elements which make up the third step forward involve *choice and control* in what prisoners do whilst in prison, as stated above. They form the basis of empowerment grounded in equality and tolerance. However, some observers may see this as a form of *confrontation or challenge* to the 'system' that can resonate through all that a prisoner may say or do throughout a sentence. A further element to be aware of is *cynicism* which can characterize the attitudes of everyone associated with educational provision in prisons from prisoners themselves who adopt a 'cynical-plus' attitude in that they are profoundly aware of their situation and the expectations that others have of them through to prison civilian staff who know that prisoners will 'go along' with any sentence plan as long as it means a reduction in sentence. This cynicism manifests itself on the part of the prisoner who 'responds' to those who represent the 'system' by colluding or conforming with their demands whilst at the same time descrying the worth of any 'correctional' programme to fellow prisoners and/or prison reformers: 'Well, look at it like this, when some of us get out, we're gonna be really smart at what we do best'.

The prisoners who adopt this attitude are mirroring the sentiments often expressed by prison officers, because these kinds of attitudes *are expected* within a prison environment. The prisoners here are resorting to the same kind of stereotyping of themselves that is also expressed beyond the prison walls, and awareness of this response to their labelling by others is important for those concerned with restoring self-esteem via education. For many in prison it seems that if you 'play the right games', you get the 'right prizes'. If you appear to agree with those who represent authority, you will benefit, regardless of what you might actually believe. It is also a way of convincing yourself that you have retained some degree of control in the choices that you make.

The way forward in prisoner education cannot be considered without recourse to prisoners and choice, control, confrontation, challenge and cynicism. Together they form the basis of understanding empowerment in appreciating how education can help prisoners and encourage them to make informed decisions about their lives. Restore choice and individual control, reduce the potential for confrontation, challenge and cynicism in the prison (Reuss, 1999, 125).

Education in prisons needs to be seen as something more than rehabilitative in the sense that it should simply assist in reducing offending behaviour. It has to be seen as something that has worth for the prisoner by the prisoner. If, as a result of attending a course in prison, offending behaviour 'stops', then all well and good; if an 'alternative future' is opened up for the prisoner through education, then all well and good; if attitudes, values, problem-solving skills and reasoning skills are enhanced, then all well and good. If social awareness and political consciousness are heightened, as they so often can be through higher education courses in particular—why is this seen as a problem? Why is it seen as a 'luxury' to provide the necessary resources, for example, for 'on-site campuses' in our prisons? Could it be that as a society for whom prison represents the ultimate form of punishment, we cannot bear the thought of intellectual 'power' shifting in favour of the offender, that we cannot accept freedom to learn for those prisoners who want to learn and for whom something might 'work' whilst doing time?

> **Duke:** This classroom is the most beautiful place in this prison. You can be yourself, you're respected, you can almost imagine that you're not in prison. (Duke, 1998)

For the most part however, the prevailing view tends to follow the pattern described by a prisoner who conducted a small study on prison education whilst serving his sentence:

> There are those prison officers, politicians, governors, Board of Visitors members, *et al* who will quite openly state that in their opinion, any form of education or training for inmates is a direct dereliction of authority, and an insidious plot by a 'Bunch of Liberal Outsiders' to pamper and indulge convicted felons who would be better 'amused' breaking rocks or digging ditches. (Richards; 1993)

Ultimately the way forward in prison education cannot be separated from a strategy that seeks to reform the penal system itself, and this in turn cannot be separated from the broader social and political context within which prisons have to operate. To achieve the policy and practice agendas we have outlined prisons have to stop being places where politicians can appear 'tough', and prisoners in turn have to be offered opportunities that have hitherto been denied to them. This is not mere idealistic posturing, but a passionate belief stemming from prolonged exposure to the practice of educating prisoners, and seeing for ourselves the transforming power of education.

BIBLIOGRAPHY for *Chapter 9*

Becker H. (1963), *Outsiders*, New York: Macmillan.

Cavadino M. and Dignan J. (1992), *The Penal System, An Introduction*, London: Sage

Cohen S. and Taylor L. (1972), *Psychological Survival*, Harmondsworth: Penguin

Davidson H. S. (ed.) (1995), *Schooling In A 'Total Institution', Critical Perspectives on Prison Education*, Westport, Conn.: Bergin and Garvey

Duguid S. (1995), 'People Are Complicated and Prisoners Are People—Using Recidivism to Evaluate Effectiveness in Prison Education Programmes'; (unpublished paper presented to International Forum for the Study of Education in Prisons [IFEPS] Conference, May 1995)

Elias N. (1987), *Involvement and Detachment*, Oxford: Basil Blackwell

Entwhistle N. (1987), *Understanding Classroom Learning*, London: Hodder and Stoughton

Fitzgerald M. and Sim J. (1982), *British Prisons*, Oxford: Basil Blackwell

Germanotta D. (1995), 'Prison Education: A Contextual Analysis' in Davidson, H.S. (ed.), *Schooling in a 'Total Institution'*, Westport, Conn.: Bergin and Garvey

Hall, S. (1980), 'Drifting Into A Law and Order Society' in Muncie J., McLaughlin, E. and Langan M. (1986), *Criminological Perspectives, A Reader*, London: Sage

Pawson, R. and Duguid S. (1997), 'Education, Change and Transformation: The Prison Experience' (submitted to *The Evaluation Review* (Forthcoming))

Porporino F. and Robinson D. (1995), 'An Evaluation of the Reasoning and Rehabilitation Program With Canadian Federal Offenders' in Ross R. and Ross R. (eds.), *Thinking Straight*, Ottawa: Air Training Publications

Reuss A. (1997), 'Higher Education and Personal Change in Prisoners', unpublished PhD thesis: University of Leeds

Reuss A. (1999), 'Prison(er) Education', *The Howard Journal*, Vol 38, No 2., May 1999

Ross R. and Fabiano E. (1985), *Time to Think: A Cognitive Model of Delinquency Prevention and Offender Rehabilitation*, Johnson City, Tennessee: Institute of Social Sciences and Arts Inc.

West T. (1997), *Prisons of Promise*, Winchester: Waterside Press

Wilson D. (1999), 'Delusions of Innocence', in E Cullen, T Newell (eds.) *Murderers and Life Imprisonment*, Winchester: Waterside Press.

Index

Abbott, P 108
Access students 85
access to prison for research etc. 28
achievement, see
    challenge/goals/success
active participation 115
Adult Education Facility,
    Nottingham University 165
ALBSU screening test 84
alienation effect of imprisonment
    85
anger management 176 179
anxiety, quelling 145
Aristotle 50 51 59
art/arts 22 117 147 154 155
    art supplies 141 145 147 150
    liberal arts 57
Ashton, J 146
attainment 146
attitude to the authorities etc 127 et
    seq.
autobiography 9 et seq. 26
autonomy 143 144 178

basic skills 10 11 19 21 64 84 115
    116 155 166
Bauman, Zygmunt 54
Becker, Howard 54
behaviour, changes in 25 34

Benson, Ian 20
black diaspora 117 et seq. 120
black people 107 et seq.
Black People in Prison: The Role of the
    Education Service 116
black prisoners 110 et seq. 116 et
    seq.
Blagg, H 114
Blakenhurst, HMP 129

'blanking off' 179
boot camps 50 60
boredom 95 103 110
Boshier, Roger 85 90 93 95
Boyle, J 86 88 98 100
Braithwaite, J 114

British Columbia 56 58 70
British Crime Survey 111
Britishness 135
budgets, see funds etc.
business studies 152 161

'can do' mentality 15
Cartesean approach 49
catching up 92 93
challenge/goals/success 95 103
    145 146 147 179
change 99 168 177 180
    measuring 71 174 177
    and see behaviour
character building 64
Chicago School 118
chief education officer 22
childhood identity 119
choice, making choices 143 et seq.
Christie, Nils 111
class aspects 88 89 93
'classroom talk' 25
Clayton, Margaret 116 132
cognitive skills/deficits 90 115 172
    174
    behavioural approach 87
    moral development 57
    skills 50 59 60 115
Cohen, S 86 100 144
colleges of further etc. education 19
communication, failure of 123
computer courses 142 151 152
confidence, raising 64 75 97 143
    146 148 167
confrontation 180
'cons' 11
Coldingley HMP 14 15
conscience 13 19 52
constructive use of time 143
contracting out /tendering 19 et
    seq. 155 166
Control Review Committee Report
    (1984) 132
Cook, Frank 12 et seq. 19
core curriculum 21 22 155
correctional enterprise 49
Correctional Service of Canada 59
    71 83

correspondence courses 151
  and see *distance learning*
counselling skills 148 150
courses, see *programmes*
creative needs 117
Creighton, Ann 140
crime and deviance 51 52 *et seq.*
  learning disability, and 58
Crime (Sentences) Act 1997 15
criminal skills, acquiring 15 16
Crossroads partnership project 89
cultural location 119
Cultural Theory (racism) 107
cynisim 180

Darwin, Charles 53 108
degree level aspirations/studies 25
  27 70 115 143 150 160 162 179
  masters degree 150 165
delay in receiving post 151
development, see *growth* 56
deviance, see *crime and deviance*
Devlin, Angela 95, 146
difference theory 55
difficulties of being a student in
  prison 151 *et seq.*
disadvantage 114 *et seq.* 155
disjunction 23 106
dispersal prisons 115 116 128 178
  179
  and see *Whitemoor, HMP, Leeds
  University project*
distance learning 138 143 154 155
diversity 121
Duguid, Stephen 9 49 70 84 115
Durham, HMP 86
Durkheim 53

education
  black issues 116 *et seq.*
  cognitive interest 90
  de-categorisation, and 99
  empowerment 9 10 19 75 114
  115 172 175 176 179
  identity, effect on and value of
  19 55 (new identity) 79 82 97
  99 106 123 130 149
  impact of 57 143

education (continued)
  improvers 75 *et seq.*
  integration 106 114 115 118
  lifeline, as 77
  long-term return 75
  luxury 181
  outside contact 90
  personal change 67
  personal control 90 94
  personal fulfilment/satisfaction
  130 133 143 148 176
  personal growth 177
  personal responsibility 143 178
  previous, effect of 75 *et seq.*
  prison(er) education 10 172
  reduced opportunities 155
  rewards of 179
  role of education in prisons 173
  sabotage 17
  self-actualisation 178
  self-assertion 90
  self-belief 167
  self-confidence, see *confidence,
  raising*
  self decision-making 143
  self-discipline 167
  self-esteem 94 99
  self-expression 144
  self-perception 123 130 131
  self-preservation 90
  self-respect 179
  theory, effect on education 51
  threat, viewed as 17
  tool for living 10 17
  transforming power/experiences
  9 10 16 23 40 118 134
  weapon of control 10 17
Educational Centre of Excellence
  (Sudbury/Foston Hall) 161
'Education, Change and
  Transformation' (Canada) 115
emotional strain of prison life 152
employment/work ethic 64 89 92
  97 103 141 145 165
Englishness 121
enjoyment 147
equality 180

escort problems 14
ethnic minority issues 106 *et seq*
    criminal justice, and 109 *et seq.*
ethnography 26 41
European Acquired Rights
    Directive (ARD) 20
evaluation 63 *et seq.* 156
    change, of 71
    pitfalls 65
evidence, need for 64
exercise and fitness studies 153
experiences of prisoners 138 *et seq.*
    158 *et seq.*
external connections 152 *et seq.*
Eysenk, H J 55

Farrington, D 123
Fitzgerald, Marion 109
FitzGerald, Mike 10
Flynn, N 175
Forster, W 87 145 147 151
Foston Hall, HMP 161 168
Foucault, Michel 54 60
Freire, Paulo 114 131
Freud 55
Full Sutton, HMP iv 67 83
funds, resources, provision of 17
    22 25 57 67 87 152 153 155
    168 181
    and see *grants*
further and higher education 25 67
    et seq. (Simon Fraser University,
    Canada) 87
Further and Higher Education Act
    1992 19 87

Galileo 50
Gartree, HMP 153
generalizability 27 44
Genet, Jean 54
Ghaill, Macan 89
Gilligan, Carol 50
goals, see *challenge*
Goffman, E 98
going straight 97
governors
    lack of control over 20
grants 138 *et seq.* 152 153 155

Greater Eligibility, principle of 114
'Great Society' movement (USA) 63
Grendon, HMP 160
Grounded Theory 106
growth, cognitive, moral etc. 56

Hall, Stuart 107 108 109 117 122
    129
hard cases 79
'hard slog', the 75 76
Harer, M D 130
Harris, Roxy 117
Havel, Vaclav 12 16
health and social care course 150
helping (teaching) other inmates
    148 160 162
higher education, see *further and*
    higher education
Higher Education and Personal
    Change in Prisoners 25
homeostasis 85 95 104
Hood, Roger 110
hope 145 179
Hoskison, John 12 14
Howard, John 87
Hull, HMP 13 17
human, feeling 143
Hume, David 50

identity
    and criminal justice/policing etc.
    125 *et seq.*
    and see *education (identity)*
Inner London Education Authority
    (ILEA) 116
inner voice, see *conscience*
Inspector of Prisons 20
instinctive benevolence 53
integration 57
international aspects 16
interpersonal skills 174
KPIs 10 19 21 176

Jefferson, Thomas 50 53 55
job finding skills 165
John, Gus 116

Kant, Immanuel 50

'keep 'em busy mechanism' 78
keeping occupied 92 95
key skills 84 153
Koestler Trust awards 154
Kohlberg, Lawrence 50
Kushnik, L 108

labelling 54 112 180
language/linguistic diversity 121
law and order politics 16
learning *in extremis* 85
'Learning in Terror' 113
Lebanon, hostages 86 102
Leeds University project 25 *et seq.*
   67 115
letters by prisoners 138 *et seq.*
Levi, Primo 86 101
Lewes, HMP 14
Liebling, A 132
lifers 26 *et seq.* 36 64 84 88 93
   100
life skills, see *social skills*
listening to prisoners 175
   and see *voices, prisoners (voice)*
literacy 10 11 21 115 155 163
Littlehey, HMP 165 168
Local Education Authority (LEA) 19
   87
Loeber, R 123
long-term prisoners 26 *et seq.* 84
   88 100 104 119 144 145 159
   174

Macpherson Report 110 112
maintaining progress 81
Mandela, Nelson 12 16
Martinson, Robert 56 177
Maslow's heirarchy of needs 167
Matlock, G 14
Matthews, Helen 19
maturity factor 77 169
Matza, David 54
maximum security aspects/culture
   36 115
   and see *HMP Whitemoor, Leeds
   University project, dispersal prisons*
May Committee of Enquiry Report
   1979 87

McGivney 88 89
Medical Model 50 56 87 174
   'New Medical Model' 115 132
Modernity and the Holocaust 54
moral aspects 52 115 134
moral vacuum 115
motivational aspects 85 95
   and see *dealing with time*
Mountbatten Report 1966 87
music 148

NACRO
   Derby 162 163
   working with 165
National Prison Survey, 1991 84 88
   92 93
New Labour initiatives 63 64
normalisation 130
'Nothing Works' 56 74 177
Nubian Link 89
'Nuff Respect' 116
numberpower 165
numeracy 10 11 21 115 155 162
nurture 52

open learning 161
Open University (OU) 84 86 88 96
   100 115 145 150 153 154 162
offending behaviour
   education as evidence of
   addressing 104
   reducing 181
order and control 64
Original Sin 55
'outsiders' 26 *et seq.* 58

paranoia 95
Parkhurst, HMP 22
Parliamentary Gaol Act 1823 87
passing the time 11
   and see *time*
Pawson, Ray 9 61
pay 14
Peel, Robert 87
peer groups 88 94 103 162
Plato 52

post-release
  behaviour 179
  education 141
Price, D 132 175
prison
  culture, effect of 15
  population 22 26
prison education
  purpose 114
  and see *education*
Prison Education Departments 9
Prison Education Participation
  Scale (PEPS) 90
prisoner(s)
  autobiography 9 *et seq.*
  choice and control 19 178
  commitment to studies 149 153
  consumer, as 11
  enthusiasm 149
  experiences 138 *et seq.*
  letters 138 *et seq.*
  perceptions of education 42
  pay 14
  students, as 149
  subjects not objects 56 61
  voice 10 12 *et seq.* 23 114
prison(er) education 10 172
Prisoners Education Trust 23 138
  et seq.
Prison Reform Trust 14
problems of being a student in
  prison 151 *et seq.*
programmes
  enhanced thinking skills 99
  formal eductaion 87
  generally 23 47
  offending behaviour 25 47 104
  175
  sex-offender treatment 99 151
  why prisoners take part 84 89
problem solving methods 115 174
psychological instability of
  imprisonment 86
psychological survival 102
psychology class 145
purposeful activity 10

qualifications 82 89 97 141 145
  159 160 161
quality assurance
  procedures/standards 22 166
Quality Mark 156

racism 106 *et seq.*
  criminal justice, and 109
  education, and 112 *et seq.*
  social theories of 107
RAND Corporation studies of
  career criminals 55
Ratcliffe, P 108 109
Reagan, Ronald 55
reasoning and rehabilitation 179
recidivism 23 46 56 57 58 115
  168 175
reconviction prediction 74
Reducing Offending etc. (Home
  Office) 89
reform aspects 52 58 60 61 65 73
regime 51 64
rehabilitative aspects 25 46 51 58
  61 64 65 66 71 77 79 117 142
  174 179 181
reasoning and rehabilitation 179
reincarceration 64
  and see *re-offending*
relationships
  family 122 152 154
  staff/inmates 64
  prison authorities 129
  and see *tensions*
remand prisoners 178
re-offending 168 174
  and see *recidivism, rehabilitation,
  reincarceration*
'Reported and Unreported Racial
  Incidents in Prison' 111
research 25 *et seq.* 91 *et seq.* 117 *et
  seq.*
  contamination 40
  methodology 36 et *seq.* 90 *et seq.*
  117 *et seq.*
resources, see *funds etc.*
Reuss, Anne 9 10 *et seq.* 19 68 178
  180
revolving door 64 77 79

Reward/Cost model of crime 114
risk of offending 115
Robben Island 17
Robson, Penny 22
Royal Commission on Criminal
  Justice 109
rule 45 (formerly rule 43) 84
Rutherford, Andrew 21

schooling 12 92 106 120 123 *et
  seq.* 147 158
security 22
sentence planning 64 104 180
sex offenders, see *programmes*
Sim, Joe 10
simple solutions, lure of 50
Simon Fraser Prison Education
  Programme 65 70 *et seq.*
SIR scale/findings 74 *et seq.*
socialisation/social controls 55 130
  132 164
social skills 21 64 174
Socrates 52
South Manchester College 20
special needs 160 164
special unit 13
spending on prison education 22
sport courses 142
staff
  attitudes, effect of 15
  encouragement 151
  enthusiasm 15
  frustrating positive initiatives 16
  positive relationships 116
State of the Prisons 87
stereotyping 180
'straights' 11
success, see *challenge/goals/success*
Sudbury, HMP 161 164
survival factor 85 98 102
  psychological survival 102
Swatsky Report 115
Sykes, Gresham 98
system 51

Taylor, L 86 100 144
Teachers Certificate 162
  and see *helping other inmates*

tendering, see *contracting out*
tensions 36
  personal 85 95
  staff/prisoners 16 19
  staff/staff 19
  and see *relationships*
theory 49 *et seq.*
therapeutic communities 58
Thorn Cross, HM YOI 20
Tilt, Richard 111
three strikes law (two strikes law)
  15 49
time
  alternative/parallel time track 88
  commodity, as 101
  concept of 87
  constructive use of 143 179
  dealing with/managing/passing
  84 86 92 98 144 160 176 179
  marking time 145
  positive use of 143
  'subjective clock' 144
tolerance 180
treatment 174 175
Troyna, B 108 113 117
Tumim, Sir Stephen 10 20

Unit for the Arts and Offenders 117
university level studies, see *degree
  level*

value of prison education 138 155
Verne, HMP The 160 *et seq.*
voice 10 12 *et seq.* 23 114 138 *et
  seq.* (letters)

Wait, Terry 86 102
Wakefield, HMP 160
Wallace, C 108 122
'Walton prison' (HMP Liverpool)
  160
Weil, S 106
West, Tessa 172
'What Works' 9 19 63 64 *et seq.* 79
  174 177
  context, effect of 79 *et seq.* 180
  factors 82

Whitemoor, HMP 22 23 84 *et seq.*
106 *et seq.* 132
'wicked people' 55
Willey, R 120
Williamson, B 85 130
Williford 173 *et seq.*
Willis, Paul 88
Wilson, D 146
Wilson, James Q 55
writing courses 142
women, lack of provision 155

Woolf Report 153 173
wordpower 165
Wormwood scrubs Pre-release
Hostel 165
Worth, V 86 88
wiping out past and future 86

X, Malcolm 174

yoga 144 148

Also from Waterside Press

Drug Treatment In Prison
An Evaluation of the RAPt Treatment Programme
CAROL MARTIN and ELAINE PLAYER
The findings of a two-year study into the effectiveness of the RAPt drug treatment programme which enables male prisoners with self-confessed problems of substance misuse to lead a drug and alcohol-free life in prison and in the community after release. The report also assesses whether completion of the programme is associated with a reduction in the likelihood of reconviction post-release. A unique and highly significant collection of information and data. 96 pages ISBN 1 872 870 26 0 **£10** plus £2 p&p (Europe £3; elswhere £6).

Scheduled for March 2001

Grendon Tales
STORIES FROM A THERAPEUTIC COMMUNITY
Ursula Smartt

Weaving first-hand accounts by members of HM Prison Grendon's therapuetic 'communities' and staff with personal research and observation, Ursula Smartt takes readers behind the scenes at one of the UK's best-known and forward-looking prisons. Her analysis of 'the Grendon experience' goes beyond straightforward description of this world famous establishment to examine the shifts (subtle and not so subtle), tensions and possibilities which underpin day-to-day life and the process of change in offenders.

By allowing the reader to listen to 'shrinks', governors, officers and a range of often high risk offenders, their recollections, self-portraits, aspirations and private thoughts, Ursula Smartt lets the reader sense the unique atmosphere of the therapeutic community itself – coming as close as it is possible for an outsider to get to an understanding of what is involved in this ground-breaking approach. The 'tales' are set within the author's own perceptions of the establishment as it goes about its daily business, resulting in a work which is both accessible and illuminating – and which also allows the reader to appreciate precisely what faces a long-term offender who has been given the opportunity to serve a central part of his sentence in conditions quite unlike those in the remainder of the English Prison System.* *Grendon Tales* is a powerful, scholarly and readable work which is destined to become a lasting tribute to this unique establishment on its fortieth anniversary in 2001. ISBN 1 872 870 96 1. Price £18 plus £2 p&p (Europe £3; elsewhere £6)

* A new prison, Marchington is set to replicate Grendon under private management in 2001

Prison Writing

A collection of original writings by prisoners and other people connected with prisons, from the United Kingdom and beyond

CONTENTS

'Razor Smith' Interview and extracts from his work *The Last Party.*
Innocent as Sin W. Maree
The Festive Season in Prison Ruth Wyner
Mellaril Mark Read
Pros and Cons S. Hewett
Slipping George Hayes
Virgo Intacta Matthew Williams
Not Today Stephen Barraclough
Looking at Life Simon Scott
Reflections/ Librarian's Tale M. Williamson
Loose Hands of Friendship Simon Tasker
One Friend Only Ian P. Downes

First Annual Waterside Edition

The Fur Coat Paul Agutter
When Wishes Come True Michael Grant
George/The Man Nobody Knew Freddy Taylor
Irish Eyes Tony Savage
Monkey Business Stephen Lewtas
Bogart's Coming out Party Ian Watson
King of the Bees John Wrigglesworth
May Day (from *This is Oxford*) Clive Benger
The Balad of Bodmin Jail Bill Hook
Winding Back Clare Barstow
Changing History Ralf Bolden
Poems by Cisse Amidou, Darren Blanchflower, John Roberts and Robert Mone
Plus **A Round-Up of Recent Books** connected to prisons and imprisonment.

Founded in 1992
Issue No 15: 2001
ISBN 1 872 870 90 2
£12 plus £2 p&p (Europe £3; elsewhere £6)

Edited by **Julian Broadhead** and **Laura Kerr**

Prison on Trial
SECOND ENGLISH EDITION (2000)

This edition of *Prison On Trial* contains all six original chapters plus a new *Foreword* and *Preface,* and a substantial *Postcript* by the author. There is also an extended *Bibliography* and a new *Index*.

Waterside Press Criminal Policy Series
Series Editor Andrew Rutherford

Prison On Trial distils the arguments for and against imprisonment in a readable, accessible and authoritative way – making Thomas Mathiesen's work a classic for students and other people concerned to understand the real issues. It is as relevant today as when it was first published – arguably more so as policy-making becomes increasingly politicized and true opportunities to influence developments diminish.

Mindful of this, Mathiesen recommends an 'alternative public space' where people can engage in valid discussion on the basis of sound information, free from the survival priority of the media – to entertain.

watersidepress.co.uk
ISBN 1 872 870 85 6

Thomas Mathiesen is Professor of Sociology of Law at the University of Oslo. He was one of the founders of the Norwegian Association for Penal Reform. His widely acclaimed works include *The Defences of the Weak* (1995), *Across the Boundaries of Organizations* (1971), *The Politics of Abolition* (1974) and *Law, Society and Political Action* (1980).

Prison On Trial has been influential in many jurisdictions. It has already been published in **Norwegian, Danish, Swedish, German, English** and **Spanish** – and is currently being translated into **Italian**. £19.50 plus £2 p&p (Europe £3; elsewhere £6)

WATERSIDE PRESS • DOMUM ROAD • WINCHESTER • SO23 9NN
Full catalogue /Orders:
☎ Tel/fax 01962 855567 E-mail: watersidepress@compuserve.com
Or visit www.watersidepress.co.uk where you can order via the Internet in secure conditions – and view over 100 Waterside publications on criminal justice and penal affairs.